THE END OF ALL THINGS IS AT HAND

A PERSONAL JOURNEY FROM APOCALYPTIC FEARS TO HISTORICAL REALITY

JACK PYLE

Philip Yancey (born 1949) is an American author who writes primarily about spiritual issues. His books have sold more than fifteen million copies in English and have been translated into forty languages, making him one of the best-selling contemporary Christian authors. Two of his books have won the ECPA's Christian Book of the Year Award: *The Jesus I Never Knew* in 1996, and *What's So Amazing About Grace?* in 1998.—He is published by *Hachette, HarperCollins Christian Publishing, InterVarsity Press,* and *Penguin Random House.*

> "I read your book and came away impressed with all the research you have done. You have an open, curious mind and spirit, so different from the dogmatism that often comes my way. I applaud you for seeking truth so diligently... Like you I have been puzzled by the book of Revelation. I love the quote from Archbishop William Temple who said, 'In God there is no unChristlikeness at all.' Yet the portrayal in Revelation, especially, brings that great quote into question, so much so that I sometimes wonder if that book should have ever made it into the canon... I learned a lot from your book although there are parts of it with which I disagree... I'm glad you're thinking. Keep it up..."

Robert Lawrence Kuhn (born 1944) is a public intellectual, international corporate strategist and investment banker. He has a doctorate in brain research and is the author and editor of over 25 books. He is a recipient of the China Reform Friendship Medal, China's highest award; he is a long-time adviser to China's leaders and the Chinese government, to multinational corporations on China strategies and transactions, and is a frequent commentator on the politics, economics, business, finance, philosophy and science of China. He is a columnist for *China Daily* and *South China Morning Post* and appears on the *BBC, CNN, China Central Television, Bloomberg* and other major media.

*"Congrats on the book! I'm so pleased...just
did another quick skim - reminding me why
I liked its 'spirit' and spunk and substance so
much the first time..."*

Dale Allison Jr. (born 1955) is **Princeton Theological Seminary's**
Richard J. Dearborn Professor of New Testament.

**"I have looked at your manuscript with inter-
est. You have read a lot, understand what you've
read, and wrestled with difficult questions.
Looks like we see eye to eye on most things.**

**Like me, it appears that your most helpful com-
panions on your journey have been books. I
appreciate that, although find it sad that so many
of us find so little honest help in the churches.**

**I wish you the best as you continue on your
journey."**

Dr. James Tabor (born 1946) is a Professor in the Department of
Religious Studies at the University of North Carolina at Charlotte
where he is a professor of Christian origins and ancient Judaism and
served as Chair for a decade. His Ph.D. is from the University of
Chicago.

**"Jack Pyle has presented here a remarkable
portrait of his lived life over several decades in
an Christian apocalyptic sect that expected the
end of the age to come by 1975. What really
makes his work stand out are the ways in which
he recounts his own deep study and research as
he became determined to search out how the
scholars and experts in the field of Christian
Origins deal with and understand the ancient**

apocalyptic movement of John the Baptist, Jesus, and Paul. The book presents something unique here for general readers as well as students of religious studies. We are able to think at once about the quest for the historical Jesus while at the same time attempting to understand sincere Christian believers and how they have attempted to quite literally appropriate the apocalyptic perspectives of the first century in the twentieth century. I believe this book will be of interest to both specialists and those of biblical background who find themselves searching the same questions."

Dedicated to our grandchildren.

ISBN 978-1-64299-919-8 (paperback)
ISBN 978-1-64299-920-4 (digital)

Christian Faith Publishing, Inc.
832 Park Avenue
Meadville, PA 16335
www.christianfaithpublishing.com

Printed in the United States of America

Colton, Amanda, Kelsey, Spencer, Peyton, Jack Cameron, and Tabby,

Let me say something to each of you about this book before you start to read it. I will tell you the end of all its contents before you start.

The end of the story is that over years of time of study I came to believe that Jesus is not coming back to the earth after the appearance of the Four Horsemen who pour out famine, pestilence, and disease upon the inhabitants of the earth. The book of Revelation states that Jesus, after their devastation, is going to kill one third of the creatures of the sea, burn the forests of the earth, poison the drinking water of the globe, and scorch the earth with fire. Billions of individuals will die along with all the sea creatures of the oceans. The ecology of the earth is to be decimated and the earth will be a smoking mess. Revelation details events of a battle of Armageddon wherein blood will run as high as the bridles of horses from bloody wars to be fought at his coming.

I don't believe that. I once did. This book is the story of how I came to believe that and the thought process over a twenty-five-year span that I stopped believing all that. My feelings are so strong that those beliefs are wrong, even though they are right out of the book of Revelation, that I wrote this book about it. Those events to occur at Jesus second coming were intended by a misguided author to apply to the Roman world in which he lived. The Roman Empire is gone, the author (whoever he was) is dead, and Jesus, who was supposed to come back then, didn't. There are millions of people living today in the country in which you live that are waiting for events to occur in the world that somebody felt was supposed to have occurred thousands of years ago. You will read of those scary events the rest of your lives. The Bible will be quoted.

You will see I wrote the book over years of time. My beliefs were so strong that Jesus was going to return in our day the way he is described in Revelation, that it took years of reading for me to change my mind and be convinced the author of a book of the Bible simply misinterpreted what was going on in his world, the same way one of the Apostles misinterpreted events that he believed were to occur in the lives of his congregations that he raised up in their day and time thousands of years ago. His name is Paul. He wrote 14 books of our new testament. He felt the kingdom was to come back then as well.

After more reading and study, I became convicted of heart that Jesus also believed and taught Paul, and all those individuals which he addressed back there in his day, that the kingdom of God was to arrive in their lifetimes, Jesus was the source of the belief of the early church the kingdom of God was to be back then, not a time in your future or the future of the earth.

If it took me twenty five years to reach all these conclusions, there is no way you will sit down and read this book and have it make a lot of sense to you. It won't. It's a book that I hope you will put in a drawer and as you continue your life's journey, marry and have children, and live a life yet to unfold before you with your own children and families, that you can pull out and read again as you will hear of wars and rumors of war, blood moons, earthquakes, famine, pestilence and disease, and daily stories out of the news that Armageddon is upon the world and that the apocalypse is now here. Jesus, I believe, will never come to this earth, nor will you ever experience a God arriving on this planet to do what is laid out in the book of Revelation or the Old Testament. I believe whatever you live to see in your lives after I am gone, the apocalypse will never come upon you and those on this earth. Those books were written by human beings proven by history to totally be wrong and misguided. That, my grandchildren, is the whole book. You don't have to wade through it. There will be no test the next time we visit.

What you might find interesting in the first few chapters now is the story of your great grandparents and how your parents grew up in the weird church they attended as a child. It is the story of how I came to believe from a child all that I believed, and it is the story of how I came to believe that Jesus is not going to come back the way I once believed. It is a story of your great grandparents and your uncles and aunts and your cousins and great uncles and great cousins.

Scary times will come in your life. Be strong, and of good courage. One thing you will never have to be afraid of is that the heavens are going to be opened one day and you find one on a white horse with a garment dipped in blood that will arrive on this earth killing and punishing citizens of the earth and destroying the ecology and marine and animal life.

This book is not all about me. It is the life of your grammy as well who was by my side through all the events in life we both experienced together before you were born. There were tears along the way, times of despair and discouragement, but the sunshine always returned after the rain, success somehow came out of setbacks, and we have always felt wonderfully blessed beyond our imagination. One of those great blessings has been to see all of you grow up. We may well live to see (who could possibly know at this point) great grandchildren one day.

I wish I could tell you more about God and Jesus. I was very aware in writing the book how inept, when I got to the end, that I would be to tell anyone about the future and what God is going to do to this earth. I just believe very strongly in what God and Jesus are NOT, as individual thinking beings, going to do, and what any god is going to do to this earth.

I think one of the most beautiful scriptures we have in the Bible are the words of Jesus. He said: "Except you become as a little child, you will in no wise inherit the kingdom of God."

It is my hope in every way that we all will one day understand and experience that kingdom with all of our families, friends, and strangers of this planet, and maybe as C.S. Lewis believed, even the pets we all knew as well.

I love you,
Grandpa

CONTENTS

Preface...13

Introduction..23

1   The Second Coming...45

2   True Believers 56

3   What It Takes to Make a Change........................72

4   Leaving It All Behind...86

5   Finding My Way..92

6   Who Is This Historical Jesus?.............................99

7   Paul Upheld and Supported Jewish Temple Beliefs.............110

8   A New Look at Jesus 119

9   Scholars' Beliefs of Jesus' Worldview 128

10 Jesus' Beliefs of the End of the Age 137

11 What the Early Church Believed 151

12 Did Jesus Not Know When the End Would Be? 158

13 Jesus God and Man 165

14 Reading the Gospels as Literature 175

15 The Gospels Can't Be Harmonized 189

16 John—A Totally Different Gospel......................198

17 Why Do 126,000,000 People Believe Jesus Will
    Return by 2050? 214

18 Summary of Quest for Jesus...........................225

19 New Horizons of the Apostle Paul 240

20 Conclusion 250

Postscript..275

Epilogue...279

Appendix: Biographies of Key Individuals Quoted 289

Notes 299

PREFACE

"Once I began to read the literature, I suffered theological confusion and anxiety, as must many churchgoers today when they learn of the quest for the first time through National Public Radio or Time Magazine, or when they browse the offerings of a bookstore, stumble onto the various titles about Jesus, and then actually read a couple. Once becoming aware of this strange new world of the critical historians, Christians may well worry whether the quest is a subject that they can, having learned about it, safely ignore, or whether it instead confronts them with facts that should amend, perhaps, significantly, their inherited religious convictions."

—Dale Allison

According to a Pew Research Poll conducted in 2010, 41 percent of American citizens stated they believed that Jesus will return by 2050. Of that number, 21 percent said he would return by that date. The remainder said he will probably return by that date. What is more surprising was a whopping *79 percent* stated they believed Jesus would return *sometime.* Those are amazing statistics.

The population in 2010 was 308,745,538. *One hundred twenty-six million* US citizens believe Jesus will most likely return by the year 2050, unless those polled have changed their minds.

That is 33 percent of the population of the country! Two hundred forty-three million American citizens believe Jesus will return sometime. If you are a United States citizen, you live in a country that is looking for the end of the age, the coming of the Son of Man, just as much or more as Jews looked for that in Jesus' own day, if not more so. This book is addressed to all people anticipating the return of Jesus to this earth in the next thirty-three years. Its subject is whether he will make it. We will see that understanding his life from a child in his culture and world is key to understanding what he believed about the future of his world. He never thought of our world.

I was part of a small sectarian church that devoutly believed Jesus was going to return in 1975. We probably used all of the scriptures individuals employ in developing their convictions of the return of Jesus. The church was the church of my parents which I joined as I grew up. I eventually became a minister within it and proclaimed the expectations of the second coming of Jesus for nearly a quarter century. I reached the point at age thirty-eight where I resigned and got out of the ministry, and after years of reading and study, I discarded most of my childhood religious beliefs. I was the quintessential person described in Eric Hoffer's book titled *The True Believer.*

The second coming is bedrock belief in the teaching and preaching of the early church, and its emphasis is found in the Gospels, Acts, and the writings of Paul. The last book, Revelation, is devoted entirely to the second coming. One can't read the New Testament and not deal with the subject of a second coming. The message of the new testament church is that of the angel in Luke who said,

> "Men of Galilee, why do you stand looking into
> heaven? This Jesus, who was taken up from you
> into heaven, will come in the same way as you
> saw him go into heaven" (Acts 1:11).

There is little doubt that Luke meant Jesus went *up* and out of sight and that as Luke wrote in Acts and Paul wrote later in Thessalonians, that same Jesus is supposed to come *down* again. Unless there is a second coming of Jesus, everything taught about his life by the early church crumbles and falls apart. They fit together or completely fall apart, including the story of his resurrection.

The resurrection of Jesus is one of the most debated subjects within Western Christianity. Christianity awaits substantiation of Jesus' resurrection. His resurrection will be proven only upon his appearance and return and a kingdom is established of which he spoke while on earth. Wolfhart Pannenberg explains the dilemma of Christians and their beliefs in his often-quoted book *Jesus, God and Man*:

> "Hence the reference of Jesus message to God's future, which has not yet definitely appeared, must have consequences for understanding his claim to authority in the sense that Jesus remains dependent upon the confirmation of his mission through the full Parousia of God's future."[1]

The book will be autobiographical. It is the only way I could write it. It involves my relaying how I came to believe what I believed and my struggles to free myself from my childhood beliefs. In the process of trying to disentangle myself from a tangled web of beliefs, I discovered there was a third quest for Jesus underway among theologians and Bible scholars. I didn't know there had been a first quest.

The so-called quests for the historical Jesus have been bantered about to have been three periods of time in history that a concerted scholastic and theological effort was made to find and come to know the Jesus of history better than previous generations.

The first quest period is the time of Reimarus (1768–1794) and stretching all the way up to and through Albert Schweitzer's production of his book *The Quest of the Historical Jesus*, which dominated modern biblical scholastic thinking of the historical

Jesus for one hundred years. Marcus Borg called him a genius. N.T. Wright calls him one of the greatest human beings of the twentieth century.

The second quest, Wikipedia says, began with the lecture of Ernst Kasemann in 1953 and lasted up until the period of the seventies and eighties when a new set of theologians and Bible scholars began again a diligent search for understanding of the historical Jesus using new criteria to research his life.

The use of the term *third quest* is said to have been coined by N. T. Wright in 1982, which would make the third quest to have a duration over a quarter century.

Our religious beliefs in this country have been developed over long periods of time in the thinking and learning process of human beings. Often it is very subtle. We gain our beliefs in many cases without thinking. They are handed to us. In discussing how I came to believe that Jesus would return in 1975, I offer it in the spirit of asking you to look at your beliefs and ask how they were formed if you think Jesus will be back by 2050 in the blazing glory described in the book of Revelation. I expected to be in the kingdom of God right now participating in a thousand-year millennial rule of Jesus after having already witnessed events millions anticipate occurring in the future, including the unleashing of the seven last plagues upon humanity. Instead I sit here writing these words on my HP laptop. I believe a lot of things being taught in church basements weekly about Jesus in prophecy classes are just as homemade as things I believed about him years ago. What happens within our culture and society if Jesus hasn't returned in the year 2050 or 3000 or year 4000? Individuals will be looking for alternate explanations of the meaning and life of Jesus, just as I did.

In my search for understanding, I discovered the "guild." The word is the nomenclature or shop talk chosen by a select group of scholars and theologians to describe themselves. They have, in several cases, spent lifetimes studying the Jesus of history. Books on the third quest for Jesus are pouring out by the hundreds. One can sift through them all. I learned one thing through the process of trying to do it. Jesus is a protected species. Christianity wants him frozen in the locker with the doors closed and sealed. To study Jesus' life as he really lived only serves to disturb all the beliefs Christendom has established about him post his death. What is important are the beliefs Christianity has made up and developed about him rather than really who he was while he lived on earth. His beliefs and outlooks amazingly are shunned. He must remain the author of our beliefs of heaven, hell, judgments, damnation, justification, grace, and the plethora of doctrines created in dogmatic theologies of churches, many of them totally contradictory to the other. To study Jesus' life could be damaging to one's faith and beliefs.

Over a twenty-five-year span, I found I had to change my inherited religious convictions about Jesus and a second coming. The process involved a lot of stops and starts, left and right turns, U-turns, confusion, angst, frustration, doubts, misgivings, and even waxing and waning fears depending upon the confidence I had in my evolving beliefs. After years of study, I got rid of fears. I believe there is no God that exists that would deprecate or impugn a diligent search for understanding of who and what he or she is. I believe, through the process, that I came to understand the Jesus of history for the first time in my life. I had proclaimed his coming for years.

Is Jesus still filled with the blazing hot anger he showed to a fig tree on the road outside Bethany? Or to people of the cities of Chorazin, Bethsaida, and Capernaum whom he condemned to burn in hell forever? Or is he like the Jesus on the cross who said,

> "And Jesus said, 'Father forgive them, for they know not what they do?'"

After returning to heaven and discovering that his father had intentionally blinded the eyes of those around him to keep them from understanding his message, is he now a much mellower Jesus? Might he be today after seeing the passage of time and all of history the world has experienced a kindlier, gentler Jesus, with a broader understanding of what is going on in the world from that which he experienced as a human being with limited understanding of the universe? Or is he waiting in the wings to destroy planet Earth and burn it with fire and dissolve our planet by fervent heat as Peter writes?

This book will discuss what Bible scholars call the "historical Jesus." It is a search for the theology of Jesus—what he believed personally about God and the future of his world, his own personal worldview, not what others came up with about him after his departure. His beliefs about himself have no connection to conferences at Chalcedon from which we get our concepts of Christology. We will also see that he personally didn't believe in the end of the world as portrayed in Revelation or the *Left Behind* series of books. Jesus wasn't the first Christian. Most of Christendom only sees him as God. His humanity, that of being, as the creeds state—"wholly man"—is never pointed out. He is only known by the second part of the phrase of the creed—"wholly God." That is the way I knew him and that is the way he is viewed by most of Christendom.

This book will be a surprising journey into the world of the third quest. Here is a summary of what you will find:

The introduction gives a biblical portrait of the father of Jesus, one who is unknown to most Christians and long forgotten and neglected. Jesus and Yahweh are the two personalities of the Bible that would be involved in the second coming, and they are described in our Christian literature.

- Chapter 1 details how the second coming pervades our collective conscious as a country and is reflected in TV scripts, movies, newspapers, billboards, and thousands of sermons weekly.
- Chapter 2 details how all my family got swept up into the beliefs of an American original sect which proclaimed that Jesus would return in 1975. Beliefs of the church were a homespun amalgamation of beliefs adopted from Jehovah's Witnesses, Seventh Day Adventists, and other groups

before it in early American history claiming to be surviving remnants of the apostolic church.

- Chapters 3, 4, 5, and 6 details how one becomes consumed in religious beliefs. It describes the process it takes to shed deeply held beliefs. Something must happen to shake you up, to cause you to question, make you a doubter and heretic, or you can never muster the energy it takes to get out of locked in belief whether a conservative, liberal, progressive, climate warmer, or Jesus freak. Its gravity field will always hold you within it.

- Chapter 7 covers Paul's beliefs of the end of the age, temple worship, and his expectations of what would happen to it.

- Chapter 8 introduces the third quest and a new look at Jesus of N. T. Wright.

- Chapter 9 is a summary of beliefs of conservative Bible scholars and theologians of the third quest, of Jesus' own worldview in their opinion.

- Chapter 10 covers Jesus' own personal beliefs of the end of the age.

- Chapter 11 details what the apostolic churches believed about a second coming.

- Chapter 12 asks the question if Jesus didn't know when the end would come.

- Chapter 13 discusses the issues of Jesus' existence. Was he God? Was he human? Which is it?

- Chapter 14 introduces how the Gospels must be read. They are literature and contain stories told by diverse people giving diverse accounts of Jesus' life and death.

- Chapter 15 points out a truth. The Gospels can't be harmonized.

- Chapter 16 illustrates that the Gospel of John contains didactic fictionalized portrayals of Jesus, which are not historical accounts of what Jesus said and did.

- Chapter 17 asks the question of why 126,000,000 Americans believe that Jesus will return in 2050.

- Chapter 18 is a summary of the third quest by conservative scholars.
- Chapter 19 presents what it appears Paul eventually believed about the end of the world and God's final plans.
- Chapter 20 is the conclusion.
- A special section includes the bios of key individuals of the third quest quoted in this book. Several of them have been lauded as "world authorities" or "world-class scholars" in their fields of study, of the historical Jesus, the New Testament, the Gospels, and Paul's epistles—the sources for our beliefs of the second coming.

Renee Descartes made a great statement about life. I personally don't think we start to learn until we reach this point. In looking back on life, I wish I had learned it a little sooner than I did.

> "If you would be a real seeker after truth, it is necessary that at least once in your life you doubt, as far as possible, all things."

Dallas Willard wisely said,

> "You are quite certainly, as I am the student of a few crucial people, living and dead, who have been there in crucial time and periods to form your standard responses in thought, feeling, and action. Thankfully the process is an ongoing one and is to some extent self-correcting."

Unfortunately, most people never get to experience what Dallas is talking about. They are true believers. True believers in politics, scientific circles, global warming, education, LGBT groups, and religion never question and never doubt, for they know. They read and absorb in their lives information that only confirms what they believe. They associate with people who likewise believe what they believe. They ridicule and mock those that believe differently. Contrary ideas and concepts are a threat. "Self-correction" never occurs in their lives. It is a world from which I escaped and I ask you if in some way maybe you are caught in a similar web of beliefs about Jesus and the future and you don't know it.

INTRODUCTION

"The paradox of Christianity always will be its conviction that Yahweh, most unsettling of all entities, whether actual or fictive, could in any sense have fathered Jesus of Nazareth, who might have been profoundly disturbed by what late-comers have reworked as his role."
                                    —Harold Bloom, *Jesus and Yahweh*

I was fifty-eight years of age when I focused on the meaning of the word *protagonist*. I am sure that I had heard it or read it before in my life, but that's when I got out the dictionary and looked up the meaning of the word. I had read the word in Jack Miles book *God—A Biography*. He had used the word to describe Yahweh of the Old Testament as being its main character. There are two protagonists of the Christian Bible—Yahweh of the Old and Jesus of the New Testament. This introduction is a brief synopsis of our two main characters of the Bible.

Yahweh. Walter Brueggemann, called by Marcus Borg, today's foremost Hebrew scholar of the Old Testament, writes in his magisterial work *Theology of the Old Testament* that

> "Indeed, the prayer of the coming kingdom in the mouth of Jesus [John 17:11] is not a prayer

for the coming of the kingdom of Jesus, but for the coming of God's rule."[1]

N. T. Wright, called by *Time Magazine* the world's foremost scholar on the life of Jesus, states that in the Lord's Prayer, Jesus is expressing the hope that God will come to rule from Jerusalem in the last days and to restore his people Israel and that only contorted exegesis can remove that element from the only prayer he taught the disciples.

Sociologist Peter Berger states in his book *Questions of Faith*, concerning Israel's God and the use of the term *God* used in the apostle's creed,

> "When the apostle creed affirms believe 'in God,' of course, it has a very specific divinity in mind—in classical Christian diction 'the God of Abraham, Isaac, and Jacob, the father of our Lord Jesus Christ.'"[2]

Wolfhart Pannenberg says the same thing in his book *Jesus— God and Man*:

> "His message can only be understood within the horizon of apocalyptic expectations, and the God whom Jesus called 'Father' was none other than the God of the Old Testament."[3]

The one spoken of as God in Jewish literature Christians call the Old Testament is the supernatural being called *Yahweh*. N.T. Wright says in his book *Simply Jesus* that the Old Testament God "is strange to us."[4] Philip Yancey explains it a little more clearly in his book *The Bible Jesus Read*:

> "Why does the Bible spend so much time on temples, priests, and rules governing sacrifices that no longer even exist? Why does God care about

defective sacrificial animals—limping lambs and bent wing doves—or about a goat cooked in it's mother's milk, and yet apparently not about people like the Amalekites? How can we make sense of the strange Old Testament, and how does it apply to our lives today?"[5]

Brevard Childs says of Yahweh,

"Although Christians confess that God who revealed himself to Israel is the God and father of Jesus Christ, it is still necessary to hear Israel's witness in order to understand who the father of Jesus Christ is."[6]

In this section, we are going to hear the witness of Israel in respect to the father of Jesus. The following information gives just a few stories about him in the Old Testament. There are dozens and dozens of similar accounts of his acts and dealings with Israel in what Christians commonly call the Old Testament.

In the first book of the Bible, after creating human beings and a beautiful world he called "good," he immediately became frustrated with the human beings he had made. He drove Adam and Eve from the garden of Eden for their natural inclination he had placed within them, which led them to eat from a tree he forbad them to eat (Gen. 3:1–8).

We get only to the sixth chapter in the book of Genesis, and we find he brought a worldwide flood that destroyed every human being except the family of Noah. He did all this because he repented that he had made humankind.

"The Lord saw that the wickedness of man was great in the earth, and that every imagination of the thoughts of his heart was only evil continually. And the Lord was sorry that he had made man on the earth, the Lord said, 'I will blot out man whom I have created from the face of the

ground, man and beast and creeping things and
birds of the air, for I am sorry that I have made
them'" (Gen. 6:5–7).

Richard Friedman writes, in his book *Who Wrote the Bible*, that
this is a strange way for God to be acting. He says that this

> "raises interesting theological questions, such
> as whether an all powerful, all knowing being
> would ever regret past actions."[7]

God doesn't tell us why he was upset with mindless creatures
such as dogs and cats and eagles and ospreys and otters and creeping
things, but he decided to kill them all. We are at this point in the
Bible story only six chapters away from God having viewed all his
creation and the author of Genesis says about him:

> "And God saw everything that he had made, and
> behold it was very good. And there was evening
> and there was morning, a sixth day" (Gen. 1:31).

Yahweh is already beginning to appear fickle. After Noah and
his family and the creaturely world disembarked the ark, God said he
would never destroy the world again. It states that he was so remorseful
for his actions that he included in his agreement animals and creeping
things and birds of the air. Perhaps the suffering of the animal world
touched his heart as the rains came down and the waters rose.

> "Behold, I establish my covenant with you and
> your descendants after you, and with every liv-
> ing creature that is with you, the birds, the cattle,
> and every beast of the earth with you, as many as
> came out of the ark. I establish my covenant with
> you, that never again shall all flesh be cut off by
> the waters of a flood, and never again shall there
> be a flood to destroy the earth" (Gen. 9:9–11).

That's good to know. But we will see there are other ways he could choose to do it.

Continuing through the first book of the Bible, we find God burned homosexuals with fire in the city of Sodom (Gen. 19). In Genesis 18, there is detailed an account that is striking concerning the actions of Yahweh before this event. On the eve of destroying Sodom and Gomorrah, Yahweh dined with Abraham on the Plain of Mamre eating the provisions of cheese and curds and veal from a freshly killed calf Abraham provided for him.

As he got ready to depart the meal and fellowship with Abraham, the Bible account says that Yahweh asked himself whether he should tell Abraham that he was going to destroy Sodom (Gen. 18:17–18). He decides to share that information with Abraham. Yahweh had heard of the wickedness of the city and chose to "go down" and see if the stories he had heard about it were true.

The narrative of the story shows Abraham carefully crafting questions to determine if his nephew Lot and his family who lived in Sodom would be killed in Yahweh's endeavors. It is an unbelievable accounting of the actions of Yahweh in the Old Testament.

To get to the question of whether God would save the city for the righteous people in it, Abraham starts off politely and obsequiously asking God if he would destroy the city if there were "fifty good folks" in the town. God tells him he would save it if there were fifty good people in the city.

Abraham continues with questions one at a time dropping the number down from fifty to ten, in what appears to be at least five different questions. God finally says he will save it for ten good people, and Abraham ceases his questions thinking that should cover Lot who must have had a family of ten or more. God told Abraham he would save it for ten righteous people living in the city.

God must not have counted as Abraham did, for he destroyed the city and turned Lot's wife into a pillar of salt for looking back on it as she walked up the hill moving away from it with her family.

In one of the strangest stories of God's actions in the Bible, we find God calling Moses to lead the children of Israel out of Egypt, and within days of having done so, God sought Moses to kill him.

The account is described in Exodus 4:2–26. After calling Moses and sending him to Egypt, God met him along the way on his journey where Moses had stopped to rest. The account says,

> "At a lodging place on the way the Lord met him
> and sought to kill him" (Exod. 4:24).

After he brought Israel out of Egypt, we find God again became so impatient with his human subjects that he threatened twice to kill every one of them and would have done so unless Moses had intervened. One of the accounts follows:

> "Furthermore, the Lord said to me, 'I have seen
> this people, and behold, it is a stubborn people;
> let me alone, that I may destroy them and blot
> out their name from under heaven; and I will
> make of you a nation mightier and greater than
> they'" (Deut. 9:13–14).

In what is called the "blessing and cursings" chapters of the Pentateuch describing God's relationship with his chosen people, Jack Miles writes in his book *God—A Biography* that the descriptions of horrors to be brought upon God's own people hadn't been matched until Dante's *Inferno* came along.

In Deuteronomy 28, a long list of Yahweh's curses is detailed by Moses, including the curse of the wombs of the women, the calves of their herds, and the lambs of their flocks. God promises to plague Israel with diseases, fevers, inflammation, scorching heat and drought, blight, and mildew. He pledges to make the earth iron and to turn the country into dust and powder. Enemies will be brought upon them and their land, and Moses tells them that God promises that

> "your carcasses will be food for all the birds of the
> air and the beasts of the field" (verse 26).

For those engaged to be married, Moses declares that God will take his bride away

> "and another will take her and ravish her"
> (verse 30).

The last sick depiction of what God will bring upon his people, Moses says,

> "The most tender and delicately bred woman among you, who would not venture to set the sole of her foot upon the ground because she is so delicate and tender, will grudge to the husband of her bosom, to her son and to her daughter, her afterbirth that come out from between her feet and her children whom she bears, because she will eat them secretly, for want of all things, in the siege and in the distress with which your enemy shall distress you in your towns" (Deut. 28:56–57).

Miles writes that

> "the sickening image of a woman fighting with her husband and children over who will eat her afterbirth is just the kind of unimaginable detail that only actual experience can provide a writer."[8]

Since most of the Old Testament was likely compiled by Ezra or Nehemiah years after Moses, they had heard stories of grisly accounts in Israel's history of scenes from horrible sieges during their many wars. We can imagine the description that might have been written had they known of Dachau and Buchenwald.

The entity or being or divinity or God promising all these events in the life of his chosen people was Jesus' father, according to beliefs of traditional Christianity. Brueggemann states concerning the God of the Old Testament that when you read of him from its pages, you always get the feeling that the ominous musical theme of the movie *Godfather* is "playing in the background."[9] His character is "cunning"[10] and he is inclined to act with "capricious irascibility."[11] He is also shown to be unmerciful and wrathful, visiting the sins of the fathers upon generations of children well past reasonableness for a merciful God. Yahweh didn't deal in terms of forgiveness of seventy times seven when he felt defied. Yahweh is what could be called ill-tempered.

The language and descriptions used by whoever wrote these passages of the Hebrew scriptures show God to be beyond our pale of understanding today as a God that we are to worship. Brueggemann says concerning the words used to tell us about the God of the Old Testament that they are metaphors.

Brueggemann writes,

> "This means that witnesses, who had other options available, who for whatever reasons chose to utter the matter in just this way, established through their utterances what is 'true' about the character of God."[12]

We can't help but get our images of him from the words they chose to describe his actions. If Paul is right, according to 2 Timothy 3:16, he stated that

> "all scripture is given by inspiration of God."

If we follow scriptural interpretation in a straight line, those very words would have been carefully crafted words selected by none other than God to reveal to us his story, his character, and his disposition. Many Christian groups believe God inspired all scripture in this way. I certainly did. According to Paul, God wrote the Bible. Those stories about him are God's own stories about himself.

Brueggemann writes concerning all the descriptions of stories we have of God in the Old Testament that,

> "...as often has been recognized, that these metaphors are open to a 'macho' understanding of the character of Yahweh, for they are associated with masculinity and virility. There is no doubt that these images for Yaweh, on the lips of Israel, have been taken to authorize masculine control that has often been heavy-handed, exploitative, and brutalizing."[13]

He continues in respect to Yahweh's character revealed in our stories of him, by stating,

> "Old Testament theology must reckon with an ominous dimension to Yahweh that falls outside any rule of law, outside vengeance as legitimate sanction."

Yahweh can be prone to a

> "play of violence that cannot be contained in any sense of justice."[14]

If Christians claim that the rather

> "devious ways of the God of the Old Testament are morally perfect then the accounts of him must either be disregarded or explained away."[15]

In a strange scene in Joshua, we see Yahweh showing up on the battlefield at Jericho with sword in hand, ready to jump into the bloody warfare of hand-to-hand combat Israelitish soldiers were about to wage. Possibly it was to make sure every Amalekite man, woman, and child was killed, as he had given orders to Israel armies.

This scene of Yahweh at work in Israel's history follows those we covered where he is shown regretting that he had made human beings, destroying humanity by flood, destroying Sodom with fire, threatening to kill Moses after calling him to lead Israel out of Egypt, and twice threatening to destroy the children of Israel after their being delivered from Egypt by his hand. Now he is armed and ready to fight on their behalf. The account is found in Joshua 5:13–15:

> "When Joshua was by Jericho, he lifted his eyes and looked, and behold a man stood before him with his drawn sword in his hand; and Joshua went to him and said to him, 'Are you for us, or for our adversaries?' He said, 'No; but as commander of the army of the Lord I have now come.' And Joshua fell on his face to the earth, and worshipped, and said to him, 'What does my lord bid his servant?' And the commander of the Lord's army said to Joshua, 'Put off your shoes from your feet; for the place where you stand is holy.' And Joshua did so."

After the days of Moses and Joshua, David, king of Israel, made the mistake of crossing Yahweh in counting the number of Israelitish men in his kingdom. Yahweh had forbidden Israelitish kings to take census counts lest they rely upon the numbers of their soldiers rather than on him for protection. Joab, David's leading general, tried to stop David from his action but didn't succeed. Yahweh's anger was kindled. David grasped his error too late.

The Bible says that God sent Gad the prophet to David. The account reads as follows:

> "Go and say to David, 'Thus says the Lord, three things I offer you; choose one of them, that I may do it to you.' So Gad came to David and told him, and said to him, 'Shall three years of famine come to you in your land? Or will you flee three

months before your foes while they pursue you? Or shall there be three days pestilence in your land? Now consider, and decide what answer I shall return to him who sent me.' Then David said to Gad, 'I am in great distress; let us fall into the hand of the Lord, for his mercy is great; but let me not fall into the hand of man.' So the Lord sent a pestilence upon Israel from the morning until the appointed time; and there died of the people from Dan to Beersheba seventy thousand men. And when the angel stretched forth his hand toward Jerusalem to destroy it, the Lord repented of the evil, and said to the angel who was working destruction among the people, 'It is enough; now stay your hand'" (2 Sam. 24:13–16).

As David surveyed the dead bodies and grisly aftermath of the actions of the Lord, he said to Yahweh,

"Lo, I have sinned, and I have done wickedly; but these sheep, what have they done?" (2 Sam. 24:17).

It was a good question. Yahweh killed seventy-thousand innocent bystanders for the sin of one man, David.

When we move into the books of the prophets, we have one description after another of the actions of God. Each of them claims to be speaking with the authority of God, and we read often introductions to their books with the words "thus sayeth the Lord!" Two apocalyptic proclamations follow, of which numerous others could be added.

Zephaniah in the Old Testament:

"I will utterly sweep away everything from the face of the earth, says the Lord, I will sweep away

33

humans and animals; I will sweep away the birds of the air and the fish of the sea."

"Neither will their silver nor their gold shall be able to deliver them on the day of the wrath of the Lord. In the fire of his jealous wrath, all the earth shall be consumed; for a full, yea, sudden end he will make and end of all the inhabitants of the earth" (Zeph. 1:2–3, 18).

In Jeremiah 4:23–26, Jeremiah states what he sees occurring in the future resulting from the actions of God:

"I looked at the earth, and it was formless and empty; and at the heavens, and their light was gone.
I looked at the mountains and they were quaking; all the hills were swaying.
I looked, and there were no people; every bird in the sky had flown away.
I looked, and the fruitful land was a desert; all its towns lay in ruins before the Lord, before his fierce anger."

Jack Miles writes in respect to all the wild utterances of Yahweh given to us from the minor and major prophets, as they are called, the following:

"Not to press any of these metaphors too far, God's conflicted personality and his checkered record do constitute the basic inventory of his developmental possibilities. To exploit that inventory, he calls on collaborators who are themselves conflicted personalities with checkered records. The three major prophets—Isaiah, Jeremiah, and Ezekiel—may be considered, respectively, the manic, the depressive, and the psychotic articulation of the prophetic messages. As for calm, sane, and moderate version of prophecy, in effect there are none. Sanity and calmness make their home not in Israel's prophetic tradition, but in its wisdom tradition."[16]

I shouldn't leave the Old Testament examples of Yahweh's antics without referencing the book of Job. In that classic book of the Old Testament, Yahweh bet the house with the devil that his servant Job would not curse God if he allowed Satan to take away all Job's wealth. And the Lord said to Satan,

> "'Have you considered my servant Job, that there is none like him on earth, a blameless and upright man, who fears God and turns away from evil.' Then Satan answered the Lord, 'Does Job fear God for naught? Hast thou not put a hedge about him and his house and all that he has on every side? Thou hast blessed the work of his hands, and his possessions have increased in the land. But put forth thy hand now, and touch all that he has, and he will curse you to your face'" (Job 1:8–11).

God took the wager. Satan went out from God's presence and took the lives with God's approval of the man's sons and daughters and their children, all his servants, the oxen and cattle, the sheep and camels, and the thousands of livestock Job owned. Job was smitten with terrible boils, and you probably know the rest of the story.

When one reads the Old Testament, N. T. Wright says, we find Jesus' father "strange." I would offer more descriptive words, like those Walter Brueggemann expresses in his book. Yahweh is shown to be in the Hebrew Bible as unmerciful, quick to anger, a flip-flopper, impatient, querulous, polemical, short-sighted, wrathful, retaliatory, and can't seem to make up his mind what he is going to do with humanity and his people Israel. He blows hot and cold.

Whether Yahweh can be characterized in this way, no one really knows for no one has ever talked with him, met him, seen him, or known him personally. We are looking at a literary creation when we read the Old Testament. Bible scholarship for years has recognized that there are no historical documents to verify any stories contained in the Hebrew Bible of Yahweh's actions and deeds with Israel nor his first-person quotes given to us. It is expressed clearly when Brueggemann states that the stories of Moses "may make use of older materials or the portrayal may be largely fictive."[17] Those would be the stories of God in all the accounts we have in the first five books. Bible scholars for years have believed that most of what we call the Old Testament wasn't assembled until the period of Ezra and Nehemiah—long past the time of Moses. An outstanding source relative to who produced the Old Testament is Richard Friedman's book—*Who Wrote the Bible?*

Brueggemann goes on to say that,

> "Of course, beyond Israel's insistence, we have no evidence that Yahweh has uttered these words. The testimony of the Bible would have us take Israel's word as certification that these promises have indeed been uttered with ensuring power and significance. Beyond such testimony, Israel can provide no warrants for the claim, and certainly historical research cannot touch the issue. Israel can only tell tales that function as vehicles for these awesome, decisive community-creating and history-generating utterances."[17]

Brueggemann summarizes Christianity's conundrum with Yahweh when he writes,

> "The truth of the matter, on any careful reading and without any tendentiousness, is that Old

36

Testament theological articulation doesn't conform to established church faith, either in its official declaration or its more popular propensities. There is much that is wild and untamed about the theological witness of the Old Testament that theology does not face. It is clear on my reading that the Old Testament is not a witness to Jesus Christ in any primary or direct sense, as Child proposes, unless one is prepared to sacrifice more of its text than is credible."[18]

Eric Voegelin, in his book *Order and History*, made the claim that Israel discovered God. He might have been more accurate to say Israel created Yahweh. He comes to us from the pages of the Old Testament. He is the father of our Lord Jesus Christ. He is the monotheistic God of the Jewish faith. He is the God to whom Jesus taught Christians to pray "thy kingdom come."

Brueggemann writes,

"Yahweh lives in, with, and under this speech, and in the end, depends on Israel's testimony for an access point in the world."[19]

Jesus. In the Old Testament, there is an interesting story of a change made in kings who ruled the ancient nation of Israel after the death of King David and later King Solomon, David's son. Rehoboam takes over after the death of his father Solomon. Naturally all his subjects were interested when he took over exactly what kind of king he would be compared to his father. When asked by a delegation of folks what kind of king he would be, Rehoboam makes a rather startling statement for his first day on the job:

"Whereas my father loaded you with a heavy yoke; my father disciplined you with whips, but I will discipline you with scorpions" (1 Kings 12:11).

When reading the New Testament, we find with Jesus that it is like father, like son. In that weird book of the Bible describing in detail the second coming of Jesus, we find an eternal house of horrors destined to unfold upon the whole world, not just the nation of Israel as it was with Yahweh and his blessings and cursings proclamations. Everyone knows generally of wars, pestilence, and disease and the four horsemen, but there is much more than that. There are trumpet plagues, vials of wrath, and bowls of wrath to be poured out upon humanity at Jesus' direction. The four horsemen and their activities are paled by angelic plagues which follow the horsemen's ventures on earth.

After the first six seals are broken, Revelation advances to what we might call the real beatings to be delivered. The whippings of a fallen world are now to be meted out by a special being. John, the author of Revelation, speaks of rich and poor, slaves and free men, kings of the earth and great men crying out saying,

> "Fall on us and hide us from the presence of Him
> who sits on the throne and from the wrath of the
> Lamb; for the great day of their wrath has come
> and who is able to stand" (Rev. 6:16–17).

Jesus, the wrathful Lamb of God, steps forward with special plagues for humanity.

In reading through the book of Revelation, we find that Jesus gives four angels power to harm the earth and the sea (Rev. 7:2–3). When the first sounds (Rev. 8:6–7), fire and hail and blood is to be rained upon the earth which causes one full third of the trees and the grass of the earth to be burned. Following that event, angels strike the oceans of the world and one-third of the oceans will be turned into blood (Rev. 8:8–9). One-third of the whales and porpoises and creatures of the sea die from the results.

After that, an angel strikes the rivers and springs and fresh water sources of the world and one full third are made undrinkable and bitter (Rev. 8:10). Following that one full third of the stars are darkened and special locusts are released upon the earth to sting humankind, creating five months of torture to the point that "men will seek death and not find it" (Rev. 9:5). A secondary plague which follows all these turns the sea into blood and "every living thing died in the sea." After that, Jesus turns up the heat of the sun upon the earth until men "blaspheme God." After reading all this detailed account of what Jesus will do, it sounds just like John has plagiarized the words of Yahweh in Jeremiah and Zephaniah we have just read.

When Jesus appears on the scene of desolation riding a white horse and "dressed in a robe dipped in blood" (Rev. 19:13), he is getting close to exceeding the shock and awe of his father in the Old Testament. John the Divine shows the whole earth, including the oceans and fish of the sea and grass and forests of the world to be an ecological disaster. Billions of human beings will be dead. Rotting carcasses will be strewn over the earth and the forests burned and scorched and the oceans will be filled with bloated and decaying marine life. The earth that he participated in creating, according to our Christian beliefs, is almost destroyed. Upon his arrival on his thigh and on his robe, he has a name written, "*KING OF KINGS, AND LORD OF LORDS.*" The Prince of Peace, The Advocate, The Redeemer, The Man of Sorrows, The High Priest, The Good Shepherd, The Savior, The Bread of Life, The Living Water, The Dayspring, The Bright Morning Star, The True Vine, The Faithful and True Witness, The Only Begotten Son, finally sets his feet on planet Earth. If we read the Bible literally, it will be a smoking mess upon his arrival, thanks to him. This is the Jesus over 126 million Americans anticipates arriving by 2050.

Jim Bakker writes in his book, *Time Has Come*, of these events and the evangelical outlook of the end of the age:

> "Hailstones weighing a hundred pounds each will pelt the earth, and yet men 'blasphemed God because of the plague of hail, because the plague was extremely severe' (16:20). No wonder that when the Lord returns he is going to create a new heaven and a new earth. This earth is going to be a mess!"

Paul wrote in one of his letters that the "whole creation groans" waiting for the joyous and celebrated day of his coming (Rom. 8:22). Paul died oblivious to how badly the creation apparently will be groaning and staggering and struggling at the end of the ages resulting from the acts of Jesus before his arrival. Paul did not live to read the book of Revelation. When Paul wrote of the creation groaning, apparently, he wrote the statement and was speaking of natural creation itself and the chaos which exists within it of hurricanes, earthquakes, floods, droughts, and cataclysmic natural disasters. Exegetes tell us that Paul was also referring to the vicious drives of natural selection in the animal world that await a time when the prophets spoke of the deserts blooming and the lamb lying down with the wolf and the nature of animals would be changed and the earth would be made into an Edenic paradise. Paul hadn't laid eyes on the book of Revelation and read the acts of the Lamb to fall upon the world before his second coming.

In the Old Testament, neither Yahweh nor Moses ever spoke of an ever-burning hell fire as punishment for lack of obedience to the old covenant. A long and blessed life was the reward for obedience. Punishment came in this life at the hand of God. It could be short and quick.

Traditional Christian beliefs tell us that when Jesus made a "new covenant," Jesus added as punishment for sinners an ever-burning hell wherein finite creatures are tortured forever for disobedience under the new covenant. Darrell Bock states in *Jesus and the Restoration of Israel,*

> "Jesus contemplated...unending suffering for those who turned their back on him."[20]

Karen Armstrong commented in her book *The History of God,* that Jesus had tried to liberate men and women from the base servitude of the God of the Old Testament, who was a "tyrant.".[21] It is most interesting that Thomas Jefferson in defending his beliefs in God and Jesus that Jefferson said that when Jesus came to this earth, he corrected the Hebrew descriptions of the actions and life of God in the Old Testament "by giving them juster notions of his [God's] attributes and government."[22]

When we look at Jesus' life described in the last book of the Bible, Jesus didn't tame or tone down any characteristics of the Old Testament God. Jesus magnified them a thousand times over! When the canon closes of the New Testament, Jesus Christ has blown away the wrathful God of the Old Testament! Who is the John 3:16 God?

In the New Testament, Jesus said, "If you have seen me you see the father" (John 14:9). Apparently, it would be so. Like Rehoboam, Jesus in the book of Revelation exceeds his father an infinity more in severity when it comes to treatment of his subjects. Despite everything said and written about Jesus and his being a metaphor of the love of God for us by Jesus showing us in the flesh God's qualities of love, grace, peace, kindness, mercy, patience, forgiveness, and tenderness, before the New Testament canon is closed, Jesus has eventually morphed into the same wrathful and capricious character of his Father in the Old Testament

John McArthur describes how humanity must deal with Jesus and Yahweh.

> "Now there are a number of different aspects to the wrath of God. There is what we could call eternal wrath because it is the punishment that God brings upon unbelieving sinners forever in hell…that's eternal wrath. And the Bible speaks often of that. There is also eschatological wrath, that is the wrath of God that is released at the end of the world described by some of the Old Testament prophets, described by Jesus Christ Himself in the Olivet Discourse and clearly laid out for us in the book of Revelation" (Sermon— John McArthur).

Calvin and Luther both taught that most of humankind was predestined to be eternally punished in a lake of fire. Calvin said,

"We call predestination God's eternal decree by which he determined with himself what he will to become of each man. For all are not created in equal condition; rather, eternal life is foreordained for some, eternal damnation for others… Therefore, as any man has been created to one or the other of these ends, we speak of him as predestined to life or to death."[23]

If the third quest for Jesus has any historical accuracy at all, when it comes to the painted picture of Jesus by evangelical Christianity, the phrase made popular years ago in space exploration and the Apollo 13 movie which followed ("Houston, we have a problem") applies to a badly needed update that needs to be made of our Christian portrayals of Jesus. It has everything to do with whether Jesus will return to this earth by 2050 believed by 126,000,000 American citizens. I found the historical Jesus didn't believe nor teach or preach Tim LaHaye's or John McArthur's end of the world scenarios nor did Jesus believe in mine.

Portrayals of Jesus' second coming have been indelibly portrayed in the *Left Behind* series. The series has been on the *New York Times, USA Today*, and *Publishers Weekly* best seller list numerous times. These books portray Jesus' second coming as one giant worldwide indescribable nightmare for humanity upon his return. This book is specifically addressed to those who anxiously await a world described in Revelation—those who seem to relish its day. I think, when you study Jesus' life as he really lived, thought, and taught, you will be disappointed to find your beliefs of the end of the world don't match his.

Another significant issue I try to raise in this book for Christendom is exactly what Walter Brueggemann points out in his book *Theology of the Old Testament*. Christian theology hasn't dealt with the God of the Old Testament in explaining exactly how he is a God of love, which Jesus came to reveal. Neither has Christianity dealt with the Lamb of God and the Prince of Peace arriving with a robe dipped in blood after almost destroying the planet. Where is

Jesus' life a metaphor of the love of God for humanity in his final acts before his arrival? Jesus arrives like the Dragon Lady atop her dragon in the current *Game of Thrones* series, spewing out death and destruction upon the citizens of the world. Between the two testaments and our protagonists, Yahweh and Jesus, it is a coin toss for which personality contains the most anger and wrath with earth's inhabitants at the end of the age. Something doesn't jive in our Christian interpretations of the Old Testament God and the person called Jesus Christ. Does Christendom really believe these are the two literary characters we all will meet one day in the second coming, if we are alive and well, on planet Earth at the second coming?

1

THE SECOND COMING

"In fact, don't believe most of what you read about the Rapture. Many Christians, particularly in North America, have been taught for the last century and a half that when Jesus returns he will come down from 'heaven' and that his faithful people (i.e. Christians) will then fly upward into the sky to meet him and be taken to heaven with him forever...But it's a complete misunderstanding. It's based on a misreading of what Paul says about the return of Jesus in I Thessalonians 4:14–17, just four verses, with the idea of a "rapture" in only one, as the basis for a complete theory of everything."

—N. T. Wright, *Simply Jesus*

October 22, 2013

None other than Billy Graham sounded the alarm again for the second coming of Jesus, having done so for over fifty years. That same week, Michele Bachman, congresswoman from Minnesota and later candidate for president, claimed the world had entered the last days.

In the same month, Benjamin Netanyahu told the United Nations General Assembly "biblical prophecies are being realized." In 2013, a poll by the California-based Barna Group found that four in ten Americans—and 77 percent of evangelical Christians—believe the "world is now living in the Biblical end times."

Graham said,

> "When Christ comes again—as he repeatedly promised to do—he will come through the heavens with glory and power, accompanied by a host of angels. All the earth will see His coming, and even His enemies will realize they have been opposing the Son of God. The Bible says, 'Look, he is coming with the clouds, and every eye will see him, even those who pierced him...So shall it be!'" (Revelation 1:7).

The year set off a new round of predictions of the end of the world. Bestselling books on Amazon included *The Harbinger: The Ancient Mystery That Holds the Secret of Americas Future*, by rabbi Jonathan Cahn, and *Four Blood Moons: Something Is About to Change*, by Pastor John Hagee. Paul McGuire, an internationally recognized expert on prophetic events, said on Fox News, "I think there is going to be an explosion of interest in the end times like nothing we have ever seen before." The same year saw the production of *Noah*, portraying the destruction of the earth by God in the flood, starring Russell Crowe. Jesus had said concerning his coming, it would be as in the days of Noah. It seemed to fit the theme of the year for things to come.

Since the time of Christ, millions of people have gone through the disappointing experience of being foiled by religious leaders who proclaim the imminent return of Jesus. The tale of my life has been lived repeatedly and will continue to be lived again and again by those who proclaim to know the return of Jesus.

There is a quiet spot located on a sixty-three-acre parcel of land in Independence, Missouri. It has nothing to do with the Harry

Truman home place in the same city but much to do with Jesus Christ. It is the location where an American-original religious group has been waiting for the return of Jesus for nearly two hundred years. It is the site of the first Mormon temple ever built.

The land was purchased in 1831 for $130. The purpose for purchase of the land was that God had revealed to Joseph Smith, founder of the Mormon Church, that Jesus was to return to that exact spot. It was the ancient location of the garden of Eden. It is to become the future location upon Christ's return for the city of Zion. In obedience to a commandment received the day before dedication on August 2, 1831, twelve Mormon men representing the twelve tribes of Israel laid a symbolic foundation stone for the city of Zion and consecrated the land for the gathering of the saints. Mormons are still waiting at the site.

Today while writing this section, an air of prophetic urgency exists with tonight's "blood moon." The Bible speaks in Joel of the moon being turned into blood in the day of the Lord. *Four Blood Moons* was published, detailing how specific moon phases were building and the moon spoken in Joel was possibly going to occur in our day signaling the return of Christ. It became a best seller, spending more than 150 days on Amazon's top 150 by April 2014. For the week ending March 30, 2014, it was the ninth bestselling paperback, per *Publishers Weekly*. Tonight is the final phase of a cycle that could bring Jesus' arrival.

Cosmologists point out that the moon turns red in color because the sun, moon, and the earth are lined up in a straight line while being in orbit. The earth blocks the light of the sun and creates a hazy red color. They can predict exactly what years these will occur. The next big blood moon which scientists easily forecast will be 2033. I have no doubt I will not see the return of Jesus this evening or next week or next year. I don't know if I will live to the next blood moon.

At the same time when turning to the WMD Superstore, it has a movie for sale giving the signs and indications of Jesus imminent return. The teaser says,

"Is the return of Jesus closer than you think? What are the most powerful prophetic signs being fulfilled in the earth today? How is the new Middle East after the Arab Spring aligning with the testimony of the biblical prophets? What are the little known prophetic signs that few are paying attention to?"

The *Daily Telegraph* had an article posted that a sect led by Chris McCann, *E-Bible Fellowship* who is an "all-around God expert," has announced that tomorrow the earth will be burned by fire and destroyed. Chris says that even though God promised he would never destroy the earth by water, he points out that God said in 2 Peter 3 it would be destroyed again not by water, but by fire. And, for some humor regarding Jesus' second coming, a sign on a small Baptist church recently read, "Jesus is coming, hopefully before the election."

If you would like to see all those groups, including the early New Testament church, that have been disillusioned with no appearance of a promised second coming, go to the Web and search "groups that believe in the second coming of Jesus."

One of them you will find is Seventh Day Adventists. Adventists gleaned their beliefs from William Miller. Miller was an itinerant preacher in the 1800s, who upon return from fighting bravely in the war of 1812, devoted himself to a study of the Bible. He found after a long and detailed study of Daniel 8:13–14 that Jesus return was approaching.

"Basing his calculations principally on Daniel 8:14: 'Unto two thousand and three hundred days; then shall the sanctuary be cleansed,' Miller assumed that the cleansing of the sanctuary represented the Earth's purification by fire at Christ's Second Coming. Then, using the interpretive principle of the 'day-year principle,' Miller (and others) interpreted a day in prophecy to read not as a 24-hour period, but rather as a calendar year. Further, Miller became convinced that the 2,300-day period started in 457 B.C. with the decree to rebuild Jerusalem by Artaxerxes I of Persia. Simple calculation then revealed that this period would end in 1843. Miller records, 'I was thus brought… to the solemn conclusion, that in about twenty-five years from that time 1818 all the affairs of our present state would be wound up.'"[1]

Several years later, Ellen G. White was influenced by his predictions and wrote her own end-of-the-world scenario in a book titled the *Great Controversy*, borrowed by Herbert Armstrong in his prophecies of the world tomorrow which became my vision of the future. White's book was a forerunner of Lindsey's book, *The Late Great Planet Earth*. She was the founder of the Seventh Day Adventist church. It is getting some publicity as this is being written in that Ben Carson, a current republican presidential candidate, is a Seventh Day Adventist. Maybe he would have made a good president but members of my church could not have voted for him for it was a belief of the church Christians should not participate in politics. Jesus' kingdom was not of this world.

The timing of White's book on the second coming of Jesus was keyed off Archbishop Ussher chronology which gave six thousand years of human history to mankind to mess around, and after that, Jesus was going to come back and straighten it all out in a thousand-year millennial rule over the earth. Ussher was an Irish bishop in 1650. He made a study of the lives of people detailed in the Bible and added them all up and came up with a period that had elapsed since creation. Bart Ehrman writes about him:

"Ussher based his calculations on the genealogies of the Bible (which state not only who begat whom, but also indicate, in many instances, how long each of the people thus begotten lived) and a detailed study of other ancient sources, such as Babylonian and Roman history. On these grounds, he argued that the world was created in 4004 BCE—in fact, at noon on October 23. It was printed widely in King James Bibles and continues to be believed by nonevolutionarily minded Christians today."[2]

We are again entering a period in history that religion is dominating our world and God is taking over its news events and headlines. We have witnessed people being burned alive in the name of God on nightly news. Beheadings, bombings, and events one after that we can hardly conceive occur daily. Iran is committed to destroying Israel. Benjamin Netanyahu, to try to reach out to the leadership of Iran, wrote on his Web site that Iran is controlled by a "theocratic tyranny." We are the "great Satan" to Muslims. You can't turn on your TV set and not hear someone addressing the topic of a religious war that is coming—Christianity against Islam—just like the crusades. The *Washington Post* has posted an editorial today after the shocking incident of Paris shootings by Muslims killing over 150 Europeans. It says that the whole purpose of mass shootings in Europe was to provoke a situation whereby "through this provocation, it seeks to set conditions for an apocalyptic war with the West." The Florida night club massacre soon followed, which involved the largest mass murder of Americans in history all done by a Muslim. Millions of Americans see all this leading to the arrival of Jesus on earth.

Weeks before the Paris shootings which electrified Europe and the Western world, then speaker of the House John Boehner tweeted concerning all that is happening in the Middle East that "the world is on fire." Tweets from Netanyahu's office warned of a "nuclear holocaust" in the nation of Israel because of the agreement. After the deal was made, John Kerry said,

> "Dubai—The United States said on Tuesday it was very disturbed by anti-U.S. hostility voiced by Iran's top leader after a nuclear deal, as both countries' top diplomats sought to calm oppo-

sition to the accord from political hardliners at home. U.S. Secretary of State John Kerry said a speech by Iranian Supreme Leader Ali Khamenei on Saturday vowing to defy American policies in the region despite a deal with world powers over Tehran's nuclear program was 'very troubling'" (*Reuters*).

Headlines today in Iranian newspapers were "Down with America—Death to Israel." A newspaper article featured the first Islamic child beheading of an infidel adult!

We have seen the world dramatically change in the last eight years. Currently ISIS is fueling Islamic radicals pushing for destruction of the West. As they die out, another will take its place. We are in a swift downward spiral economically as a country with huge national debt out of control despite a booming current stock market. Our culture as a nation is becoming weird and bizarre with an assault being made upon traditional views of sexuality, marriage, and the family structure we have known. Going to the toilet in public becomes confusing to some. The world has a refugee crisis not known since World War II.

In the meantime, Christians are looking for the return of Christ to solve problems. NSA is building the largest spy center in the world. The Mark of the Beast appears to be on the horizon, some feel. You can't turn on Fox News without seeing multiple ads for prepping for an apocalyptic event. A financial collapse is coming. Build a shelter to protect yourself. Change your currency into gold. Get ready—Jesus is coming. The wrath of God is soon going to be poured out. He has had it, and this whole world is about to have unleashed the king of kings who has been waiting in the wings for his second coming to finally rule the world. *Forty-one percent of our population believes this.*

Dr. Natasha O'Hear is lecturer in Theology and Visual Art at ITIA, St. Andrews, United Kingdom. Her research interests center on visualizations of biblical texts and the book of Revelation and the use of biblical terms gleaned from it, to describe daily events in newspapers, TV, movies, and our speech. Hardly a day goes by that one doesn't hear the words *apocalyptic, Armageddon, apocalypse,* or other descriptive term, all pulled from the book of Revelation. The latest example at the time of writing, almost beyond belief, was a statement in the *New York Times* of Hillary Clinton stating regarding the choice for president. She said, "I am the only person standing between you and Armageddon."

As if biblical sounding words aren't rolling off the press fast enough, a recent article appeared in the *Daily Telegraph* dubbing New Zealand "apocalypse island" for the rush of mega wealthy persons to the island purchasing acres of land and building safe places for when the world falls apart. New Zealand is supposed to be a place to survive a nuclear winter.

Movies, one after another, portray galactic battles between the forces of good and evil. Individuals warn of the end of the world through climate change, nuclear war, nanotechnology, or some other kind of manmade disaster.

When Jesus walked the earth, he believed that he was living right where people feel they are living today in expecting his return in 2050 except he lived in 30 AD. As 126,000,000 people believe Jesus' return is imminent, Jesus believed that in his day, God's return to establish his kingdom was imminent and he taught his followers its expectation as we will see from this book. It isn't a Sunday morning sermon one hears today.

Rudolph Bultmann, a German theologian, rocked the Christian world in 1957 when he published his book titled *Jesus Christ and Mythology*. Bultmann was a German theologian who lived through Hitler's rise and fall, World War II, the holocaust, and the horrors of that period in history. He wrote,

> "It is possible that the Biblical eschatology may rise again. It will not rise in its old mythological form but from the terrifying vision that modern technology, especially atomic science, may bring about the destruction of our earth through the abuse of human science and technology. When we ponder this possibility, we may feel the terror and

anxiety which were evoked by the eschatological preaching of the imminent end of the world."[3]

There couldn't have been a more prescient or prophetic statement. It was written almost thirty years before Hal Lindsey's book *The Late Great Planet Earth* burst on the scene. Bultmann was dead wrong on one part of what he wrote, for mythology of old has taken over the American mind in respect to the end of the world. He hadn't read the *Left Behind* series nor Hal Lindsey's books nor *Four Blood Moons* nor dozens of others, which all are newly woven mythical creations of the second coming based on Revelation and the prophets of old. It was forty years before the block buster series *Left Behind* arrived resulting in sixty-five million book sales. These books are saturated with mythology. All are laced with terror and anxiety and intended to make your pulse race visualizing mythical events occurring at the return of Jesus. It is better than *Star Wars* and *X Men* combined.

On the other side of the ledger, we have all the cries we hear daily of gloom and doom and destruction because of science creating a nightmare of some type which will bring the end of the world, whether global warming or robots taking over the earth, a nuclear winter, or nanotechnology devouring us. It has spawned prepper television reality shows and prepper movements across the country. Killer pandemics, World War III, martial law, solar mega storms, asteroid strikes, and societal chaos are some of the other things that preppers are worried about.

The *Charlotte Observer* reported recently that,

> "Three decades after his PTL empire near Charlotte crumbled amid financial and sex scandals, Jim Bakker is back on TV with a different, darker message:
>
> The Apocalypse is coming and you better get ready.
>
> Ready to be judged by God, sure. But the main mission of "The Jim Bakker Show" – broadcast from a Christian compound deep in

the Ozark Mountains of Missouri – appears to be to sell you fuel-less generators, doomsday guide-books and freeze-dried food with a shelf-life of up to 30 years."

In 2003, Bakker launched a new ministry called Morningside, located near Branson, Missouri. Bakker has also created a new PTL Network, which is an acronym for Prophets Talking Loud. Bakker's ministry has focused on the "prepper" movement, putting an emphasis on the sale of survival food, equipment and health products. Mixed with survivalist sales pitches are doomsday prophecies. His predictions often focus on supposedly imminent threats from the government or acts of judgment from God. In his book titled *Time Has Come*, Bakker states that he believes the country should prepare to experience and live through the great tribulation to soon strike the world. He believes the system of "Babylon" described in Revelation to be most likely New York City and that it will fall in one hour, either by an asteroid strike or terrorist nuclear bomb. His views of impending doom are not too different from mega wealthy individuals purchasing land in New Zealand to escape the apocalypse they see coming upon the world from whatever source that may bring it about.

Commercial business enterprises are not going to miss out on making a buck on the end of the world scares we are witnessing. *Fox News* announced today on their website:

> "If you've ever fretted about what to snack on during an apocalypse, Costco has got you covered. The wholesale superstore has rolled out a $6,000 food kit featuring 36,000 servings of food that can feed a family of four for a year, according to its online listing."

The second coming of Jesus and the end of the age are central to more of the political and social climate of this country than we would like to admit. It pervades our collective conscious as a nation.

Look at the bumper sticker on the car in front of you while driving or read the road signs as you travel along the road, all blaring messages about a judgment day and Jesus' return and your place in it if you don't repent. Bumper stickers have warnings posted to beware of driverless cars. By the time this book will be published, there will be dozens of events crowding out the last one pointing to the second coming.

One of the most recent events in the world portending prophetic fulfillment for those on a countdown to Jesus return, has been President Trump's announcement to move the U.S. Embassy from Tel Aviv to Jerusalem. A modern day Sanhedrin, made up of Jewish leaders in Jerusalem, advocating the building of a third temple, importuned Trump to follow in the footsteps of Cyrus, King of Persia 2000 years ago, and assist in building a final temple in Jerusalem. Religious activists, Jewish and Christians see this as a first step in establishing a temple that Christians believe Paul's book of Thessalonians, tells them will be defiled before Jesus' return.

When you study what Jesus believed and taught while on earth and what he believed about himself as he lived as a human being, you will find his beliefs rule out that he personally believed the world was soon coming to an end as John the Devine describes it in the book of Revelation and we have in the *Left Behind* series and we see in all the Hollywood productions.

2

True Believers

"Mass movements are usually accused of doping their followers with hope of the future while cheating them of the enjoyment of the present."

"No faith is potent unless it is also faith in the future; unless it has a millennial component. So, too, an effective doctrine: as well as being a source of power, it must also claim to be a key to the book of the future."

—Eric Hoffer, *The True Believer*

Before the return of Jesus, Revelation 12:9 says that the whole world will have drunk the Kool-Aid of Satan. In my previous church experience, we gloated in the belief that wasn't us. It was everybody else in the world.

True believers drive political and religious groups. They live among us. There is no more nirvanic state, no more peaceful state, no greater exhilaration, and no higher high than to be a true believer and drink the Kool-Aid. It is wonderful to know that you know that you know the "truth." It's better than drugs. That is the world of political, scientific, educational, personal, and religious movements.

If you have ever been one, you hopefully wake up realizing one day you were snake bit, poisoned, drugged, placed under a spell, and somehow awakened out of it all to live to tell the story.

I graduated high school in the lethargic and long forgotten east Texas community of Big Sandy, once a dynamic and flourishing town with an economy feeding off jobs provided from gushing oil wells in Kilgore, Gladewater, Longview, and surrounding towns. I lived there with my parents not for anything the community offered but for revelation from God. In a 440-acre plot east of Big Sandy, we believed God had chosen to place his name upon a parcel of land covered with scrub oak trees and sand burr patches. It was mostly occupied by armadillos and scorpions and yellow jacket hornets, which I frequently was stung as a kid while mowing the grass planted around a large redwood Quonset-looking building used for congregational meetings of our church. God allegedly had made it known to leaders of our church this was a special spot where God chose to dwell.

The shaping of my religious life was that of my parents, as it is of every child born in this world. My father was a graduate of the University of Arkansas. His graduation year was the same year Hitler started bombing Poland, and the world was soon into World War II. Upon his graduation, he became a teacher and began his teaching career by riding a mule several miles one way from his home to teach eight grades in a one-room country schoolhouse.

In the mid-1940s, my mother and father found themselves searching for God and answers for a world which saw World War II ingenuity and genius gift mankind with the ability to erase human life from the planet. The world experienced some of the worst human atrocities known to humanity in the holocaust. Countries were rocked with a war like none other on earth. After the world was educated to the power and explosive capability of the bombs dropped on Hiroshima and Nagasaki, the statements of Jesus concerning the end of the age that "except those days were shortened, no flesh would be saved alive" (Matt. 24:10) convinced my mother and father they were living in the end times. Contrary to the words of the wise preacher in the book of Ecclesiastes, there was something new under the sun. The atomic age had begun.

Biographer David McCullough, writing of President Truman in his book titled *Truman*, stated that upon Truman's learning at Potsdam of the explosive capability of nuclear weapons, President Truman wrote in his diary Wednesday, July 25, 1945, that this weapon might be the "fire of destruction"[1] prophesied in the Bible. Truman also felt during his presidency when he was witnessing the return of Jews to Palestine, that it was a possible adumbration of the events leading to the second coming of Christ, and it influenced his decisions in expediting the founding of the nation of Israel. In a ceremony in the White House after US recognition of Israel as a state, Truman stood listening with tears running down his cheeks when Chief Rabbi of Israel, Isaac Herzog, said to him, "God put you in your mother's womb so you would be the instrument to bring the rebirth of Israel after two thousand years."[2] This was, for prophecy watchers, a sequential step to occur before the return of Christ.

Even though Truman felt we possibly live in Bible times and he had possibly just seen the fire of destruction prophesied in the Bible at the explosion of bombs on Hiroshima and Nagasaki, he penned a note to his staff before his departure from the White House, which read,

> "It is part of my responsibility as Commander in Chief of the Armed Forces to see to it that our country is able to defend itself against any possible aggressor. Accordingly, I have directed the Atomic Energy Commission to continue its work of all forms of atomic weapons, including the so-called hydrogen or superbomb..."[3]

Albert Einstein warned that annihilation beckoned. Prophecy watchers saw this as the world moving one step closer to the time to be fulfilled when Jesus said, "except those days would be shortened no flesh would be saved alive." In case you don't have an apocalyptic church background, this phrase of Jesus is considered to define exactly when the end would come of which Jesus spoke in the New Testament. The end of the world was to be a time when human kind could destroy itself. Jesus is supposed to come before that happens. His second coming must be hurried by God to prevent human annihilation. Apparently as we have seen in the introduction, the human population on earth at his coming would need to be saved alive so that Jesus might almost destroy them himself in the great tribulation.

That statement of Jesus concerning the shortening of time, it is said, even later in life to have influenced the mind of President Ronald Reagan, who "was known to express frequently his conviction that we find ourselves at the very brink of the Last Days."[4] Reagan had read Hal Lindsey's book *The Late Great Planet Earth*. Nuclear proliferation had grown to the point in Reagan's days that even presidents' minds were being influenced by Jesus' words in Matthew's Gospel.

The *Late Great Planet Earth*, written by Lindsey, was first published in 1970. Following it were two other books by Lindsey based on prophetic interpretation of scriptures in the Bible, titled *Satan Is Well and Alive on Planet Earth* and *Countdown to Armageddon*. By the 1990s, twenty-eight million books had been sold of his original book, most of them sold in the United States. Lindsey's final "predictions" were that he felt Jesus would return and the end of the age would occur in the 1980s, with prophetic events occurring in the world as he saw it. So far, he has only missed it about a quarter century plus.

These viewpoints of presidents of our country concerning the end of the age were years later to prejudice founders of the Jesus Seminar in their search for the historical Jesus. One of the ambitions of the group in their studies, they said, was to steer our national leaders away from end-of-the-world scenarios by pointing out this really wasn't the message of the historical Jesus. Their advice to Ronald Reagan was that for him to follow apocalyptic foreign policy decision-making wasn't good for the country.

The Jesus Seminar found instead that Jesus was a wandering hippie type, a "subversive" secular sage, who had nothing to say about the end of the world and a judgement day coming. Possibly the moral beliefs of Robert Funk, who founded the Jesus Seminar, might have influenced him from interpreting the Jesus story, in that he advises that Christians should "endorse responsible, protected recreational sex between consenting adults."[5] Funk found Jesus to be "irreligious, irreverent, and impious."[6] Funk also wrote that Jesus "did not pre-scribe behavior or endorse specific religious practices."[7] In the next couple of chapters, it will be shown that Jesus fully endorsed, sup-ported, and urged citizens of his world to continue in the religious practices and beliefs they had grown up with in Israel.

During the 1940s, my mother and father began to listen to a radio-church evangelistic program called the *World Tomorrow*. Long before FCC rules and changes on radio frequency and the airwaves, back when there were no cell phones nor Internet nor FM radio, they listened at night from a big superpowered radio station with the call letters of XELO booming signals out of Mexico that reached way up into the hills of Arkansas. The program called *The World Tomorrow* was the proselyting outreach of a small religious group that was then called the Radio Church of God. The program heralded the soon coming millennium and a new age just around the corner, a time when the lion would lay down with the lamb. Once TV was utilized to evangelize others, the program opened with a Hollywood shot of a massive lion laying down beside a lamb. You couldn't see the large pain of glass between the two of them. Years later, the name of the church was switched to the Worldwide Church of God. The small cultish church was led by its charismatic leader Herbert W. Armstrong and later his son, Garner Ted Armstrong. You can go to a Web site and "Google" the names and read until your eyes pop out. You may find it interesting.

I remember my dad listening to Herbert over the radio when I was six years of age. He was smoking at the time. I recall it clearly because while he was sitting with his ear to a radio about half the size of our refrigerator, he dropped a burning cigarette he was smoking on my bare leg while I was sitting in his lap. The year was 1947. That is my first remembrance of Herbert Armstrong. He influenced my life and my family's life forever.

By the time 1953 arrived, Mom and Dad were seriously involved in changing directions in life and breaking away from the beliefs of their own mother and father and the community in which they lived. They stopped attending a small Church of Christ in north central

Arkansas and turned to Herbert Armstrong for the keys of what life is all about.

My father owned and was operating a hardware store in the little town of Yellville in north central Arkansas not far from the White River Development, made popular by Bill and Hillary Clinton and recently was discussed again in the 2016 election as Hillary ran for president. Since Herbert taught that Saturday was the Sabbath day and was a day of rest with no business to be conducted, Dad started to close the store on Friday evening before sunset and all-day Saturday. Not only did he close his store, he took out a full-page advertisement in the small county newspaper in Marion County. In it he stated his reason for closing the store was that Saturday was the day of worship for true Christians instead of Sunday.

Upon publishing the advertisement, he received a letter from his local pastor of the Church of Christ warning our family of taking the first steps toward eternal punishment by keeping the seventh day of the week as a Sabbath day for a day of worship. My mother and father had become guilty of turning their backs to grace.

> "Norvel, these enclosures are a 'last ditch effort' to try to help you and your wife to regain your faith and footing before it is eternally too late; it might be futile on my part, but anyway, I'm supposed to try—and I am convinced that to do it with the pen is more effective than orally, but I'll be glad to talk with you personally if you so desire.
>
> The step you have taken is usually the first step in the direction of utter repudiation of New Testament Christianity in its entirety.
>
> Let me urge upon you people that unless you do correct your error you are going to have much to regret for a long, long time.
>
> Most sincerely,
> O. L. Mankamyer"

The enclosures which were referenced by his local pastor were an article he had written titled "Which Day Shall We Keep, the Lord's Day or the Jewish Sabbath" and an article on *Saturday Adventists*.

The article by their pastor contained mindless theology quoting certain scriptures as proof that Jesus did away with the Sabbath and the law, something of the nature one finds in tracts left on your auto windshield while shopping. One of the most ridiculous statements in what was written was his pastor quoting Jesus statement on the cross where Jesus said, "It is finished" (John 19:28–30), and stating that what Jesus meant to say was that his death was to be the "end of the law" or end of law keeping of Christians. The law was nailed to the cross and our sins with it. Grace had begun and all one needed to do for salvation was to accept Jesus Christ as personal savior. This was Jesus whole purpose for his life and death.

We will find when we study Jesus life that he had no forethought at all for stopping or negating Sabbath keeping by any action he took upon the cross, either for Jew or Gentile. He didn't have in mind doing away with the Jewish Sabbath, abolishing the temple and animal sacrifices and ritual, and freeing the people of the nation from its religious laws and practices, which is common understanding of Jesus' life and purpose to millions who sit in church each week. His mind was far from it. Neither was atonement theology on his mind, which is his dying for the sins of humanity for time immemorial. His purpose of casting himself into the hands of authorities of his day which resulted in his crucifixion was totally different from what I have believed and most of all Christianity currently believes. We are told that Jesus most likely saw himself as a martyr for his cause and his death a continuation of martyrdom of a long line of Israel's prophets before him who were calling out to the nation for reform.

An example, getting a little ahead of ourselves at this point, is a statement of N. T. Wright, to whom I have referred already and will refer throughout this book due to his attribution as the world's foremost scholar on the historical Jesus:

> "Jesus' beliefs, therefore, remained those of a
> first-century Jew, committed to the coming king-

dom of Israel's god. He did not waver in his loyalty to Jewish doctrine. But his beliefs were those of a first-century Jew who believed that the kingdom was coming in and through his own work... He believed in the coming kingdom of Israel's god, which would bring about the real return from exile, the final defeat of evil, and the return of YHWH to Zion."[8]

"What Jesus was offering, in other words, was not a different religious system. It was a new world order, the end of Israel's long desolation, the true and final forgiveness of sins, the inauguration of the kingdom of God."[9]

"I also agree, of course, that Jesus, like Jeremiah, regarded the temple as God-given; there is no question of his suggesting it should never have been built in the first place, or that worshipping in it was wrong."[10]

Many third quest scholars tell us that Jesus believed that the kingdom of God would arrive in the lifetime of his listening audiences of his day. Raymond Brown says in his outstanding book *Death of the Messiah* that the earliest traditions of Jesus do not show him as viewing his death as a sacrifice for sins of the world. His whole focus was upon Israel and an attempt to usher in the kingdom of God in his day. Brown writes,

"The oldest account of the crucifixion as the earliest step in the Passion tradition, was not acquainted with the meaning of the death of Jesus on the cross as an expiatory offering or expiatory death."[11]

In this book, we will discuss in detail the conclusions of scholars and theologians on the life of Jesus. The pictures and mental images we all received as a small child in Sunday school classes totally clash with the real Jesus who lived and was killed by Roman authorities.

With a public verbal squabble in the small town where we lived over which day is the Sabbath, it was just a few months before business in the store totally dropped off resulting from people in the community boycotting it. People wouldn't shop in a store which closed for church on Saturday. Sunday was supposed to be everyone's day of worship. Our time as a family in Arkansas was coming to an end.

One evening, Dad gathered me and all my brothers and sisters in the living room of our home and announced that we were going to be selling our home and moving. Our family was soon to become devoted disciples of Herbert Armstrong.

A few days after our family meeting, cars began to appear outside our home located on a gravel road about a mile outside of town. I was twelve years old. Crowds gathered all over the property. An auctioneer showed up, and I listened as he went from one item to another on our property rattling off numbers until he would finally shout: "Sold to the individual standing over here!"

Everything we had, Dad and Mom sold. We had shotguns, rifles, sporting gear, and a bunch of stuff besides our family beds, dressers, tables, chairs, lamps, quilts, blankets, furniture, and pots and pans. I had a pig I was raising for a 4H club project which we sold, as well as a family saddle horse used for riding and plowing our garden on the property. The end of the world was coming, and we didn't have any need for earthly possessions.

After the auction was over and we said good-bye to all our relatives in the community, we strapped a large metal trunk on to a luggage rack on top of an old Nash Rambler, and with everything we owned loaded into it, we left Yellville and headed to Pasadena, California, home to Herbert Armstrong. We looked like the Joad family from John Steinbeck's novel *The Grapes of Wrath*.

Nothing became more important in our lives than the religion of the Worldwide Church of God. I was consumed in it 24-7. In 1959, I entered Ambassador College in Pasadena, California, a church school designed to train ministers for church pastors. In 1961, I went to London, England, and finished college in beautiful facilities in a fairy tale-like setting that would have made a movie set for *The Chronicles of Narnia*. I graduated in 1963—the same year C. S. Lewis died and JFK was shot. Both died on the same day that year.

It is pitiful that I didn't even know C. S. Lewis while I was living in England. I had never read a single book of his. I have every one of them, and I dig one out occasionally from my book closet. I didn't know of him because the educational institution of which I was part never pointed anyone within it to sources of information outside concerning Christianity for fear of someone being influenced by them in any way. One might see error or find fault with the teaching of the church. All my reading and studying was pouring over church pamphlets, booklets, college class notes, sermons of the ministry, and digesting the indoctrination of the special purpose we alone had on earth to do the work of God.

In 1964, I was ordained as a minister of the church, a dream fulfilled from my high school days. Over the next sixteen years, my wife and I ministered to congregations of the church group in Chicago, Illinois, Peoria, Illinois, Champaign, Illinois, Memphis, Tennessee, Tupelo, Mississippi, and St. Louis, Missouri.

In 1979, my world dramatically changed. My wife and I were in Tucson, Arizona, staying in the Double Tree Inn at a special meeting of all ministers of the church. I can recall those events clearly thirty-seven years later because it had such a profound impact upon my life.

All my brothers and sisters and their spouses and mom and dad were there. My father at the time was an elder in the church. I had two brothers who were ministers in the church and three sisters that had married ministers of the church. The meeting in Arizona was an emergency session set up by the leaders of the church for trying to get back control of the church from the state of California. Doctor Phil talks about a time in his life in the third grade that it was changed forever by a fight with a third grader. My life was changed significantly by steps that I took.

Weeks before the meeting, our church had been taken over in a legal action by the attorney general of the state of California. The California attorney general by court order had seized financial assets of the church. State Troopers in squad cars swooped on to the property located just two blocks from the start of the annual Rose Parade in Pasadena, walked up and down the halls of the church offices and facilities, and took control. The church had literally been confiscated. The California attorney general, Deukmejian, had issued legal documents authorizing state appointed officers to seize the bank accounts of the church. As they arrived at the church headquarters, they presented official documents to the receptionist at the front desk of the administrative building housing executive offices of the church. They stated that the church was no longer financially managed by Herbert Armstrong, and Steven Wiseman, a retired judge appointed by the state attorney general, was to take over all "financial matters." He was the appointed trustee of the state of California to handle tithes and offerings of the church because of financial abuse of money and assets by Herbert Armstrong, its leader and founder. News outlets loved the story.

Overnight, an appointed judge took charge of a $150,000,000 plus annual church income, which financed its corporate jet fleet, minister's salaries, three colleges, millions of dollars of properties around the world, and a printing and religious broadcasting empire as large as any religious group in the country. It far exceeded the scope and operations of Billy Graham and most radio and TV evangelist groups. It was bizarre. It was embarrassing. It was unbelievable! It was like Jimmy and Tammy Faye Baker before Jimmy and Tammy Faye.

Its eighty-two-year-old founder, Herbert Armstrong, was charged by the state with criminal misuse of funds. Fearing he was going to be arrested and jailed, he had fled Pasadena, California, where he lived and moved out of state to Tucson, Arizona. Tithes of the membership were all collected locally in churches and diverted from local banks in Pasadena to circumvent outside control of the financial operations of the church by the state. Herbert called an emergency meeting of ministers of congregations from across the country. We all caught planes and were in attendance with ministers that came in from around the world. The church in size and scope had come a long way since the small redwood building surrounded by yellow jacket hornets and armadillos in Texas twenty-five years before.

I found myself sitting in that audience that year asking myself what on earth am I a part of? What have I gotten into? I was thirty-eight. I thought about all my past life, that of my mom and dad, and all my family. I had spent my entire life in the church as had all my brothers and sisters. I knew nothing but the ministry. All my family was in the church. How could I leave it?

By the age of twenty-three, I had been pastoring churches. I was a minister making decisions and doing things that were way beyond the maturity and grasp of a twenty-three-year-old. I thought I had answers for everything in the Bible. I felt I was one of a rare group of individuals known as "ministers of God," a term among ourselves stressing our significance out of billions of other human beings living in darkness. We believed that we were God's one and only "true" church. All other churches were deceived and tools of Satan. I have a list of apologies I hope to personally make one day to the people to whom I ministered.

We all lived in a biblically inspired bubble creating our own make-believe world. We read scripture after scripture from the Bible taking passages from both the Old and New Testaments that applied specifically to us, we thought, as God's chosen servants. Sermon after sermon would be given detailing the future and events soon to happen in the world. All of them were based upon scriptures we interpreted to be applicable to us. Time and again, I would leave church meetings riveted by fiery explanations of events unfolding in the world before my eyes. I see these same outlooks within groups today who think they are called of God in a similar manner to do the work of God. They are locked into the same mental outlook. They also feel they are living in the end times and are living biblically today and are addressed in the pages of scripture. It is characteristic of churches that get bit by the bug and sold on their own enlightenment and live thinking they understand reality and what is going on in the world. Like the song of Manfred Mann years ago, they become "blinded by the light."

The Worldwide Church of God was an exclusive group. The church taught that Christians didn't exist outside its membership. Unless you were a baptized member of the church and professed its beliefs and doctrines, you were not going to gain salvation or be in the kingdom of God. Salvation was only for those souls who "came into" the church. I believed that wholeheartedly for years and baptized members into the church only after their confession of faith that they believed the same.

Sunday worship was considered satanic. We didn't eat pork, shrimp, catfish, or any "unclean foods" referenced in Leviticus. A rigid tithing system was enforced of its membership—not one-tenth—but three separate tithes copied from instructions to the Levites in the Old Testament. One of them was to be set aside for funds to attend seven annual religious festivals of the church, instituted by God for the children of Israel, in the Old Testament. The Jewish calendar was used to calculate observance of the "holy days," as they were called. Celebration of birthdays was a sin, and women could not wear make up. Easter was taught to be pagan. We didn't keep Christmas. All these practices were efforts to live as Jesus lived. Allegedly God condemned make up in the Old Testament. Jeremiah 10 spoke of the evils of a Christmas tree.

In the early '50s and '60s, it was prophesied by Herbert, that Jesus would return by 1975. Prior to 1975, Germany was to become the leader of a United Europe and wage war against the United States. Ten kings were to rise which would be a loose political and military organization of European nations. It was to be a brief political union of states for the Bible spoke of the image as having feet of clay and exist only for a short time.

The rise of Europe and the resurrection of the Holy Roman Empire was always an exhilarating topic after Bible study evenings on Friday nights. We went so far as to name the *Beast* (Rev. 15:5). Franz Joseph Strauss was to become the political leader of a resurrected Holy Roman Empire and later to be cast into the lake of fire with the false prophet. Strauss died of old age years ago.

While a student, I worked in what was called the *News Bureau*. My job along with a team of other students was to "watch world news" for all signs pointing to the end of the age and the return of Christ. We would print up a summary sheet of events all over the world that were pulled off a UPI teletype machine clacking away in the office where we were huddled in our mission and work. We gleaned newspaper articles for wars and rumors of wars, earthquakes, famine, pestilence, and disease—all prophetic signs of the immanency of the return of Christ. The summary sheet was to me sort of like the president's daily briefing given to him each day explaining what is going on in the world. I became excited when sitting out in an audience during a Bible study group when a minister in front conducting the study would pull out a production we titled the *News Bulletin* and begin to read of events occurring portending all that we believed about the end of the age.

The church believed that 33 percent of the US population was to be carried captive to Europe after troops from a United States of Europe landed in the country. Thirty-three percent of the US population was to die by famine before arrival of German troops. Thirty-three percent of the population was to be killed by a military assault when German and European troops invaded our country. By interpreting selected passages in the Old Testament, it was believed that only a tenth of the US population was to survive and they were to be transported back to Europe as slaves.

For years after the collapse of Germany and the ending of World War II, it was common chatter and conversation that Hitler had possibly survived and made it out of Europe by submarine to South America and would return one day to unite Germany again at the head of a revived Holy Roman Empire. The passage in Revelation 13 which spoke of the beast "being dead, and made alive" referred to Hitler suddenly appearing out of nowhere creating an appearance that the beast had been resurrected. This "fulfilled" the passage speaking of the beast "being dead and being made alive again." Hitler, we felt, would show up to lead a resurrection of the Holy Roman Empire. It wasn't too far-fetched from the movie in 1978 starring Gregory Peck, *The Boys from Brazil.*

The keys to understanding the placing of America so pivotal to all prophetic understanding, was the esoteric belief of *British-Israelism.*

That was a belief that the United States and British Commonwealth were spoken openly in the Bible in the passages of the prophets. The United States were composed or made up of descendants of Manasseh, one of the sons of Joseph. Britain was identified as Joseph's second son who was named Ephraim. All the other tribes of Israel which had been missing from the time of Jesus were scattered over Europe, with France being Reuben, and other European states being descendants of one of the other twelve sons of the ancient patriarch Jacob. It was a viewpoint of life sort of like "manifest destiny" which propelled Western expansion in the United States, the extermination of Native Americans, the Buffalo, and events in the developmental history of our nation so vividly portrayed in Ken Burn's outstanding series on *PBS* titled *The West*. *British-Israelism* was of course another adopted or borrowed belief that God had revealed only to Herbert.

The Catholic Church was taught to be the great spiritual whore of Revelation and the pope was the false prophet to come, later to be thrown by Jesus into the lake of fire along with the beast. The great tribulation was to be unleashed and finally the seven last plagues were to be poured out upon a sinful world as God crushed it into nothingness. Just before the pouring out of the seven last plagues, the church taught that's it's members were all going to journey from the US, or wherever they were around the world, to a place in Jordan called Petra, an ancient city built in rose-red rock caves. There the church was to be protected from the wrath of God on a fallen world. It was a variation of the rapture of course. We had no clue how we were going to all get there. That wasn't really discussed. A supernatural event wasn't ruled out. All we knew was a passage from Isaiah that we would be borne upon the "wings of eagles," whatever that was supposed to mean.

At the end of three and a half years of tribulation and after the seven last plagues had been unleashed, the two witnesses would be killed in the streets of Jerusalem after a newly built temple was desecrated in Jerusalem by the political leader of Europe. The very final event was a great earthquake which was to divide the city of Jerusalem in half. Christ was to return and place his feet on Mt. Olivet and begin the millennium. We were to live and reign with Christ on earth. We wrote the book for Hal Lindsey and Tim LaHaye.

Here, I sat in 1979 in a meeting in Arizona with the old man's and my prophetic visions a shamble and everything I had grown up believing not quite turning out the way I thought it was supposed to turn out. Jesus hadn't returned. Stores were still stocked with food. German boots hadn't set foot on US soil. My church had been confiscated by the attorney general of California. I found myself exactly where Malcolm Muggeridge explained people find themselves when marking signs and special events and tying those events to the return of Christ. In his book *Jesus* published in 1975, he says,

> "As I write these words apocalyptic intimations are multiplying, to the point that many see the last days as soon to be upon us. For believers, Christianity has thus been a condition of continuing alertness. No state of mind could be more appropriate to our human condition, enabling us, as it does, to see each day as perhaps marking the end of Time—as each issue of a newspaper must have a lead story of Olympian significance, and then, once published, fades away to nothingness, useful only to light fires and wrap fish, while another issue with another lead story of Olympian significance comes off the presses."[12]

I had drunk the Kool-Aid.

3

What It Takes to Make a Change

"Sects paint outsiders as ignorant of the 'obvious' truth of the subcultural worldview. For the 'native' the world has been divided from birth into a sharply dualistic scheme—those on the inside who dwell in the light of truth, and those on the outside dwelling in the darkness of ignorance. (If that ignorance results from a deliberate rejection of the truth, the outsider is not just to be pitied but must also be condemned.) For the convert, coming from the pool of the ignorant, this entails a bifurcation of biography. The convert's life is reinterpreted in terms of a period BC and a period AD—that is before and after the conversion."

—Peter Berger, *In Praise of Doubt*

In baptizing individuals into the Worldwide Church of God, I often would use the term in talking with them prior to the act of baptism by asking them, "When did you come into the truth?" This would-be BC and AD in Berger's language. When I used the term in communicating with them, the term of "when did you come into the truth" was a common term or expression used in inquiring as to when a nonbeliever's eyes were opened and they were converted to the "truth." "Coming into the truth" was a short phrase denoting when they were convicted in heart to believe everything taught by Herbert Armstrong. All true believers spoke the lingo in their meeting and conversations with other members at church and making their acquaintance at church festivals. They hadn't lived until they arrived among the enlightened people of God. The world outside the group was made up of the walking dead spiritually.

The purpose of the church was to do the "work"—again, an inside term we all understood as meaning that no other group was authorized or ordained by God to proclaim the Gospel truth to a deceived world. We were sole representatives of God on planet Earth. I would hear a sermon refer to our place in the world occasionally where someone would speak of "God's ministers" and their work, and it would make me shudder in grasping the significance of my life. Our worldview of our purpose was so intense that we often would drive between cities for Bible studies, church services, or anointing's at high rates of speed well above the speed limit, feeling our work placed us above the law. Unlike the *Blues Brothers*, we knew we were on a mission from God. We must always be about the business God had ordained us to carry out. It was an around the clock job. We knew nothing else. Dale Allison describes in detail groups just like us who periodically appear on the planet in his book *Jesus of Nazareth— Millenarian Prophet*, pages 61–64.

In the year 1975, instead of the sounds of trumpets shattering the eardrums of miserable souls as God's seven vials of wrath were being poured out on sinners there was trouble within the flock. Rumors of sexual liaisons with young coeds on campus by the churches' flamboyant presenter on its worldwide TV and radio evangelistic programs were turning out to be true. Mike Wallace on *Sixty Minutes* conducted a damaging profile of profligate and lavish spending of the founder and his son who both spent their time flying around the world in a Gulfstream II and Falcon Jet lavishing gifts upon others to curry favor and status for themselves. They were spending tithe money of poor church people that I ministered to weekly who had to cough up 10 percent of their income monthly while they lived in poverty in many cases.

For years, it had faced various crises that had been weathered. All of them had been explained by Herbert, to prove who we thought we were—God's chosen people. Satan, we were told, was obviously attacking us to prove and test us, the old standby message always pulled out when a crisis would strike. It's the devil. This had been my third or fourth cycle of attacks of Satan trying to succeed to break up those spreading God's true message to a fallen world—a familiar damage control message with religious cults and groups when their leaders are caught in improprieties. Oral Roberts's senior decried the attack of Satan upon his son in 2006 when it was found that his son was spending tithe money and financial contributions to support his jet set living lifestyle outside of preaching the Gospel. The devil was at work, Oral stated.

The last day of the conference, I realized I wasn't one of them anymore. I wasn't there to get back "our" church. I knew inside it wasn't my church any more. I resigned the ministry and got out of a church that was teaching what it was teaching and doing. I couldn't go on encouraging people anymore to give and tithe to an organization that was using money and scamming them for their leaders to maintain their own lascivious and luxurious lifestyles. I knew the financial circumstances of people compelled to cough up 10 percent. On the last day of the conference, I met with the church's superintendent of ministers and turned in my resignation as a minister.

It wasn't long after returning home to St. Louis, a letter arrived asking for my ordination certificate, all church documents, and I was ordered in a letter "in the name of God," for me to return a lease car provided to me by the church. My wife and I were disfellowshipped—an official act of the church where letters were sent out to members of congregations asking all members to not eat or associate with me or my wife. It was a form of shunning like the way Amish religious groups do to a reprobate member or excommunication done in the Catholic Church years ago. My parents who lived at the time in a church owned home on church property in Texas were forbidden by Herbert to allow me and my wife and children into their home. We were anathema to the group.

I wish today I had made that decision years before I made it. I was able mentally inwardly to make excuses for not leaving the church after discovering sexual dalliances of its leaders and witnessing them bilk people in the name of Jesus in obtaining money and financing their egotistical endeavors. It had been instilled in me from a kid that the Bible is filled with examples of leaders who sinned and made mistakes and were placed in positions of "authority" and the biblical example is that we shouldn't rebel against those God had placed to rule over his people. Paul had made clear that it is God who places people in positions of authority and we should be subject to them despite their sins. David and his adultery with Bathsheba was used as an example of a leader sinning or falling short of being an example and his remaining as king. God smiting Miriam with leprosy for criticizing the administration of her brother Moses is another example. Miriam criticized her own brother and was smitten by God (Num. 12:1–10). There were numerous other examples that I myself quoted and used to try to stem shrinking membership when members began to desert the church after hearing of life conduct and examples of its leaders.

There was one major reason that I finally was able to sever the umbilical cord and break the gravity field in which I was gripped. It was the push I needed. The key event in my life that drove me to leave the group, involved the church's practice of healing. The church believed in divine healing, as do many churches in this country. Just down the street from where my wife and I live now and where I regularly walk our little Yorkie, there is a church. On the sign outside the church is posted the weekly schedule. Wednesday at 9:00 AM is a healing service. It is an episcopal church. Many mainstream churches are offering this service as part of their outreach to their communities. I know those prayers for healing include all the help they can get from the medical world. That wasn't the case in my church.

In 1974, while I was ministering to a congregation in Memphis, a twelve-year-old boy died from ruptured appendix in his parent's home without medical treatment. Just a few days before his death, I had been in his home, counseling his father and mother who lived in Olive Branch, Mississippi. It was evident that he had appendicitis. All the symptoms were present and he had experienced appendicitis in the past. We prayed together that God would heal him. Before I left their home, the father asked me if he should take him to the hospital. I told him that I would get back to him.

On that same day, I followed a procedure we were asked as ministers to follow with cases of members with severe illness. I called the superintendent of ministers of the headquarters church in Pasadena and asked him how I should advise the family. He stated, "If they are going to trust God, they are going to have to be willing to do so even to his death." Being a loyal dedicated believer and minister, at the time, I gave them that advice.

I will never forget the early morning call a day later and hearing that sobbing father on the other end of the line say, "Tim is dead." They were so poor they didn't have a phone in their home. The father had run barefooted for a half mile down a gravel road to a next-door neighbor's house to make the call, after helplessly watching his son expire.

One other child's death also occurred in that same Memphis congregation, not long afterward. A young couple experienced the blessing of a beautiful baby girl, only to discover within hours that she was born with an RH negative blood factor. When a child is born with this disease, treatment is very simple. Blood transfusions are given to offset the impact after birth of being taken from the mother's womb, and then doctors perform a simple operation and reroute the blood flow of the baby. It is fixed for life.

Instead of doing this, the parents did what they believed they were to do as members of the church. They called me as an instrument to God for what they needed—a miracle. I arrived at the hospital to find a tiny little baby slightly blue-gray in color (in 1970, a child born in this way was called a "blue" baby) that looked ever so helpless as she lay in a hospital bassinet. I took out a vial of olive oil which I always carried and prayed, along with her parents, that God would heal her. I had not experienced the lame rising and walking, or the deaf hearing, because of my prayers. I don't think I have ever been more intent and sincere in asking God for anything than when I placed my hand on her tiny forehead and anointed her with a drop or two of olive oil.

As I left the hospital, the staff on duty began to impress upon the father the seriousness of her condition and state that she urgently needed a blood transfusion. She would need an operation to reroute her blood flow to ever be normal. She could possibly die. The church taught also that blood transfusions were a sin, much like Jehovah's Witnesses. Jehovah's Witnesses believe that the Bible prohibits ingesting blood and that Christians should not accept blood transfusions or donate or store their own blood for transfusion.

Her father was a true believer. Sometime during the night, he came into the hospital and carried the infant home. He believed he was obeying God in what he did. She died within a couple of days.

There were hundreds of deaths over a twenty-year span within congregations across the country that were similar in nature during the time I was a minister. It was generally not discussed or publicized, for it represented nonresponse on God's part due to "lack of faith" by the minister and parents, and it raised legal issues for all parties.

In witnessing, the results of my inability to heal the sick, I was beginning to focus on the fact that I wasn't special, neither was the group of which I was a part gifted with healing. The air was beginning to seep out of my balloon. Reality had set in. I had begun to realize that I wasn't a part of a group of individuals who walked the earth and could look down upon the crippled and tell them rise and walk, which as remnants of the apostolic church, many felt we should be able to do. I had been called often to St. Jude's in Memphis to pray for those smitten with leukemia. I saw no miracles occur resulting from my prayers. I didn't have the gift of healing.

Because of all my experiences in the church, I was agonized over what I saw as a double standard in the practices of leaders of the church. I personally knew Herbert and other ministers were seeking and getting medical treatment for sickness and diseases they suffered. Herbert had an RN around him 24-7 taking care of any medical needs he had.

Several months before the conference, I had written him a personal letter asking him how he could go on teaching to congregations that the use of medical professionals was a sin when he himself was receiving medical care.

During our four days of meetings of the group, Herbert had remained allegedly in ill health in his residence in Arizona. I don't think he was that sick or ailing during the conferences. He wasn't present in meetings because at the time, he just didn't want to take the heat of the political and emotional state of the church ministry. Everyone was asking how the church was in the mess it was in.

As I write these words and look back upon events that occurred in my life thirty-six years ago, I understand the death of both these children were attributable to what I did as an individual to assist in preserving beliefs that their parents held, which led them to denying medical treatment to their children which could have saved their lives.

Those two children never got to grow up. In the case of the tiny baby, her entire life was snuffed out. Both of those children could be somewhere in marriages with children and grandchildren of their own today. Those parents would be experiencing the joy of all that.

The Associated Press ran an article today as this is being written, detailing the death of an infant resulting from parents who believed in divine healing and declined medical treatment for a newborn. It involved a small sect with less than a thousand members in the Oregon and Idaho area. Prosecuting attorney's in the state charged the parents with murder and criminal mistreatment. The infant was born prematurely at the parent's grandparents homes where three midwives and church members were present at the time. Being premature, the lungs of the infant child were not fully developed and the child had only a short time to breathe unassisted. As it gasped for air, no one had called 911.

As I read the article, I naturally thought of those two children and events in my life. I feel for the parents going through what they are doing in their individual faith and beliefs in the choices they are making. It is a terrible situation for the courts, parents, family, and all people involved when faced with the issues of freedom of religion in our country when it is over the medical treatment of children. I understand it from all sides.

My whole family personally experienced a similar tragedy. In 1979, I had a twenty-one-year-old brother who died under somewhat similar circumstances, where he trusted in God for his healing. I have never experienced in my life since that time something that was so emotionally painful as his death and all the circumstances surrounding it. What I had seen and experienced in ministry and its pains and hurts became a part of my life deeply and personally, the same year I got the courage to walk away from it and free myself from the mental and psychological bonds with which I had been bound. I lived it and will share it with you to again illustrate how religion grips the heart and soul of all of us as human beings.

My brother's name was Joe Dan. Joe was the youngest child of seven living children of my mom and dad. On an unseasonably warm October day in 1978, high in the Colorado Rockies, I was deer hunting with my brother Joe Dan and my brother Ray and several friends. We had stopped for lunch at an agreed spot, after spending the morning hunting. While eating and catching our breath, my brother Ray asked Joe, "What is that spot on your neck?" He had a purplish-looking spot on his neck.

After getting back from the hunt and his going to the doctor, he was diagnosed with melanoma cancer. Joe had grown up from the time he was a baby inside the church. To turn to medical doctors for medical treatments he considered a sin. He chose faith in God and to not be operated upon. He knew no other beliefs. He died October 31, 1979, at twenty-one years of age, just six months or so after he was diagnosed with cancer.

A couple of months prior to his death, we were all visiting as a family in the home of my brother Ray in Oklahoma. One morning after breakfast together, the topics became quite heated. Ray had just chosen a few weeks earlier to resign the ministry, as my brother Dennis and I had done earlier that same year. Conversation in the family due to the intensity of our lives together always drifted around to doctrinal subjects and what we felt was wrong with the church.

As we talked that day, Joe was lying on the couch in the living room listening to all of us argue and debate each other. I vividly can recall the scene and especially the words he spoke. While lying on the couch in the living room with his head heavily bandaged, he said, "I wish you guys would quit talking about the church."

How many times in life I found myself so inadequate for the moment? I can look back over twenty years that I spent in the "ministry" of the church and I was so unprepared for the deaths I faced, funerals I performed, and moments and times that I had the opportunity to minister. I wish I would have said so many things that I didn't have the words nor wisdom to say at the time. I look back and I don't think I could have changed the minds of anyone, for they were true believers. Changes must take place within for someone to see themselves, their lives, their error, and correct things in and of themselves. I could not change the mind of my own mother and father in any way in the steps I took.

Before we all departed Oklahoma and returned to our respective homes, my father on an occasion asked me and my two brothers to sit down with him privately at the dining room table. He said as accurately as I can recall, "I want to speak to you guys as a minister of God. I believe that God has placed this cancer upon Joe as a trial and test for all of you, in hope that you will come to your senses and come back to God's church."

Those comments stung. I could not expect anything different from my dad. He had drunk the Kool-Aid as well. He was entrenched in religion and a true believer, and he could think no other way. My father's world, in one sense, was being turned upside down. His youngest son was dying of cancer, he felt, because his other sons were forsaking God's true church. He feared for our spiritual lives and made a gallant effort to prevent us from leaving the church and losing our salvation, in his thought world.

One feels so helpless to watch another slowly die. It is agony. I have never seen a medical journal picture that portrayed the ugliness and grotesqueness of the cancerous growth that eventually passed up through Joe's neck and on to the side of his head. One side of his head was consumed in black cancerous cells, making his head almost half again its size. His neck muscles grew so weak he could hardly hold up his head. I suspect, even though he was looking for God to heal him, he knew he was most likely going to die. The human psyche never knows when it will cross the threshold and move from life to death, but I would suspect it gives one dripping thoughts on quiet nights, of truth and reality. I would think when he saw himself in the mirror that he wished secretly he could die. But, if he did, he never spoke of it. He remained optimistic on the surface that God would heal him.

One day, about thirty days before his death, he wanted to go shopping. His neck muscles were so weak and the cancerous growth on his head so large, he was like a tiny baby whose head weaves and bobs until they get neck muscle strength sufficient to hold their head erect. Dad wanted to assist in any way he could. Out in the garage, he had some orange life preservers hanging on nails pegged in the wall. They were left over from church summer camp used for boating activities. He came up with the idea of using one of them and cutting a piece of plywood and making a vertical neck brace out of it by sticking the plywood strip vertically through his life preserver then using duct tape to secure it. With the board sticking up behind Joe's neck and wobbly head, a bandana was used to tie around his head and around the strip of board. This gave him support to hold up his head as he walked.

As we were shopping that day, I saw stares as we walked with him about a store he had chosen to shop. He bought gifts for every one of his brothers and sisters, as if he was realizing internally he was most likely going to die. He wanted to leave them something. I enjoy a great Caesar salad and love to make them. Joe knew that. In every house, my wife and I have lived for the past thirty-five years, we have a special spot where we place a large three-legged walnut salad bowl he bought that day. We use it for special occasions, and every time we use it becomes a moment to remember the life of a spirit that truly was unique before God.

Joe died on Halloween day 1979. He left behind a beautiful young wife. He had been married just over a year. His funeral service was one of those typical services where the whole congregation turns out. My mother and father were admired by all. Members had borne their pain and hurts, not just of sickness and disease, but they were aware of family members who were leaving God's true church and sons resigning the ministry of that church.

I stood at the gravesite and looked around at the hundreds of people who had gathered in a peaceful little cemetery outside Gladewater, Texas. I knew most of them, although I no longer was part of the church. After the minister had spoken his last words, I walked away and stood by a tree and cried. I didn't care who saw me. I didn't just cry for the loss of my brother. I was feeling the pain inside I knew that was agonizing my father and mother. I hurt for them knowing how they felt. I couldn't talk to my father or mother and discuss with them their feelings. We had forsaken them, and above all, we had, they felt, forsaken God. I hurt for all of us, so torn and so divided over God, his purpose, his will for us, salvation, and whether we would ever find again the peace we had seemed to enjoy when we were all "in the church." My father died eight years after Joe's death. During his last eight years of life, I never discussed religion again with my father. For twenty-five years, it had consumed our lives as a family.

On the tombstone of my brother Joe, Dad later had inscribed the words I HAVE KEPT *THE* FAITH. *The* was underlined to signal to all his adult sons and daughters who had left the church, that our brother had died in the true church of God doing the will of God. I still occasionally visit that gravesite for it is the site of both my parents and my brother. Memory can instantly take me back thirty-seven years ago, to the exact feelings I had that afternoon as I stood and watched individuals throw dirt over his casket and bury it.

I realize I have talked extensively of my life so far. I have shared my personal life with you of my past religious outlook for several reasons. It is impossible to communicate clearly sometimes without an author doing that. You can easily see my bias, prejudice, and where I come from in what you are reading. My experience is shared in detail to try to illustrate how we all get locked into beliefs one way or another in our journey in life about a lot of things. It isn't just religion, we get seized in scientific, political, sexist, gender issues, climate warming, and a hundred other ways we establish "beliefs" about something in life and effectively become true believers, just as much as I was.

I hope by my clearly giving the life story of families seeking God you can make some comparisons to your own experiences in life relative to your beliefs about God and Jesus. I have spoken openly and honestly about my life in order that you might understand how religion takes over one's thoughts and actions. Religious beliefs have been handed down to all of us in this nation which go back for thousands of years.

There may be some who read this that may pity my ignorance and that I was contributory to the death of those children. I understand that. You may shake your head at the stupidity of individuals in a religious group. I can't fault you and you would be right. Twenty-five years after the death of those children, through a mutual friend of the families involved, I tried to reconnect and apologize for the part I played in their lives contributing to the death of their children. I was told in very clear terms they had no desire to see me, hear an apology, or discuss what occurred in their lives. I understood that as well.

I can tell you one thing for sure from my life's experiences. I know and understand religion and what it does to individuals, families, groups, churches, and nations. Our nation, through immigration and powerful religious forces within a dynamically changing world, is rapidly being driven to the point that religion will consume it. It isn't going to back off. We see it in the cultural wars tearing our country apart which are all based on religion. The divisiveness we see over marriage, sexuality, homosexuality, transgender changes, the Ten Commandments, standing for the national anthem, use of the word Christmas in the public arena, male and female designations, whether we are a Christian nation—all is driven by religion. Christianity is in a struggle for survival in a country that was founded upon freedom of religion and was founded on Christian values and principles.

For young and old, rich and poor, male and female, mothers and fathers, brothers and sisters—religion does exactly what Jesus said it does:

> "Think not that I am come to send peace on
> earth: I came not to send peace, but a sword. For
> I am come to set a man at variance against his
> father, and the daughter against her mother, and
> the daughter in law against her mother in law"
> (John 10:34-3).

After leaving the group, I found I also faced exactly what Peter Berger describes above of those who join churches or clubs or political and scientific groups and become true believers. Once you depart the fold, you become the enemy.

I was condemned in formal communication by the ministry of the church and I was "turned over to Satan for the destruction of the flesh." Announcements were made in the churches in St. Louis that I had pastored which stated that I had left the church. Members were not to be seen with me and my wife nor speak to us. Everyone knew the routine and no one knew it better than I did. I had disfellowshipped individuals as a regular part of protecting the flock. It was now being protected from me.

This practice of turning one over to Satan allegedly came from Paul in his statements in one of his letters where he used this term. It was an approach taken with one who forsook God's true way of life in Paul's day and the term had to do with the hope that one who sinned and was committing acts contrary to practices of the church would come to their senses by finding it was better to be on the inside with God than outside with Satan. Maybe there was some tinge of "cursing" individuals for having bolted from the community—at least it was that way in the church of which I was a part.

I stayed in the Worldwide Church of God long past the time I should have. I was literally fearful—afraid to leave the church. I believed at one time that Herbert Armstrong was the incarnational spiritual embodiment of the biblical Elijah in the flesh today with a warning message for people at the end of the age before the return of Christ. It was a form of incarnational theology. He was literally viewed by church congregants and myself, as a second Elijah, appearing on earth before Christ's return. I feared for my chances of eternal life in thinking of leaving the group. I was upon leaving somewhat for me on the scene of *Pascal's Wager* in reverse, in my thoughts. Was I rejecting God should I leave my church?

Something must happen to shake you up, to cause you to question, make you a doubter and heretic, or you can never muster the energy it takes to get out of locked in belief whether a conservative, liberal, progressive, climate warmer, or Jesus freak. Its gravity field will always hold you within it. The mental control it has on your life is unknown to everyone except those who have had an experience to have been shackled and chained to a belief system and somehow escaped and broken free of its mental tentacles.

I set about to find employment. It was, for five months, a shock to my system. I made up a resume that I thought might influence a personnel manager but soon found it didn't. Unemployed ministers of a church under investigation for scamming its members wasn't a real winner in the job market. I found two great books that anyone will value if you are ever without a job and trying to find employment— they are authored by David Bolles and still in print. They are *What Color Is Your Parachute* and *The Three Boxes of Life*. I found a kindred spirit. He had left the ministry after he witnessed the untimely death of his younger brother and afterward felt he didn't have the answers he needed to teach others about life and its tragedies.

That change was made in my life thirty-seven years ago. Instead of explaining the acts of God in the universe as a profession, I began a new profession selling insurance for "acts of God," the standard term in all insurance policies used to describe tornadoes, hail, wind, hurricanes, floods, and earthquakes. I began to sell insurance to protect people from God, not provide them a place of safety in Jordan before God's deliverance of the seven last plagues on earth.

4

LEAVING IT ALL BEHIND

"Faith organizes and equips man's soul for action.
To be in possession of the one and only truth
and never doubt one's righteousness; to feel that
one is backed by a mysterious power whether it
be God, destiny or the law of history; to be convinced that ones' opponents are the incarnation
of evil and must be crushed; to exult in self-denial
and devotion to duty—these are qualifications
for resolute and ruthless action in any field."
—Eric Hoffer, *The True Believer*

Hoffer's quote sounds like the world scene today in which we all
live. Everyone is screaming out that they only possess truth, or true
"worldview" or true "viewpoint" or "understanding" whether gays
and lesbians, climate changers, liberals, conservatives, Muslims,
leftists, democrats, republicans, or radical evangelicals. Everyone is
screaming and no one is listening to the other. It all comes from their
interpretation of a worldview. Everyone feels they are in possession
of the "truth."

God had not spoken to found the Worldwide Church of God.
As to everything I had been a part of in the past, eventually the

Worldwide Church of God totally unraveled over time. The mistakes it made in treatment of its members caught up with it. Individuals discovered Herbert wasn't Elijah on earth after his death and that both he and his son were all too human rather than vicars for Christ possessing divine insight to the plan of God on earth. Ted Armstrong died several years after his dad. It is now the church of dead men.

Afterward, political battles among the ministry to take over the church have produced over 250 splinters of the original Worldwide Church of God. It has split and split again with each new break off involving someone feeling he or she possesses a little more truth and enlightenment than another group. Many have splintered off to get back to the faith once delivered by Herbert.

The dissolution of the church took a terrible toll on the lives of people who lost their way in life after losing faith and conviction in their having found and lived within the true church. Friends of mine I had known since college days that had married and started families at the same time my wife and I had been married, were shattered. Some turned to a life of crime. Suicides occurred among a few. Many were mentally crippled and just not able to walk away and live in the real world and now live within religious groups they have embraced to handle life.

My mother and father are dead. My mother lived until ninety-nine, and up until 2013, she witnessed all the changes in her church over a fifty-three-year span. All during that time, she continued to keep the Sabbath day, observe Jewish Holy Days, refrain from eating pork, and following the beliefs of her church. She eventually saw every one of her children and their spouses and all her grandchildren leave her church. She found that Christmas began to be kept by various ones of her family and that shrimp and pork was consumed in diets at home. Mother never criticized any one for how they lived. She asked God often to put angels for protection about each child and grandchild and eventually great-grandchildren. She prayed for others in her church, sent cards when they were sick and made calls to them. She got a computer and got on email and had a mailing list far larger than any I have ever had as friends, to which she sent notes of encouragement or cheer regularly. She did all this after being born into a rural Arkansas family and environment with no electricity, no running water inside the home, a wood cook stove in the house, no car, no TV, an outdoor toilet, and she made some of her dresses as a young girl out of flour sacks kept after purchases of flour in bulk by the family. Her mother and father and her brothers and sisters lived off the land or farmed for a living.

Above everything, she diligently watched world news, read the *Drudge Report*, and poured over everything daily she could find while looking for signs of the return of Jesus, even though he had been supposed to return in 1975. If she saw something, she frequently called me at home, and I would hear her voice as she would ask, "Are you watching such and such a program? If not, you ought to be." It was usually something on *Fox News* of wars and rumor of wars, famine, earthquakes, and Jerusalem disturbances—signs of Jesus' second coming.

There are millions and millions of Americans that are doing the same thing daily my mother did—watching for the return of Jesus. Millions more are watching for the rapture which is a sort of crazy event we are all supposed to witness one day if alive when it occurs.

The rapture is described by Jerry Falwell in a sermon he gave before his death:

> "What is going to happen on this earth when the Rapture occurs? You'll be riding along in an automobile. You'll be the driver, perhaps. You're a Christian. There will be several people in the automobile with you, maybe someone who is not a Christian. When the trumpet sounds, you and the other born-again believers in that automobile will be instantly called away—you will disappear, leaving behind only your clothing, and physical things that cannot inherit eternal life. That unsaved person or persons in the automobile will suddenly be startled to find that the car is moving along without a driver and suddenly somewhere crashes. These saved people in the car have

disappeared. Other cars on the highway driven by believers will suddenly be out of control, and stark pandemonium will occur on that highway and every highway in the world where Christians are called away from the driver's wheel."

Jerry Falwell was found dead on the floor of his office in 2007.

The *Left Behind* series of books is all about what is supposed to happen when the church is raptured, which occurs prior to the return of Christ and prior to the great tribulation to come upon the world. Of course, it will be a rapture of selectively chosen people which is clearly explained inside the series. One criteria of being chosen is that you first believe in the rapture.

Susan Garrett wrote in her book on the historical Jesus, titled *No Ordinary Angel*, this portrayal of the rapture:

"The first novel in the series opens with the Rapture of the true church. This is the anticipated event when Jesus returns and whisks all who are born-again Christians into heaven (together with all young children, including fetuses), according to an interpretation of I Thessalonians 4:16–17. The Rapture initiates the seven-year period of the Tribulation, which is the overarching time frame for the entire series of novels."[1]

There are fifty shades of gray out there in churches across this country of those 126 million people that believe in Christ's return by 2050 that hold similar end time scenarios as the Worldwide Church of God and LaHaye's books. They look for ten kings to rise just as I looked, and every week prophecy classes are covered in churches across the land detailing all the things they believe are to occur in this world in the countdown to Armageddon. The great majority of it is taken from the book of Revelation and those statements of John the Devine when he spoke of the end of the age.

One will find in looking at their beliefs that they have that all really have been given to us as it was in my life. Mark Twain made the comment,

> "We have no thoughts of our own, no opinions of our own: they are transmitted to us, trained into us."

This is true of all societies and human experience in general. As we age and arrive in our twilight years of life, it is difficult to penetrate our psychic makeup and ask ourselves what we really learned for ourselves or what beliefs we ever gained that were our own and not those given to us by others throughout our lives. C. S. Lewis said regarding the experience of being born and living and existing in this world that

> "our experience is colored through and through by books and plays and the cinema, and it takes patience and skill to disentangle the things we have really learned from life for ourselves."

When a search is made within our souls for what we believe and how we came to believe all that, one finds it is someone else's faith upon which our beliefs are based. William James expressed man's plight when he wrote,

> "Our reason is quite satisfied, in nine-hundred-ninety-nine cases out of a thousand of us, if it can find a few arguments that will do to recite in case our credibility is criticized by someone else. Our faith is faith in someone else's faith, and in the greatest matters this is mostly the case."

You get out of a cult, you get out of a club, you get out of a group, you get out of a church, you leave one political party and join another, only when you get disillusioned with it and it doesn't make sense to you any more. You never make changes in your life until you question what it is you believe about life. Your worldview must be totally turned upside down. We only change our beliefs about anything through questioning, doubting, and examining. We should spend our lifetime doubting almost everything we have believed. Most likely it has been wrong in some way. History shows it is most often the doubters and heretics who have led us to truth. It is true in religion. It is true in science. It is true in all our endeavors to understand the universe and world around us. When you start the process to examine how you came to believe what you believe, you will find how difficult it is to look inside your mental construct of your beliefs and find those things you believe that were original to you in what you believe. As Daniel Taylor wrote in the *Myth of Certainty*,

> "Once in operation, a belief system processes all information, all evidence, on its own terms, appropriating that which verifies its outlook and defusing or ignoring anything else."[2]

5

FINDING MY WAY

"The quest for the historical Jesus refers to academic efforts to provide a historical portrait of Jesus. Since the 18th century, three separate scholarly quests for the historical Jesus have taken place, each with distinct characteristics and based on different research criteria, which were often developed during each specific phase. These quests are distinguished from earlier approaches because they rely on the historical method to study biblical narratives. While textual analysis of biblical sources had taken place for centuries, these quests introduced new methods and specific techniques to establish the historical validity of their conclusions."

—Wikipedia, Third Quest Historical Jesus

It was several years after leaving my church that I had any interest in delving into the Bible again after being grossly disappointed in the experience I had with religious groups. The pressures in my life were to get out and find a way to make a living, make the car payments, pay the mortgage, put food on the table, and provide for our three children. My wife and I wanted to keep them in West St. Louis County schools where we were living at the time and let them grow up and be normal rather than freaked out in a fringe religious group as both of us had grown up. Eventually after leaving the group, something brought me back around to picking up the Bible again and searching for answers and understanding.

There were several issues that I had to work through in what I believed. When I walked out and began a new life, many of the beliefs I had learned were deeply ingrained, far more than I conceived they were as I discovered over years of time. If someone had asked me what the big bang was, I wouldn't have had a clue. I hadn't heard of Fred Hoyle or the Big Bang, the theory of the universe being the size of a period at the end of this sentence just a few billion years ago. When we deal with infinity, a few billion years is just a short time ago.

At a time of thrashing around and trying to find myself, I recall reading one of J. P. Moreland's books titled *Love God with All Your Mind* wherein he referenced difficulties he had with the earth being billions of years old. That clashed with Archbishop Usher's chronology that told us the earth is six thousand years old. It conflicted with Moreland's beliefs about creation and the story and account we have in Genesis. At the time, I was struggling with the same thing.

Moreland made a great comment in the book wherein he asked himself and his readers how it is that we can know what it is that we even believe on any subject. He stated in his study of the Bible and the subject of the age of the earth as to how old that it is that he got up one day thinking it was one way and he got up the next day thinking it was the other. Then one day he began to wake up believing that the earth is billions of years old and not six thousand years old and science was correct on the age of the earth. He also said in all his studies that when a person begins to believe something, when he alternates between two positions, that when we reach a threshold of 51 percent, he or she is probably beginning to lean in a direction of that as what he or she believes. There were subjects I vacillated fifty-fifty for years. Most of the time what I had been taught won out. It was comfortable, and who likes to make changes?

I grew up believing the earth was reformed and shaped and rec-reated in six days and nights, for I was taught this. I believed Moses wrote the first five books of the Old Testament, for I was taught this. I took every statement in the Bible where it is said that Yahweh spoke as being the words of the preexistent Son of God or the Logos.

An example would be Genesis 1:26 where it is stated, "Let us create man in our image." Jon Levenson says in his book *Creation and the Persistence of Evil* that "there do seem to be other divine beings… to whom God proposes the creation of humanity."[1] I believed the Genesis account to be a conversation between God the father and another being who was preexistent and who became God the son in the incarnation.

These words were spoken words coming from the mouth of God which for me were just as real as the statement that still can be replayed in my mind spoken in July 1969 by Neil Armstrong which I heard at thirty-one years of age as Armstrong spoke from the moon: "One small step for man, one giant leap for mankind." I never thought about the fact that when God created the earth, there wasn't any human being around to hear what he said. I assumed God later told Moses (he had visited with him forty days and forty nights on Mt. Sinai) what he said at creation and many of the other things Moses allegedly wrote about him.

I slowly came to see there is no possible way anyone would have been on the spot at creation and be able to know exactly what went on in the cataclysm that produced the earth. Our Genesis account isn't exactly true science as to how the earth got here.

C. S. Lewis expresses it most clearly in his book titled *Miracles*.

> "No philosophical theory which I have yet come across is a radical improvement on the words of Genesis, that in the beginning God made heaven and earth. I say 'radical' improvement on the words of Genesis—as St. Jerome said years ago—is told in the manner of a popular poet, or as we should say, in the form of a folk tale. But if you compare it with the creation legends of other

peoples—with all those delightful absurdities in which giants to be cut up and floods to be dried up are made to exist before creation—the depth and originality of this Hebrew folk tale will soon be apparent. The idea of creation in the rigorous sense is there fully grasped."[2]

I felt that we were to keep the Sabbath day, just as Jesus had when he walked the earth. I didn't eat unclean foods. I believed the end of the world was ahead. I adopted all the outlooks and views of my parents and those around me and my church. I devoutly believed.

The challenge I faced after rejecting my church was to take everything that I believed relative to doctrines and dogmatic explanations of scripture, salvation, and what I believed was God's plan and purpose, and question and examine everything that I believed. I can't describe how difficult it is to search inside the human mind to ferret out the bricks and mortar that went into the mental construction of my ID or person with all it's beliefs about life and the world around me—my mental reality structure. It requires a great deal of mental effort on the part of anyone to change mental images and concepts developed over a lifetime. Often, I thought, "What the heck, who cares?"

Human beings don't like our belief's questioned. We all like to remain at ease in our outlooks and viewpoints and worldview. We don't like to be under stress about what it is that we believe. It is easiest to let life ride. I felt like my mental compass was being turned upside down as I faced one set of beliefs after another set of beliefs that I found I had to discard. It was unsettling and uncomfortable time after time to give up what I believed for I felt that I had read the Bible and researched it and used scriptural basis for the formation of my beliefs. Again and again, I found my concepts and understanding of "doctrine" were wrong. The mental pictures I had formed were so imbedded I found it almost impossible to alter them.

While having to find my place in the world and struggling to find reality in the world of religion, job pressures and earning a living occupied most of my time. I reference this because for several years,

I hardly picked up a Bible to read it. Twenty-five years of my life had been spent reading from it one way or another daily if not doing it for nothing more than picking it up and trying to say something comforting for someone standing beside a grave resulting from tragic accidents, premature deaths, old age, and all the causes of death common to humanity.

Economic survival was at stake for me and my family, and my life was consumed in having to face realities of the real world I had never known before, such as struggles to find and hold a job, build a business, start an insurance agency, meet payroll and expenses, and of pressures unknown from where I had been in life.

My wife and I had friends we would occasionally go to church with by invitation. By in large, we didn't make a habit of attending any church. Around the house, if I read the Bible, everything came slithering back to me like ghosts of the past. I had a leather-bound Oxford Bible I had bought in England while a student that I had given sermon after sermon from its pages. I had stood at gravesides and read all those comforting passages from it when trying to support grieving families facing death. It was marked in blue, yellow, and red crayon and had notes in pen all through it. After getting out of the church, I found that every scripture I read, all that I could see or hear from its pages were the sound of voices from fiery sermons I had heard or an explanation that I got in a Bible class about the verse that I might be reading. It was right there in black ink in marginal notes I had penned in it. I didn't want to read the Bible because it brought back so many negative memories.

Finally, after years, I threw the Bible away. I had carried it and read from it for a quarter century. I started all over in my life to read the Bible and absorb what it says rather than everything I thought it said before I read it. It was an amazing experience to shut out voices in my head when I read the Bible.

At the time I pitched it, I had been consumed in reading all of Philip Yancey's books. I had been reading at the time his book titled *The Bible Jesus Read*. In it, he quoted Kathleen Morris from her book titled *Amazing Grace*. I took hope that I was in good company in my journey from a statement of Morris that Yancey quoted. She wrote,

"Many people these days feel an absence in their lives, expressed as an acute desire for something more than a spiritual home, a community of faith, but when they try to read the Bible they end up throwing it across the room. To me this seems encouraging, and a good place to start, a sign of real engagement with God who is revealed in scripture."[3]

It was several years before I began to mow my lawn on Saturday without a guilty conscious. D. A. Carson's book *From Sabbath to Lord's Day* is an outstanding book about the Christian obligation of observing any day as a Christian.

A year or two later, I crunched down on some shrimp not knowing I needed to peel the scales off first. Having scales, it cleared the excluded list in Leviticus except that it had no fins, which made it forbidden by Leviticus. By this time, I wasn't trying to be an Israelite.

After years reading dozens and dozens of books to dig my way out of the myopic and dysfunctional ignorance in which I lived in a cultish religious environment, I read one day a reference to Jesus and a term used in a book I was reading. A statement was made that biblical scholars were now in the so-called third quest for the historical Jesus. I didn't know there had even been a first quest.

I found myself in the same audience of people that Dale Allison describes in his book *The Historical Christ and the Theological Jesus*,

"Remarkably, many pew-sitters are happily oblivious of what has been going on in the thinking world for two and a half centuries. They have somehow avoided most or even all the serious intellectual commentary on the Gospels since the Enlightenment. Perhaps typical are the two churches I grew up in, one Presbyterian, one Congregationalist. Never in Sunday School or from the pulpit did I hear anything of the modern debates surrounding Jesus and the Gospels."[4]

For sure, I had never heard anything in the cult of which I was a part. I had no concept that I was living during the third quest to understand Jesus. I had missed the first two quests.

In the next three chapters, we are going to take examples of incidents or stories of Jesus' life which are recorded. They show him dong very strange things. The purpose of this is to show that Jesus lived as a Jew of his day. He believed things Jewish people of the day believed. He believed in a future for the people of the nation at the time not some far off time into the future of the world. His mind wasn't on scenarios taken from the book of Revelation. He wasn't trying to change the Sabbath day to Sunday and make available ham sandwiches for the multitudes. All this will be to show you the real Jesus of the Bible, his world, his environment, and what was going on in the religious world in which he lived. We will then move on after that to Bible scholars and theologians' beliefs from the third quest for Jesus.

6

WHO IS THIS HISTORICAL JESUS?

"Sanders' next major book was *Jesus* and *Judaism*, published in 1985. In this work he argued that Jesus began as a follower of John the Baptist and was a prophet of the restoration of Israel. Sanders saw Jesus as creating an eschatological Jewish movement through his appointment of the Apostles and through his preaching and actions. After his execution (the trigger for which was Jesus overthrowing the tables in the temple court of Herod's Temple, thereby antagonizing the political authorities) his followers continued the movement, expecting his return to restore Israel. One consequence of this return would involve Gentiles worshiping the god of Israel. Sanders could find no substantial points of opposition between Jesus and the Pharisees, and he viewed Jesus as abiding by Jewish law and the disciples as continuing to keep it (cf. e.g., Acts 3.1, 21:23–26, for their worship in the Temple)."

—E. P. Sanders, Wikipedia

In the early 1950s, I would go with my dad on Sunday morning to visit with my grandmother. It was right in the middle of all the changes impacting my family. As a twelve-year-old, I was barely able to understand what was occurring in what my father was doing. He was making major changes in his life in standing up for his beliefs and his study of the Bible. To this day, I admire greatly the steps he took that became for me an inspiration for committing oneself to what you believe. He was misguided in choices just as I was, but he truly did all he did to obey God as he felt he should, just as my mother did. My mother and father were wonderful people that I consider Christian as much as I do any person I know or have observed in the world. So were my grandparents.

To introduce you to the historical Jesus, we will be discussing in this book I want to relay an account of the formation of beliefs of my parents and grandparents and exactly how those came about, including the way mine were developed. It is typical of the way religion enters the life of most people as they grow up.

I don't remember too much about my grandmother. What I do remember are the conversations my dad would have with her on those Sunday morning visits. They would always argue about the Bible. My grandmother was keeping up with all the small-town talk and she wasn't on the side of her son. She had grown up attending various small little churches closest to places where her family had lived and survived in the communities of Arkansas.

It is humorous as I look back on it for my grandmother chewed tobacco. Between bursts of emotional anger over a topic of disputation, she would pick up an old red empty Folgers coffee can that she kept next to her rocking chair and spit into it while catching her breath between bouts of dissension between the two. My father was trying to convince my grandmother that the things he was reading and studying were "truth," and I am sure my grandmother was trying to convince my dad that she was right about what she understood about truth as well.

There is one phrase or line my grandmother always used. It was, "Norvel, I don't care what the Bible says. You can't convince me that

Saturday is the Sabbath day!" She was a staunch believer of her local Baptist church.

My grandmother's viewpoint is exactly the way most people form their beliefs. There is an aphorism: "Don't confuse me with the facts. My mind is already made up." No matter what the Bible says, people don't change their minds on cherished beliefs.

My father had grown up just like my grandmother. He adopted hand-me-down religion. We all grow up assuming the religion of our parents when we were young. People have said the "accident of birth" creates our religion. Most nations grow up continuing to believe the religious beliefs of their parents. South Americans grow up to be Catholic. We speak of "Irish" Catholics. Muslims grow up to be Muslims. Mormon children grow up to be Mormons. Hindus grow up and become Hindus. And as sociologist Peter Berger says regarding societies growing up and accepting the religious traditions of their forefathers that they don't make changes until they finally reach the point where they ask,

> "I should find out more about my faith, or even more sharply, I really ought to learn what we believe."[1]

When my father started to study the Bible, he found that what Jesus did and said was totally different from what he believed Jesus had said and done. He found that Jesus was a Jewish boy. That wasn't emphasized in his church. Jesus was a Christian—not a Jew. Instead, my father found Jesus was circumcised on the eighth day. Jesus' mother went in to be purified through a series of detailed procedures required by Jewish ritual law. Jesus grew up observing Jewish customs and traditions.

My father discovered that Jesus kept the Sabbath day, not Sunday, nor did Jesus ever intimate that the Sabbath day was to be changed to Sunday, contrary to the arguments of his former Church of Christ pastor. Jesus kept Jewish holy days. This was never talked about in his church. Jesus never ate pork, and he refrained from eating unclean meats. It would have set off a revolt as Ed Sanders points out in his books. There is no mention of one resulting from his cleansing pork and shrimp and his walking the streets of Jerusalem eating a ham sandwich. We can be assured he did not do that.

I quoted N. T. Wright earlier who stated that Jesus stood steadfast within the Jewish traditions and religious beliefs of his day. To give you examples in the New Testament of Jesus' beliefs and actions, let's look at a couple of examples. We will move on after that to the example of Paul. These examples show us in detail the historical Jesus few Christians know. All his beliefs tie in to the point of the whole book—what Jesus believed about the end of the age during his lifetime. Contrary to Funk's comment that Jesus didn't prescribe any religious beliefs as such, we find he absolutely did.

Jesus instructed those he encountered in the society of the day to offer appropriate sacrifices as required under the law of Moses in respect to the temple and priesthood. He was aware his own parents had done the same after his birth as they were instructed from Leviticus (Luke 2:22–24). In the case of a leper Jesus healed, his words of instruction to him were to "offer the gift that Moses commanded, for a testimony to them" (Matt. 8:1–4).

E. P. Sanders, whom I will also quote often for his highly acclaimed works on Jesus' life, says that the account of the healing of the leper by Jesus

> "bears on one of the most important questions about Jesus, namely his stance toward 'official' Judaism: the nation of Israel as a political entity; the Temple; the priesthood; the law; the fasts; the Synagogues."[2]

To show that this was not a one-time-only approach of Jesus relative to the temple and Jesus loyalty to the system and rituals and procedures, there is one other Gospel account where he healed ten lepers. When Jesus healed them, he likewise instructed them to "go and show yourself to the priests" (Luke 17:11–14).

Jesus knew the steps these individuals would take. He totally endorsed it and believed in it and made no steps to condemn the worship of God through the temple sacrifices and priestly ordinances of the Levitical system. Jesus expected either a new temple or a renewed temple soon and prophesied of its arrival. Instead of Jesus stopping temple worship, Jesus expected a continuation of the temple system he grew up with from a child.

There was a decisive reason for Jesus doing this and telling them to take the action which he advised them to take. Lepers had to follow specific rituals to be assimilated back into the community. There were a series of temple requirements to be followed by each of them to be able to merge socially back into the community after being healed. These steps enabled them to avoid continued ostracizing and shunning. They could become citizens of the community once more by approval of the priests after they had been ridded of leprosy by following sacrificial rites of the law of Moses.

Leprosy was believed to be contagious in Jesus' day. The community quarantined lepers. In reading all the accounts of the Old Testament, their treatment was quite sad even up to the time of Jesus. In the Old Testament period, lepers had to live in leper camps. They wore tattered clothing. When individuals outside the camp walked by the encampment filled with fellow lepers, they all in unison cried out "unclean, unclean" to signal the passersby to avoid them and pass on their way.

> "The leper who has the disease shall wear torn clothes and let the hair of his head hang loose, and he shall cover his upper lip and cry 'unclean, unclean.' He shall remain unclean if he has the disease; he is unclean; he shall dwell alone in a habitation outside the camp" (Leviticus 13:45–46).

I assume some of the dress and garb and even requirement of growing the hair long was to create a person with a Halloween look to scare children and individuals to assist in keeping them away from leper camps. In one scene in the movie *Ben Hur*, a graphic portrayal is given of how lepers were shunned and ostracized.

Jesus knew, if omniscient as God, exactly what he was instructing these lepers to do. He as preexistent God would have written the script through the pen of Moses in that he inspired it all, in that Paul said that all scripture was written by inspiration of God.

Yahweh had instituted all the ritual himself in the Old Testament. The leper was going to have to pay for two birds in the cleansing ritual and two male lambs and one female lamb. The leper was to shave his head, his eyebrows and his whole body when presenting himself to the priest at the temple in Jerusalem. I will quote in the entirety the verses which explain the final act a leper was to perform to be pronounced clean once again.

> "Now on the eighth day he is to take two male lambs without defect, and a yearling ewe lamb without defect, and three tenths of an ephah of fine flower mixed with oil for a grain offering and one log of oil; and the priest who pronounces him clean shall present the man to be cleansed and the aforesaid before the Lord at the doorway of the tent of the meeting" (Lev. 14:10–12).

The only difference from the instructions in the book of Leviticus was that for the leper in Jesus' day, there was no portable tent or tabernacle to appear before. The leper in Jesus' day instead walked up to one of the most magnificent and beautiful buildings or edifices known in the world of Jesus' life—Herod's temple. Historians tell us Herodian renovations began on the temple in 19–20 BC and continued until the early '60s AD, thirty years or so after Jesus' death. Its splendor was world renown at the time. It sat high on a hill in the city of Jerusalem, where the Dome of the Rock or Temple Mount resides today. In Jesus' day, it had acres and acres of beautiful grounds elaborately landscaped surrounding it.

Priests worked there daily offering and burning sacrifices, which were "clean" animals or birds described by Moses in the book of Leviticus. Some of the meat of sacrifices was eaten by the priests. Smells of sacrifices being burned and cooked were as common as wafting inviting smells we might get while walking the streets in any restaurant row in a major city of the world. The temple, with all its sacrificial rites and daily ritual, was the religious and social and financial center of the national life of the nation of Israel. It also served as a quasi department of health of the day which governed whether you could even enter the premises to worship. These lepers had to substantiate they were not diseased to be able to worship within it and live freely in the community once more. Jesus dined with a man called Simon the Leper in one scene in his life. He had been cured of leprosy or possibly had been healed by Jesus.

Jesus most likely believed that once each year, on the Day of Atonement, his father Yahweh, personally entered the holy of holies, that revered area of the temple where God was reputed to reside. Jesus had read of those occasions in the Old Testament. Not even Jesus could go in there. Only a chosen Levitical priest could do so. That special priest on the Day of Atonement wore a bell and a rope tied around his leg which extended outside under a curtain which surrounded the area for a special reason. If the priest had a heart attack and died while performing his services in the holy of holies, he could be dragged out. No one could go in to rescue him.

Stop for a moment and reflect on what we have read. If our Christian beliefs are correct about Jesus, he was the preexistent Lord to whom the leper in the Old Testament account was instructed to appear ("shall present the man...before the Lord at the doorway of the tent"). Jesus would have been the Lord at the doorway of the tent if Jesus was incarnated several thousand years later as Christians believe.

Jesus didn't try to point out to the leper that this was all to be done away. He didn't take the opportunity to say, "Don't go offer the gift that Moses commanded since I don't deem that important or necessary any more under my administration." Instead he told the leper to go offer the sacrifices as a "testimony" to the priesthood of Jerusalem.

Since Jesus had just told the leper that "see thou tell no man" (Matt. 8:4) of the healing and to be quiet about it, it is obvious Jesus was showing his total support in the covenant of Yahweh and a temple and its system of worship, conducted in a place which Jesus called several times in the Gospels, "my father's house." In another place in the Gospels, Jesus told the public and his disciples that they should obey all the commands of the priests and those who were their religious leaders in the community. Jesus wanted, apparently, to have the priests know he wasn't a dissenter or rabble rouser or trying to change the religious system or old covenant or put them out of a job.

> "Then spoke Jesus to the multitude, and to his disciples, saying, the scribes and the Pharisees sit in Moses' seat; all therefore whatsoever they bid you observe, that observe and do; but do not ye after their works; for they say, and do not" (Matt. 23:1–3).

Those things that priests of the day would have bid Jesus' disciples to "observe and do" would have been the keeping of the seventh day as a Sabbath, abstaining from eating unclean foods described in Leviticus 11, observance of all the annual Sabbaths, and adhering to all the rules and regulations of the Old Covenant regarding the whole sacrificial system carried out in the temple.

What is clear in this recorded action and speech of Jesus is that Jesus wasn't tearing down, opposing, changing, altering, disrupting, terminating, and extinguishing the religious structure given to the nation of Israel through the temple. Jesus called the authority that emanated from the priesthood with a term they all understood. It was called "Moses seat."

Catholics have a very good comparison in their belief that the pope is the Vicar of Christ. By Jesus preaching and teaching and advising them to continue in their structure and outlook they had grown up with as Jewish people, Jesus wasn't trying to change everything he knew from a child.

E. P. Sanders states in his book *Studying the Synoptic Gospels* that years after Jesus had been killed that the attitude toward the temple of the early church had nothing to do with it being changed, altered, done away, or disparaged. He says,

"The general attitude of the disciples in Jerusalem seems to have been that they should spread the word that Jesus was Messiah and that faith in him would save, while waiting for God to do something; more precisely, while waiting for the return of the Lord."[3]

It appears we are hearing the voice of Jesus here when he speaks words of support and continuation of the temple and its services and functions for the nation of Israel and those words in the Gospels we find are something he most likely said. They are scriptures we can take that gives us a view of Jesus' outlook, the contents of his messages, and Jesus' own thoughts in the way he viewed the temple and religious system in which he grew up from a child. It is what he learned. It is what he believed. He confirms the outlook most of those to whom he spoke possessed and how they viewed that beautiful edifice on the hill where the Dome of the Rock is located today.

Sanders says that this example of Jesus instructing those lepers he healed to honor the laws of Moses, tells us the way Jesus thought and viewed the world around him. He writes,

"The case of the leper is the clearest instance in which Jesus is represented as affirming the Temple, the priests and the purity laws, but it is unambiguous. Here Jesus shows himself in agreement with and obedient to the sacrificial and purity laws."[4]

Most likely if you are an evangelical Christian, you probably were taught that Jesus spoke about changing all this and "doing away" with the law of Moses, just as my father was taught. Jesus was very much a proponent of the religious system built around Herod's temple, including Sabbath keeping, holy day observance, and rituals of sacrifices as prescribed in the Old Testament. Jesus is never represented in the Gospels as speaking of a new covenant with Israel or a spiritual group he was founding to oppose or reject the religious system Jesus had grown up knowing from a child.

Sanders writes concerning theological beliefs Jesus was going to change everything in his world and set a new way of worship of God the following:

> "Had Jesus thought that the entire systems were corrupt, that the priests were criminals, that sacrifices were wrong and should be done away with—or anything of the sort—we should have more material pointing in that direction. The temple was central to Palestinian Judaism and important to all Jews everywhere. To be against it would be to oppose Judaism as a religion."[5]

I found that one of the criteria or rules of engagement by scholars in the current quest for the historical Jesus is to study the life of Jesus in the world in which he lived and grew up. Just as every human being is a part of the community and the nation of his birth and childhood, so was Jesus. He was a part of his own world and day and age and time in his thoughts, actions, and beliefs. John Meier says regarding the daily religious life of Jesus and his family the following:

> "For these Galilean Jews of the countryside, fidelity to the Jewish religion meant fidelity to the basics spelled out in the Mosaic Law: circumcision, observance of the Sabbath, observance of kosher food laws, and pilgrimage to the Jerusalem temple, whose sacrificial ritual during the great feasts was the high point of the annual cycle of their religious life."[6]

Robertson points out in a *Harmony of the Gospels* that most likely Jesus participated in the ritualistic killing and sacrifice of a lamb for his last night on earth in the Jewish custom of Passover. It would have been one of thirty or so times Jesus would have remembered doing so from a child. As Jesus spoke on his last night as a human being, he now saw his final evening with the disciples as his last time. Jesus felt he most likely would be killed as prophets of old were and John the Baptist. As he ate and drank with them, he told them he would not do it again with them until the kingdom was here of which he spoke frequently. Jesus anticipated its arrival just around the corner.

A priest at the temple would have slain the lamb eaten by Jesus and the twelve in his last night on earth. In respect to the law and "law keeping," Jesus said in another place, "Not one jot or tittle of it will pass." Harold Bloom states inside his book *Jesus and Yahweh,*

> "No Jew known at all to history can be regarded as more loyal to the covenant than was Jesus of Nazareth."[7]

Far from being recognized as a Bible scholar and known as a literary critic, Bloom accurately nails the historical Jesus presented in the New Testament. No Bible scholar or theologian who reads the New Testament honestly could deny nor refute that simple statement no matter how hard he or she may try. We will find that Paul carried on with beliefs of Jesus of his day regarding the temple and its significance and the laws of Moses, so called. This is important in understanding what Jesus believed about the end of the age and what was going to occur in the future. Paul and Jesus both believed the temple was to continue and the coming reign of God was just around the corner. A temple was to be a critical part of both their futures. They saw no changes in respect to its functions and daily administration by Levitical priests.

7

PAUL UPHELD AND SUPPORTED JEWISH TEMPLE BELIEFS

"Only those who carry the teachings of the cat-echism back into the preaching of the Jewish Messiah will arrive at the idea that Jesus was the founder of a new religion. To all unprejudiced persons it is manifest that Jesus had not the slightest intention of doing away with the Jewish religion and putting another in its place."
—Albert Schweitzer, *The Quest for the Historical Jesus*

"If we are to locate both Jesus and Paul within the world of first-century Judaism, within the tur-bulent theological and political movements and expectations of the time (and if we are not then we should admit that we know very little about either of them) then we should face the fact that neither of them was teaching a timeless system of religion or ethics, or even a timeless message about how people are saved. Both believed themselves to be actors within the drama staged by Israel's God in fulfillment of his long purposes. Both, in other words, breathed the air of Jewish eschatology."

—N. T. Wright, *What St. Paul Said*

In respect to the temple and its sacrificial system which Christians believe today that Jesus taught was to be changed and abolished, the apostle Paul walked into it thirty years or so after Jesus death to offer sacrifices in fulfillment of the law of Moses! This is sort of a "whoa" statement for millions of Christians who sit in church each week. They have probably never in their lives heard a sermon from the book of Acts giving the account of Paul's actions in his life thirty years after the resurrection and the reasons he did what he did.

Not only do we find that Jesus followed and lived by and encouraged others to follow the laws taught his race, we find Paul, being a Jew himself, did the same. He taught Jewish Christians to obey the law of Moses and that never changed in his lifetime. He never changed in his outlook of the special place the Jewish people have with God in a covenant relationship.

We find the account of Paul in the book of Acts. The resurrection was thirty or more years past. When Paul was making his last visit to Jerusalem described in his life journeys by Luke, the elders of the Jerusalem church explained they had a problem. Rumors were coming back to Jewish Christians in the city of Jerusalem that Paul in Asia Minor was preaching the temple at Jerusalem was to be done away by grace coming on the scene and all the sacrificial system and customs of the Jewish Christians were to be abolished. The elders, James as the chief apostle, asked Paul in a similar fashion to make a testimony as Jesus had asked the leper.

In Paul's case, it was a testimony for Jewish Christians at Jerusalem. That testimony was that Paul wasn't doing what was rumored about him. Acting upon their request, Paul walked into that same gorgeous temple on the hill to offer sacrifices along with four other men who had taken Nazerite vows. Luke records,

> "Take these men and purify yourself along with them and pay their expenses, so they may shave their heads. Thus, all will know that there is nothing in what they have been told about you but that you yourself live in observance of the law" (Acts 21:24).

Paul was to join in all the ritual sacrifices and services in all the procedures along with them so that individuals would know "you yourself live in observance of the law." Thirty years after Jesus' death, Paul did exactly what he was asked to do to show his support for the temple and all its ritual. Paul himself continued to live, a quarter century after his conversion, by the law of Moses. We do find that when Paul worked among Gentiles he ate with them freely which was contrary to Jewish social customs. When among Gentiles, he followed social practices to win them over to his message. None involved living contrary to Jewish laws and precepts but only had to do with being seen with Gentiles in table fellowship and Gentiles eating meats that had been sacrificed to idols. It was very like all the Jim Crow stuff and black and white restrooms and lunch counter separation this country grew up with. Paul wasn't eating pork as a Jew when he ate and mixed socially with Gentiles.

Luke says,

> "So, Paul associated himself with the men next day; he had himself purified along with them and went into the temple to give notice of the time when the days of purification would be completed—the time when the sacrifice could be offered for each one of them" (Acts 21:26).

Luke is showing that Paul even years after his conversion held to keeping of the Sabbath day and those beliefs within the temple worship of Jews that were common to those of Jesus. In his book *From Sabbath to Lord's Day*, by D. A. Carson, the statement is made:

> "Particularly in his portrait of Paul, Luke wants to demonstrate that despite allegations to the contrary, Paul remained in continuity with Israel, and that includes continuity with the law."[1]

We have no reason to believe that Paul didn't expect all the sacrifices and system of worship connected with the temple rituals and ordinances to continue for a thousand years into the future. Paul expected Jesus to return to the city. Ed Sanders says that Jesus saw a new temple or cleansed temple as part of the kingdom of God. Sanders writes:

> "Jesus, like virtually all other first-century Jews, assumed that there would still be a Temple."[2]

Ed Sanders says the same of Paul in his book *Studying the Synoptic Gospels*:

> "In Romans 8 Paul looks forward to the time when the creation itself will be set free from its bondage to decay (8:21)...Paul, in short, supports the idea of a new or transformed creation in a way that makes his cosmic expectation compatible with the synoptic passages which point to a new creation and a new society."[3]

In chapter 10, we will see that Paul was preaching and expounding the imminent return of Jesus to earth. Paul didn't foresee the future as John the Devine in the book of Revelation. Jesus didn't tell Paul anything about the contents of a future book he allegedly was to inspire to be written sixty or so years later on the small island called Patmos which is now part of the nation of Greece and most famous for being the location of both the vision of and the writing of the book of Revelation.

Paul most likely saw the future, as scholars point out, solely from a typical Jewish expectation of the coming of the messiah that he learned from a child. He saw the future as Jesus saw the future in his ministry and preaching. It would involve God ruling from Jerusalem and the Gentiles from around the world flowing into the city in the worship of God as described in the prophets. As Tom Wright points out above, Paul breathed the air of Jewish eschatology. Paul looked for a change in the natural order of our world. We see no thoughts ever expressed by Paul that he believed the temple was to be destroyed and torn down. It was not part of his futuristic expectations in any of his writings available to us. The Gospel accounts had not been read by Paul. Jesus had never made clear to Paul the temple was to be destroyed with no stone left unturned.

Second Thessalonians 2:3 indicates that Paul believed the temple in Jerusalem would be still standing when Jesus returned. It shows that certain events had to occur before Jesus' coming. He says,

> "Let no one in any way deceive you, for it will not come unless the apostasy comes first, and the man of lawlessness is revealed, the son of destruction, who opposes and exalts himself above every so-called god or object of worship, so that he takes his seat in the temple of God, displaying himself as being God" (2 Thess. 2:3).

The temple on the hill in Jerusalem is referred to as "the temple of God." From everything we have covered, it is evident by context that the passage is referring to the temple in Jerusalem that was yet standing in Paul's day.

Dozens and dozens of churches, including the remnants of the Worldwide Church of God, use the statement in 2 Thessalonians, that in the end time, a human being will sit in a temple at Jerusalem, claiming to be God, as one of those points on a countdown list of prophetic events to occur before Jesus' return. The temple, according to LaHaye's book, which is referenced in this verse, is not interpreted to be the temple in Paul's day but a future temple yet to be built. Hal Lindsey's books all point out that a future temple is to be built in Jerusalem. So do hundreds of other similar books that detail events in the countdown to Jesus.

A time or two before my mother's death, I got calls at home, in which she would refer me to a newspaper article indicating that land had been purchased somewhere in Israel or stones were being quarried in some spot in the world by Jews, for construction of that temple yet to be built before Jesus can return. Or it would be an article she had found that someone had just discovered that perfect red heifer on a farm some place in the world ready to be offered to cleanse the sanctuary upon its inauguration. She believed, just as I did at one time, a new temple, spoken of in the Bible, was to be built in our day.

All those of course turned out to be false alarms. We can be sure with tensions in the Middle East between Iran and Israel, any attempts to build a temple will invite Iran to lob some of their yet to be built nukes into Israel. I think this is one alleged prophetic item that can be taken off the countdown list.

Paul believed that mortals would put on immortality upon Jesus' return. Jesus, he believed, would come "down" to the earth and bring dead saints who had been resurrected with him. With his expectation of the churches of God participating in the establishment of God's rule on earth, he most likely saw the temple in Jerusalem, as being the place from which God would rule. For Jewish Christians, it was part of their religious heritage and beliefs. Paul fully acknowledged and gave support to them for continuing worship of God in the sacrificial system and procedures connected with the temple. He showed them he had no beef with it and for the nation of Israel it was not anti-Christian or weak and beggarly or whatever terms we might use to describe them for them to continue religious practices in it.

Larry Hurtado writes in his book *Lord Jesus Christ* of Paul's beliefs:

> "Paul held together fiercely two things that most
> of Christianity subsequently came to regard as
> incompatible: (1) He confirmed the continuing

ethnic identity of Jews and the continuing special significance of 'Israel' (by which Paul always
refers to a group made up of Jews): and (2) he
affirmed the necessity for all people to obey the
gospel and, through faith in Jesus, to receive
God's eschatological salvation."[5]

In chapter 19, we will get to Paul's beliefs about the arrival of
God's kingdom on earth and how it would impact the society of his
day. We will discover what Paul believed about the nations of the
world and their futures at the time. We will find conflicted concepts
he held about what was really occurring in his life, his ministry, and
the works of Peter and other apostles. It is enlightening and doesn't
include the concepts of dogmatic theologies of the Christian religion
when it comes to salvation of souls as covered in the preface of this
book.

As to what happened later to the temple, Paul had neither a
crystal ball view nor prophetic insight from Jesus it was going to
be destroyed by Roman legions within a dozen years or so after his
appearance in it to offer sacrifices. If Jesus spoke of it being torn
down Paul doesn't seem to be aware of any of the so-called prophecies
of Jesus that it would be razed with no stone remaining. Paul had not
read the Olivet prophecies. They had not been written.

Raymond Brown writes that most Bible scholars have discarded
the concept that Paul was the author of Hebrews, one of them being
the contradiction shown in this step that Paul took in supporting
the temple system of worship. Brown, in his book *The Churches the
Apostles Left Behind*, says that "few Bible scholars hold the belief" that
Paul wrote Hebrews. The reason—it's complete abnegation of the
Jewish religious system of priest, temple, and sacrifice. Brown says,

"The style of Hebrews is totally different from
Paul's and there is nothing in the apostles writing to match the radical critique of Israelite cult
that is at the heart of Hebrews. In Romans 9–11
and 15:16, Paul shows himself far more preserva-

tive of Judaism and its cultic language than does Hebrews which would replace the OT sacrifices, priesthood, and tabernacle."[6]

We see that all this remained very important to Paul and he didn't condemn any part of it as Larry Hurtado points out.

Since Paul had to pick up the tab for the expenses he had agreed to purchase for everyone,

> "a year-old male lamb without defect for a sin offering, a ram without defect for a fellowship offering, together with their grain offerings and drink offerings, and a basket of bread made without yeast, cakes made of fine flour mixed with oil, and wafers spread with oil"[7] (Num. 6:14).

Outside the area on the temple grounds, a huge commerce existed in the buying and selling of livestock and birds and grains which were an integral part of the requirements under the Mosaic law for an individual to bring for sacrifice to the priests. Jesus had called it a den of robbers and overthrew the money changers' tables used to make coinage for divergent Jewish citizens appearing to offer sacrifices. He told those who sold the pigeons, "Take these things away; you shall not make my fathers house a house of trade" (John 2:16).

Most likely Jesus was angered due to the abuse of profit making by those who attached themselves to the temple site for monetary greed. Jesus viewed it as a residence of his father Yahweh. In this action, Jesus didn't condemn the worship nor the law of Moses but the attitude of those abusing the system and using it for a selfish business enterprise. As Sanders states in the beginning of this chapter, this act of Jesus ultimately was the key that led to his crucifixion. Dale Allison writes in respect to Jesus overthrowing the money changers' tables that he was either upset with the abuses with the money changers or it may have been a symbolic gesture of some kind on Jesus' part.

Christianity hasn't been given a picture of the one who walked the streets of Jerusalem in his day and time. A "theological" Christ has overshadowed the historical Jesus who preached and taught in its streets and what Jesus believed about his world and the future of ours. He didn't speak of founding a church within the nation of Israel. Jesus believed things most Christians don't imagine he believed. His outlook as to his purpose in life as he saw it is totally different from the way we have all learned in our churches. Jesus set about to usher in the kingdom of God. So did Paul.

John Meier says regarding Jesus preaching and message to Israel that

> "Jesus the Jew addressed his fellow Israelites and sought to gather all Israel into the community of the end time. It was apparently only at the consummation of Israel history that he thought Gentiles would be brought into the kingdom (see, e.g., Matt. 8:11–12 par.). He was not interested in creating a separatist sect or a holy remnant a la Qumran, and he never sent his disciples on a formal mission to the Gentiles. The idea that his special religious community within Israel would slowly undergo a process of separation from Israel as it pursued a mission to the Gentiles in this present world—the long-term result being that his community would become predominately Gentile itself—finds no place in Jesus message or practice. While the early church as we know it would not have arisen with the ministry of the historical Jesus as a necessary precondition, the ministry of Jesus taken by itself did not create the early church."[8]

Coming from a Roman Catholic priest and scholar and one devoted to the primacy of Peter and all the scriptures supporting the establishment of the office of the Pope with all its authority and stature for the church, this is quite an honest admission on his part.

8

A New Look at Jesus

"Forget the 'titles' of Jesus, at least for a moment;
forget the pseudo-orthodox attempts to make
Jesus of Nazareth conscious of being the second
person of the Trinity; forget the arid reduction-
ism that is the mirror image of that unthinking
would be orthodoxy."
—N. T. Wright, *Jesus and the Victory of God*

All through the Gospel accounts, scholars and theologians tell us we have passages of Jesus warning of the soon coming arrival of the king-dom. Jesus constantly gave cautions and warnings to watch and be ready, for it would come in an hour that they might not be aware. He expected at any time a great crisis. So did the apostle Paul. Instead of preaching an altar call of just believe and accept the Lord, they lived in different times with different thoughts and saw the end of the age or a cataclysm approaching. Paul felt the dead would be raised and the world changed and the wolf would lie down with the lamb and the ecosystem would be changed to cause the deserts to blossom and yield agricultural products in abundance. It's groaning would be brought to an end.

The single theologian-scholar among those of the guild or third quest for Jesus, is N.T. Wright, whom I have quoted already several times. He has written numerous books, lectured, taught, and been one of the most active voices in attempts to explain the historical Jesus through the lens of today's Bible scholarship. His beliefs are best summarized in *Jesus and the Victory of God* and *Surprised by Hope*.

Like a jousting knight in armor, Wright has charged into the field of third quest scholars with a wrecking ball to try to give a totally different interpretation of the life of Jesus of Nazareth. He has challenged all comers. He has bashed those of the so-called Jesus Seminar which has given us a picture of Jesus as a wandering cynic or sage in his day with nothing to say of an apocalyptic future. As was pointed out in chapter 2, the Jesus seminar has come up with a Jesus who gave no warnings of impending disaster ahead, a coming of Yahweh, or judgement soon to face Israel.

Wright believes that Jesus viewed his life and his death being solely for the nation of Israel. It has been labeled 'restoration theology.' Instead of the traditional Christian view summarized in John 3:16 of Jesus dying for the sins of the world and for all humanity for all time, in what we know as atonement theology, Jesus instead was attempting to fix the broken relationship with God and Israel under the rubric of the Old Covenant. Jesus efforts were to repair and restore the old covenant, not create a new one. His purpose in his preaching and teaching in life was an attempt to bring about a condition whereby Israel would "return from exile," which is a metaphor for Wright of Jesus restoring the covenant relationship between Israel and Yahweh.

We find all through the Gospels Jesus shows he didn't think about people of the world beyond the boundaries of the national state of Israel as he knew it and he was never addressing us as people of the future in his messages. On numerous occasions the Gospel writers speak of Gentiles who came into Jesus' life and asked to be able to involve themselves with his message in some way. His approach to them is quite abrupt and it is very clear he didn't see them as having an immediate part in the kingdom message he proclaimed. On one occasion, he refers to Gentiles as dogs. In sending out the disciples with their message of the coming kingdom, Jesus told them not to go to any Gentile cities with the message of hope for the future. Albert Schweitzer got it right when he wrote of Jesus:

> "Jesus shared Jewish racial particularism wholly and unreservedly. According to Matt. 10:5 he forbade his disciples to proclaim the coming of the kingdom of God to the Gentiles. Evidently, therefore, his purpose did not embrace them. Had it been otherwise, the hesitation of Peter in Acts 10 and 11, and the necessity of justifying the conversion of Cornelius, would be incomprehensible."[1]

In *Jesus and the Restoration of Israel*, Darrell Bock explains Wright's views.

> "The center of Wright's assessment of Jesus prophetic kingdom announcement involves three claims that emanate from Jesus' self-identification with the task of Israel; the return from exile, the defeat of evil and the return of YHWH to Zion. For Wright, Jesus saw himself as the 'leader and focal point of the true, returning-from-exile Israel'; this meant that he was the Messiah, 'the king through whose work YHWH was at last restoring his people.'"[2]

All this means that Jesus spoke to his world, not ours. His message wasn't timeless and for all generations. He didn't speak to future generations in his messages. Alister McGrath goes on to say about what Wright's interpretation means for traditional Christian beliefs.

> "The individualism that has been so characteristic of much of evangelicalism, particularly in North America, is called into question. Since a

set of individualist assumptions, probably ultimately deriving from the late Renaissance, evangelical interpreters of Scripture have tended to
assume that the biblical message is addressed to
them as individuals, dealing with issues such as
personal sin, personal destiny and an individual
relationship with God."[3]

Wright summarizes his beliefs of Jesus' intent when he states,

"He was identifying himself with the sufferings
of Israel…The symbolism and story-telling of
Jesus make sense only within this Jewish world,
but they play their own strange and unique variation on their dark theme. What Jesus did and said
stands out a mile from what early Christianity
said about him and his execution, but early
Christian atonement-theology is only fully expli-
cable as the post-Easter rethinking of Jesus essentially pre-Easter understanding."[4]

When Jesus spoke at the Last Supper, he passed a cup and spoke
the words,

"And when he had taken a cup and given thanks,
He gave it to them, saying, 'Drink from it, all of
you, for this is My blood of the covenant, which
is poured out for many for forgiveness of sins'"
(Matt. 26:27–28).

Wright believes Jesus thinking was his sole consideration of the
nation. Wright says,

"Once again we must stress in its first-century
Jewish context, this (i.e., 'forgiveness of sins')
denotes, not an abstract transaction between

human beings and their god, but the very concrete expectation of Israel, namely that the nation would at last be rescued from the 'exile' which had come about because of their sins. Matthew is not suggesting that Jesus' death will accomplish an abstract atonement, but that it will be the means of rescuing YHWH's people from their exilic plight."[5]

Alister McGrath, in summarizing the beliefs of Tom Wright concerning atonement theology, writes in *Jesus and the Restoration of Israel* this comment:

"The death of Jesus can indeed be thought of as being 'for others,' but it is to be understood as having corporate significance for the people of Israel, not individual significance for sinners. Wright argues that the death of Jesus is linked with the notion of the covenant, so that Jesus can be seen as a redemptive representative of Israel, bearing her specific curse and making it possible for her as a people to achieve her intended destiny."[6]

McGrath goes on to point out that

"notions such as the forgiveness of sins are not to be interpreted as global and timeless construal's; they are specifically related to the history of Israel and thus have concrete referents (the return from exile) within that history."[7]

On a typical Easter Sunday morning one will hear sermons on radio and TV, of how Jesus suffered and died on the cross for your sins and mine, often with emotionally descriptive words like—'while nails were being pounded into his flesh, Jesus was thinking of you and me as it was taking place.' If what Wright and other third questers tell us, Jesus was most likely solely thinking of himself and the pain he was experiencing. We had not been born yet and certainly had committed no sins. Jesus couldn't see two thousand years into our world nor would he even know of our existence. His concern was the nation of Israel and Yahweh's appearance in his world.

Wikipedia says that the length of time before a person dies could vary from hours to days, depending upon how someone was hanged on the cross, the individual health and stamina of the person, the scourging or beatings the person may have experienced before being hanged, and other factors. Death could result from heart failure, blood loss, shock, sepsis of wounds, dehydration, and more commonly by asphyxiation resulting from the weight of the body collapsing down on the lungs not enabling the person to breathe. Jesus' body eventually took over his thinking. He thought of nothing but the pain and agony he felt.

All this, we have been taught, Jesus went through to do away with the old covenant and establish the new. He did it for you and me. He died for the sins of humanity once and for all. Wright and other Bible scholars believe it was the exact opposite. Jesus hoped his death would be the way for Israel and God to continue the special relationship between Yahweh and his people under the old covenant, not dissolve it! That was Jesus' mission in life. It was restoration theology.

Alister McGrath says that Wright's books and reinterpretation of Jesus aims and purposes would mean a major revision of evangelical thought of Jesus' life. One will find it extremely hard to accommodate this Jesus in the thinking process. I find it is almost impossible to think of the death of Jesus in any other way than John 3:16, for all my life I was taught this. One's mental gyroscope will begin to spin to accommodate this Jesus. Limiting the thoughts of Jesus, to just the nation of Israel, decimates the indoctrination Christianity has received for generations in respect to Jesus death on the cross. McGrath writes in *Jesus and the Restoration of Israel,*

> "Wright has thus lobbed a hand grenade into the world of traditional evangelical theology."[8]

McGrath says for evangelicals that,

> "Wright obliges us to read the New Testament again and to take the profound risk allowing our most settled ideas to be challenged in the light of the Biblical witness."

McGrath goes on to say that if Tom Wright and Ed Sanders, another world-recognized scholar of the historical Jesus, are correct in their views of Paul and Jesus, that the icon of the reformation, Martin Luther, is wrong. Major paradigm changes are ahead for cherished traditional Christian views held of Jesus if either Sanders' or Wright's views have lasting impact upon theology.

Wright says further that on that last night when Jesus sat down with the twelve that

> "there should be no doubt but that Jesus intended to say, with all the power of symbolic drama and narrative, that he was shortly to die, and that his death was to be seen within the context of the larger story of YHWH's redemption of Israel. Those with Jesus who shared the meal received 'the forgiveness of sins,' that is, the end of exile."[9]

Schweitzer says something similar. He states of the last supper of Jesus the following:

> "The Lord's Supper, again, was no new institution, but merely an episode at the last Passover meal of the kingdom which was passing away, and was intended 'as an anticipatory celebration of the Passover in the New Kingdom.' A Lord's Supper in our sense, 'detached from the Passover,' would have been inconceivable to Jesus, and not less so to his disciples."[10]

Regarding the trinity or baptizing in the name of the father, son, and holy spirit that Jesus is claimed to have spoken to the disciples, John Hick points out in his book *The Metaphor of God Incarnate* that

> "Conservative New Testament scholarship today does not suggest that Jesus thought of himself as God, or God the son, second person of a divine trinity, incarnate; and so we cannot reasonably suppose that he thought of his death in any way that presupposes that. It is more believable, as a maximal possibility, that Jesus saw himself as the final prophet precipitating the coming of God's rule on earth, than that he saw it in anything like the terms developed by the church's later atonement theories."[11]

Concerning whether Jesus believed he was the Son of God and whether he walked around believing and teaching that he had come down from heaven to die for the sins of the world, James D. G. Dunn writes in his book *Jesus and the Spirit*,

> "The evidence permits us to speak only of Jesus' consciousness of an intimate relationship with God, not of awareness of metaphysical sonship, nor of a 'divine consciousness,' (far less consciousness of being 'second Person of the Trinity'!). Even to speak of consciousness of 'divine sonship' is misleading. And certainly, to speak of an awareness of preexistence goes far beyond the evidence."[12]

What does this have to do with when Jesus will return? It has everything to do with it. We are looking at Jesus' own beliefs regarding his work, his message, his relationship with Israel, and what he expected and intended to do while on earth. It doesn't involve the outpouring of death and destruction in the book of Revelation covered in the preface of this book and the bizarre portrayal of the end of the world described in the contents of the *Left Behind* series. It wasn't upon his mind. Our pictures we gained of Jesus about his dying for the sins of the world and returning after letting humankind go about life until his wrath has built up over the world's sins and return to pour out death and destruction, isn't the way Jesus thought and felt. Those pictures of Jesus have been given to us by interpreters and those who have built our theologies post Jesus' death.

We will turn to third quest scholar's beliefs of the coming of the kingdom of God.

9

Scholars' Beliefs of Jesus' Worldview

"Jesus, Luke would have us understand, was expecting a single great crisis, which would mean death for himself, a searching test for his disciples, and judgment for Israel, and this event, contrary to all appearances of defeat and failure, was to be the great triumph prophesied by Daniel (7, 13), in which God would bestow world dominion on the Son of man, the symbolic representative of the people of God."

—N. T. Wright, *Jesus and the Victory of God*

Third quest scholars tell us Jesus never spoke of the new covenant as described in Hebrews or even implied one was in the works through his life or that was the purpose for his life.

We find instead of Jesus speaking about a future end of the age years away, Jesus spoke about and preached and warned of a first coming of Yahweh in his own day. His message had been the message of the Old Testament prophets before Jesus for a thousand years. Jesus saw himself as a prophet of the end time, meaning, the final fulfillment of all the promises God had made to Israel throughout their history as a nation and their being a covenant people with him. Wright believes that Jesus never spoke of his return and "such stories are the invention of the early church in the persons of the evangelists or their sources."[1]

As we go forward, we will see that other third questers do feel that Jesus did speak of his return and it led to the beliefs of the early church that he was to return and the belief was that as well for the apostle Paul.

Jesus message followed specific themes. He thought like many Jews of his day in regard to the future and what God was going to do. Sanders says

> "evidence points towards Jewish eschatology as the general framework of Jesus' ministry that we may examine the particulars in the light of that framework."[2]

Jesus was a Jewish eschatologist with an apocalyptic message of his day. The best definition I can give you of Jewish eschatology is that of Dale Allison in his book *Jesus of Nazareth Millenarian Prophet*. Allison says,

> "Herein I shall, with reference to Jesus and early Christianity, use 'apocalyptic' to designate a cluster of eschatological themes and expectations— cosmic cataclysm, resurrection of the dead, universal judgment, heavenly redeemer figures, etc.—that developed, often in association with belief in a near end, in postexilic Judaism."[3]

Allison says of Jesus' overall presentation of himself and his life in the Gospels that "he was rather an eschatological prophet who typically but not invariably spoke and acted in the light of his eschatological expectations." Those expectations were that the rule of

Yahweh, his father, was soon to begin in the lifetimes of those who heard him.

Wolfhart Pannenberg writes concerning Jesus' expectations,

> "Measured by the imminent nearness of these events of the end, it must have been a secondary significance for Jesus whether he himself would have to endure death before the end came. The truth of his proclamation did not need to depend upon this. One way or the other the ultimate confirmation of his message through the imminent fulfillment of all history with the appearance of the Son of Man on the clouds of heaven was immediately at hand."[4]

Pannenberg says, along with that, Jesus "expected the resurrection of the dead and judgement."

James D.G. Dunn summarizes what he believes Jesus believed about himself when he preached and taught and walked upon the earth. In his often quoted and referenced book *Christology in the Making*, he says,

> "We find one who claimed to be inspired by the Spirit of God, to be a prophet in the tradition of the prophets, but more than that, to be the eschatological prophet, the one anointed by God to announce and enact the good news of God's final rule and intervention."[5]

In the book titled *Jesus Proclamation of the Kingdom of God* authored by Johannes Weiss, editors Richard Hiers and Larrimore Holland state,

> "The great majority of European New Testament scholars have accepted Weiss and Schweitzer's

conclusions that Jesus expected the Kingdom to come in the near future."[6]

Jesus was a Jew with Jewish outlooks and beliefs of his day gained from the time he was a child. Individuals of his day expected and anticipated the arrival of the kingdom of Yahweh. Wright says,

"No solution which claims to be talking about history can ever undo this basic move."[7]

E. P. Sanders says about Jesus beliefs:

"The hard evidence is this: he talked about a kingdom; his disciples expected to have a role in it; they considered him their leader; he was crucified for claiming to be king…The proclamation of the coming judgment was accompanied by the prediction that God was about to redeem Israel, as promised by Isaiah (Mark 1:6 also Matthew and Luke)."[8]

If Jesus believed everything was happening in his day, it is only logical that he would have seen the prophecies of the Old Testament as occurring in his day and time, such as those that speak of a time of great tribulation and stress, the pouring out of the wrath of God upon his people, and those events which evangelicals all see ahead of the world before the arrival of Jesus in 2050. Dale Allison in his book *The End of the Ages Has Come* points out that Jesus did interpret events that way and so did Paul.

Allison details that many New Testament Bible scholars believe that the death and resurrection of Jesus were seen by Paul as a start of those whom Jesus said will be resurrected soon (John 5:28–29). Paul expected the resurrection to occur in his lifetime as we see in those statements of Paul in his letter to the Thessalonian church. Before that momentous event, Paul also knew certain things were prophesied to happen. Great tribulation was to strike Israel.

In 1 Corinthians 15:23, Paul calls Jesus the "first fruits of those who have fallen asleep." Allison says as well as many other Bible interpreters that Paul believed and felt that Jesus' "death was assumed to have been a death in the great eschatological tribulation."[9]

In support of his outlook, Allison quotes among others James D.G. Dunn in his book *Jesus and the Spirit* who writes concerning the reference to Jesus being the first fruits of those to be resurrected, that Jesus' resurrection

> "denotes the beginning of the harvest, the first swing of the sickle. No interval is envisaged between the first fruits and the rest of the harvest."[10]

Dunn goes on to explain his concepts of Paul's thoughts by stating that

> "Paul saw himself fulfilling an important and essential role in the last act of the history of salvation. This is sufficiently clear from Rom.11:13ff.; 15:15ff, Gal. 2:7–9; Eph. 3:1–10. His ministry is to the Gentiles."[11]

Paul, Allison believes, saw all the events occurring in his life and the life of the church as being part of events occurring in the great tribulation which was to precede the general resurrection.

Paul speaks when he admonishes against getting married and having families it is because of "the present distress" (1 Cor. 7:26). It has the same sound as those warnings of Jesus in the Gospels about the future where we see passages about people having to flee and not returning to the house for anything or their running and hiding to escape the wrath to come. The urgency in the mind of Jesus was so vital that he constantly spoke dramatically about the necessity to respond now and do urgent things to be ready to get into the kingdom, for it is was coming imminently. He spoke of not even getting married to make it into the kingdom. In Luke 20:34, Luke writes,

> "And Jesus said to them, 'The sons of this age marry and are given in marriage; but those who attain to that age and to the resurrection from the dead neither marry or are given in marriage.'"

Paul phrases all his cautions in language about being married in the similar way Jesus is quoted in Luke. Paul said that it would be better if couples don't get married. He stresses why. Paul says in 1 Corinthians 7:28–29, "I mean; the appointed time is very short." Before the second coming, great tribulation was to strike the earth in Paul's mind. Apparently, Jesus saw it much in the same way when he emphasized that individuals put aside marriage due to the urgency and tribulation which was soon to arrive. Some, Jesus said had made themselves "eunuchs for the kingdom of God's sake." Jesus lauded them for their decision.

Allison says that Paul offers his counsel that those unmarried in his day and age and time

> "remain in the unmarried state—on the presupposition that the present experience of the Corinthians is an eschatological experience: it partakes of the messianic woes." Allison says, "The final time of trouble will prove to be especially arduous for the married (cf. Mark 13:17 and Luke 23:29)."[12]

These thoughts of Paul reflect all the thoughts of Jesus given throughout the Gospels' warning of the time to come and the times to fall upon the citizens of Jerusalem. Jesus' outlook was a continuation of the message of John the Baptist who spoke of the axe already being cut into the tree and that individuals came to him to flee from the wrath to come.

Paul speaks of the end right around the corner.

"In 2 Thessalonians 2:7, he writes that the mystery of lawlessness is 'already at work.' That is, the rebellion whose advent marks the final apostasy has already entered the world, even though in full manifestation belongs to the future."[13]

We have already seen that Paul felt that all his world would end ultimately with some individual sitting in the temple in Jerusalem declaring himself to be God (2 Thess. 2:7–9). Paul's take on the future relative to the temple being defiled probably came from Jewish traditions and beliefs about the time of the end and the account in Daniel of the defilement of the temple referenced by Daniel.

Mark records Jesus as having said,

"But when you see the desolating sacrilege set up where it ought not to be (let the reader understand), then let those who are in Judea flee to the mountains" (Mark 13:14).

Paul saw all this as occurring before the second coming of Jesus which would bring the resurrection of the dead of those members of his churches and all would occur in the lifetimes of those members of his congregations. Allison points out that all Paul's language, even that including of how the whole creation groans and waits for the end of the ages, conveys his outlook that all these events were beginning to be fulfilled in his day and time. They were living in that period leading up to all the final events they saw that were to come before the dawning of a new age. Paul saw himself living in a time capsule as people do today believing Jesus will return in 2050. He believed his congregations were living during the great tribulation to come upon the world prophesied in the Old Testament. He interpreted events occurring in the world to be those events to occur before Jesus second coming.

Jesus' own outlook would have involved his preaching and teaching of the soon coming arrival of his father's kingdom. His entire mental outlook and frame of mind when it comes to the end of the age was that it was to occur in his day and time and the lives of his audiences.

In *Jesus and the Future*, Richard Hiers summarizes what appears to be Jesus' outlook toward the immediate future.

> "Jesus evidently believed that all of his contemporaries, except, perhaps, the Twelve, would have to pass before the throne of judgment. He proclaimed neither the traditionalist message of forgiveness to all who believe, nor the liberal gospel of the inherent value of the human soul...The historical Jesus evidently did not visualize the continuation of the world beyond the lifetimes of his own generation; he was not issuing a program for life in the world for succeeding centuries; and he did not set forth a 'system' of ethics, 'sublime' or otherwise."[14]

Unknown to my father years ago, when he began to read the Bible to discover what Christ said and did and when he decided to close his store on Saturday to follow the example of Jesus, he had begun a quest for the historical Jesus and didn't know it. My father had never heard of Albert Schweitzer or Johannes Weiss, but he discovered a truth of those who quest to understand Jesus. Jesus can only be understood by his history and who he was from the time he grew up because he grew up just like every one of us as a child. Jesus got religious beliefs from his parents, his society, his synagogue, his community, and his world.

Concerning the future and a second coming of Jesus, third quest scholars tell us Jesus looked solely in his day for a first coming of his father, the one we know as Yahweh. Wright says that if we are to understand both Paul and Jesus, we must view them and their speech and messages in the day and time in which they lived. They addressed their world, not ours.

Sanders says about Jesus:

> "In temporal terms, the context of Jesus' movement runs from John the Baptist to the early Christian community. John the Baptist was a preacher of repentance in view of the pending judgment and Jesus began his public career by accepting his baptism."[15]

A study of the historical Jesus has everything to do with the second coming. If third quest scholars are correct, Jesus expected everything to occur in his day and time, not ours, or sometime in the future of the world.

Before proceeding, I want to quote Peter Berger from his book *Questions of Faith*. Berger is not a theologian but a world-recognized sociologist. I have quoted him earlier in a statement he wrote about Thomas Jefferson. Berger made a cursory study of the historical Jesus. Here is a summary of his conclusions as a sociologist searcher.

> "Still, despite many disagreements, there is near-complete consensus among New Testament scholars (including most of those who would adhere to Protestant or Catholic orthodoxy) about one point: 'Neither Jesus himself, nor his immediate followers, nor the Synoptic Gospels thought of him in terms of the Church's later teaching—that is, as divine, as the second person of the Trinity, or as the being affirmed in the great historic creeds.'"[16]

In chapter 10, we will cover what Paul and the early church believed about a second coming of Jesus. It was viewed through the eyes of the prophetic beliefs of the Jewish race when Paul lived and Jesus preached.

10

JESUS' BELIEFS OF THE END OF THE AGE

"Even if those texts did not exist we would have essentially the same problem with Jesus' eschatology, for what is problematic is the implicit time limit which pervades the whole."
—Ben Meyer, *The Aims of Jesus*

"Expectation of the imminent second coming of Jesus is also found in the gospels. The thirteenth chapter of Mark, often called 'the little apocalypse,' speaks of 'signs' that will precede the coming of 'the Son of man.' The chapter reaches its climax in these words attributed to Jesus: 'But in those days, after that suffering, the sun will be darkened, and the moon will not give its light; and the stars will be falling from heaven, and the power in the heavens will be shaken. Then they will see the Son of Man coming in clouds with great power and glory. Then he will send out the

angels, and gather his elect from four winds, from
the ends of the earth to the ends of heaven.'"
—Marcus Borg, *The Meaning of Jesus*

Jesus encouraged decisive action on the part of his hearers concerning getting ready for the kingdom and trying to be a part of it in those strange scriptures where he said that in order to make it into the kingdom that if it is necessary that one should cut off their hand, foot, or pluck out an eye. He spoke as if there would be individuals who would go into the kingdom missing a hand or foot in his day.

In his book *The Aims of Jesus*, Meyer points out that the scriptures in the Gospels tell us Jesus believed the kingdom was literally to be set up in his day. Meyer says that "imminence, swiftness, certainly typified the whole."[1]

Ben Meyer is saying above, that when we review scriptures one at a time concerning what Jesus believed, we find he expected an imminent arrival of the kingdom. Our problem (to deny Jesus didn't believe it was imminent) is the enormity of scripture written of Jesus' ministry that indicates that time is short, the end is coming, get ready, prepare, act now, it is all soon going to be over. It wasn't just Jesus' beliefs but those of his closest disciples and the beliefs of Paul, which he claims he got from Jesus.

Concerning the whole modus operandi of Jesus, to use a football term, he operated constantly in "hurry up offense." So did all his disciples that he sent out to preach and warn the nation of the soon coming judgment of God. As Bible scholars point out, the whole theme of Jesus speech was get on the stick, get with it, take decisive action, God's judgment is coming now, not two thousand years into the future.

From the time Jesus began his ministry after being baptized by John, it was Jesus' outlook toward the future. Jesus even told the seventy in their missionary journey that when they go into a city and get no response to walk out of it and shake off their sandals signifying their rejection and that nothing awaits the people of those cities or houses but judgment for their refusal to hear their message. It was eternal punishing in a lake of fire.

Jesus' ministry began out of the ministry of John the Baptist. Jesus fully supported John's message which was saturated with imminence, a fiery judgment, and the soon coming arrival of God's kingdom to Jerusalem. Jesus fully endorsed all John had to say about that kingdom, going on to laud John after his death by saying that among "those born of women there has been no greater person." Jesus' followers practiced water baptism which was a rite he obtained from John. It symbolized the washing away of sins to prepare for the judgment of God to come and to spare people from the anger of God to be poured out before his arrival on earth. Jesus fully endorsed John, was baptized by him, and scholars tell us, followed John for a while before starting his own ministry. John brought a message of the imminent arrival of the kingdom of God and the great tribulation before that event.

All those accounts detailing and explaining the message of John and Jesus, supports Sanders', Wright's, Schweitzer's, Allison's, Meier's, Pannenberg's, and Schillebeeckx's views that Jesus believed it would arrive in the lifetimes of his listening audiences.

A list follows taken from several books of the New Testament that shows that Jesus expected the kingdom of God to arrive. Jesus expected at that time the resurrection of dead and judgment to occur upon Israel. He told the twelve they would sit upon thrones judging the twelve tribes of Israel which he foresaw would return to Jerusalem. Jesus expected to rule with the twelve in that kingdom. They would rule from Jerusalem. Gentiles would partake of the benefits of God's rule. Jesus expected to drink wine again with the apostles in festive occasions within that coming kingdom.

We start with the direct words of Jesus in Revelation, who at the time of writing of the book, is resurrected and with God in heaven. In Revelation, John quotes Jesus in the first person. This is approximately forty-five to fifty years after Paul wrote to the church in Thessalonian's about the second coming. Jesus' mind has not been changed since returning to heaven concerning the arrival of the kingdom. The first verse explains the purpose of the whole book.

- Revelation 1:1 says, "The revelation of Jesus Christ, which God gave him to show his servants what must soon take place."
- Revelation 1:17 says, "When I saw him, I fell at his feet as though dead. But he laid his right hand upon me, saying, 'Fear not, I am the first and the last, and the living one; I died, and behold I am alive for evermore, and I have the keys of Death and Hades. Now write what you see, what is, and what is to take place hereafter.'"
- Revelation 1:3 says, "Blessed is he who reads aloud the words of the prophecy, and blessed are those who hear, and who keep what is written therein; for the time is near."
- Revelation 1:8 says, "Behold, he is coming with the clouds, and every eye will see him, everyone who pierced him; and all tribes of the earth will wail on account of him, Even so, Amen." John seems to write as if those who pierced him (Romans) are still around at the time, whether he thinks the actual piercer is still alive doesn't matter. He seems to think of "them" being present on earth as he wrote.
- Revelation 22:6 says, "And he said to me, 'These words are trustworthy and true, And the Lord, the God of the spirits of the prophets, has sent his angel to show his servant's what must soon take place, and behold, I am coming soon.'"
- Revelation 22:12 says, "Behold, I am coming soon, bringing my recompense, to repay everyone for what he has done."
- Revelation 22:20 says, "He who testifies to these things says, 'Surely I am coming soon.' Amen, Come, Lord Jesus!"
- Matthew 16:28, Luke 9:27, and Mark 9:1 says, "For the son of man is to come with his angels in the glory of his Father, and then he will repay every man for what he has done. Truly, I say to you, there are some standing here who will not taste death before they see the Son of man coming in his kingdom." This verse stresses judgment to soon come upon that generation in Jesus' audience. The NIV translates

the passage that the Son of man is "about to come." All this was viewed as present day for those that were addressed, not an indefinite time into the future.

- Matthew 10:23 says, "When they persecute you in one town, flee to the next; for truly, I say to you, you will not have gone through all the towns of Israel, before the Son of man comes."
- Mark 13:30, says, "Truly, I say unto you, this generation shall not pass away before all these things take place." Raymond, Brown, on page 73 of his book *Jesus God and Man*, states,

"In the present context of these things would have to include the coming of the son of man described in 13:26…A. Vogtle, in the latest Catholic treatment of the logion, agrees with Taylor and a host of Protestant scholars that the original reference of 'these things' was the destruction of the temple mentioned in 13:2–4. All efforts to explain away the temporal limits of the saying by claiming that 'this generation' refers to the existence of mankind are refuted, in my judgment, by the closely parallel saying we cite next."

- Mark 9:1 says, "Truly, I assure you, there are some standing here who will not taste death before they see the kingdom of God come with power." Raymond Brown, in his book *Jesus God and Man*, states about these verses:

"Matthew 16:28 offers an interpretation of what Mark's last clause implies; it reads: '…before they see the Son of man coming in his kingdom.' In order to avoid the implication that the Parousia will take place while some of Jesus' hearers are alive, some scholars question Matthew's interpretation and suggest that the saying does not refer to the Parousia, or that it is inauthentic or a secondary rewriting of Mark 13:30 and referred to the destruction of the temple…However, the reason that causes many scholars not to regard them as 'ipissima verba' or at least to claim that they were not originally a reference to the Parousia is the theological thesis that Jesus could not have been mistaken about the time of the Parousia, which, de facto, did not take place during the lifetime of his hearers" (pp 74–75, *Jesus God and Man*).

- Mark 13:13–17 says, "And you will be hated by all for my name's sake. But he who endures to the end will be saved. 'But when you see the desolating sacrilege set up where it ought not to be' (let the reader understand), then let those who are in Judea flee to the mountains; let him who is on the housetop not come down, nor enter his house, to take anything away; and let him who is in the field not turn back to take his garment. And alas for those who are with child and for those who give suck in those days! Pray that it may not happen in winter." Jesus is here speaking of all those events in the tribulation which would precede the kingdom. Scholars point out that it is completely obvious he was addressing those events to occur in the lifetime of those to whom he spoke. He speaks of everyone hanging on until the end. That would be the end of the age as Jesus saw the future. There are numerous of these types of warnings to his audience.
- Matthew 23:34–36 says, "Therefore I send you prophets and wise men and scribes, some of who you will kill and crucify, and some you will scourge in your synagogues and persecute from town to town, and upon you may come all the righteous blood shed on earth from the blood of innocent Abel to the blood of Zachariah the son of Barachiah, whom you murdered between the sanctuary and the altar, Truly, I say to you, all this will come upon this generation."

Jesus sees all these events of the tribulation to come upon his audience. He states that all will come upon *this* generation, not a time into the future thousands of years away.

- Luke 12:49 says, "I came to cast fire upon the earth; and would that it were already kindled!" Scholars point out the statement of frustration here of Jesus. There are two theories of thought. One is that he was frustrated it hadn't yet occurred. The other was a wish that it would soon come. This is a pretty common thought with those who set dates and nothing happens. I experienced it constantly as events in the world unfolded in 1975 and nothing expected occurred. Many Christians today, expecting the second coming, often express exasperation that Jesus hasn't ended all this world's problems with his return. Even Willie Nelson expressed frustration of Jesus having not yet returned when he sang one of his recent songs, and in it, he asked Jesus to return and for him to bring John Wayne with him.

- Luke 21:34–36 says, "But take heed to yourselves lest your hearts be weighted down with dissipation and drunkenness and cares of this life, and that day come upon you suddenly like a snare; for it will come upon all who dwell upon the face of the earth. But watch always, praying that you may have strength to escape all these things that will take place, and to stand before the Son of man." Richard Hiers writes in *Jesus and the Future*:

> "They must be ready at all times, lest 'that day' come suddenly, finding them unprepared. 'That day,' the day of Judgment before the Son of man, can come at any time, and when it comes it will do so universally and unmistakably; 'It will come upon all who dwell upon the face of the whole earth.' The admonition to 'pray that you may have strength to escape all these things that will take place' refers to the peirasmos or tribulation

expected in Jewish and other Christian sources before the coming of the new age."[2]

- Luke 23:27–31 says, "And there followed him a great multitude of the people, and of women who bewailed and lamented him, But Jesus turning to them said, 'Daughters of Jerusalem, do not weep for me, but weep for yourselves and for your children. For behold, the days are coming when they will say, Blessed are the barren, and the wombs that never bore, and the breasts that never gave suck!'" It is obvious again, Jesus is speaking of that generation which would be in the tribulation before the end of the age. He spoke to them and hurt for their small children who would face what he believed was to occur yet ahead.
- Mark 1:14 says, "Now after John was arrested, Jesus came into Galilee, preaching the gospel of God, and saying, 'The time is fulfilled, and the kingdom of God is at hand; repent and believe in the gospel.'"
- Matthew 3:1–2 says, "In those days came John the Baptist, preaching in the wilderness of Judea, 'Repent, for the kingdom of heaven is at hand.'"
- Matthew 3:7 says, "But when he saw many of the Pharisees and Sadducees coming for baptism, he said to them, 'You brood of vipers! Who has warned you to flee from the wrath to come?'"
- Matthew 4:17 says, "From that time Jesus began to preach, saying, 'Repent, for the kingdom of heaven is at hand.'"

Ben Meyer writes in his book *The Aims of Jesus*, "Like John, Jesus preached repentance and baptism in the face of imminent judgment and stood as witness to the conversion of the repentant and its ritual sealing in water…That Jesus not only responded positively to the Baptist's call to the nation but actively shared in it as an ally already stamps his horizons as 'eschatological' and 'preparationist.' Moreover, intimate association with the Baptist's movement argues participation in his aim; the reconstitution of Israel in view of the eschaton."[3] Meyer goes on to point out that Jesus saw John as the messenger preparing the way for him and the establishment and arrival of the kingdom of Yahweh. Meyer quotes Malachi which gives a prophecy of the role John was to play. John fulfilled the role of a second Elijah and the scripture from Malachi 3:23 was used to identify who John was: "Behold, I will send you Elijah the prophet before the coming of the great and terrible day of Yahweh, and he shall turn the hearts of fathers to their sons and the hearts of sons to their fathers lest I come and smite the land with a curse" (Malachi 3:23).[4]

- Mark 3:13–14 says, "And he went up into the hills, and called to him those whom he desired; and they came to him. And he appointed twelve, to be with him and he sent out to preach." Bible scholars point out that there is no piece of information that is more historical than Jesus choosing twelve individuals, later called apostles. The number 12 involved a symbolic reference to the twelve tribes that Jesus expected to be reconstituted in the land. Again, Ben Meyer makes clear the understanding common to Bible scholars as to why he did and what he expected in the future from the twelve.

"The historicity of the deliberate act of choosing twelve disciples to participate most intimately in his mission (Mark 3:13; 6:7–13; Matt. 19:28) is beyond reasonable doubt…"[5]

He points out as many other Bible scholars do that choosing of the twelve was very deliberate on Jesus' part and it symbolized the reconstruction of Israel and the twelve tribes over which the disciples believed some of them would sit as rulers.

- Matthew 19:28 says, "Truly, I say to you, in the new world, when the Son of man shall sit on his glorious throne, you who have followed me will also sit on twelve thrones, judging the twelve tribes of Israel."
- Matthew 26:29 says, "I tell you I shall not drink again of this fruit of the vine until that day when I drink it new with you in my Father's kingdom." Most all exegetes point out that Jesus had reference to a period in the near future. Table fellowship and the eating of meals is shown in the Gospels to be something that Jesus believed would physically and literally occur. He wasn't using symbolic language nor metaphors.
- Matthew 26:64 says, "You have said so, But I tell you hereafter you will see the Son of man seated at the right hand of Power, and coming in the clouds of heaven." These words most likely were not actual words of Jesus. No one was present to hear them. They do express what the early church believed.
- Following is a translation from eight different versions of the Bible. There were hundreds of Bible scholars involved in the translations. These are provided to show that Paul clearly stated that he got from Jesus information about Jesus imminent return. E. P. Sanders says that "the saying as he quotes it is very close to sayings ascribed to Jesus in the gospels."[6]
- *New English Bible*: "For this we tell you as the Lord's word; we who are left alive until the Lord comes shall not forestall those who have died" (1 Thess. 4:15).
- *New International Version*: "According to the Lord's own word, we tell you that we who are still alive, who are left till the coming of the Lord, will certainly not precede those who have fallen asleep."

- *Today's English Version*: "This is the Lord's teaching that we tell you: we who are alive on the day the Lord comes will not go ahead of those who have died."
- *Jerusalem Bible*: "We can tell you this from the Lord's own teaching, that any of us who are left alive until the Lord's coming will not have any advantage over those who have died."
- *Living Bible*: "I can tell you this directly from the Lord: that we who are still living when the Lord returns will not rise to meet him ahead of those who are in the graves."
- *Revised Standard Version*: "For this we declare to you by the word of the Lord, that we who are alive, who are left until the coming of the Lord, shall not precede those who have fallen asleep."
- *New American Stardard Version*: "For this we say unto you by the word of the Lord, that we who are alive and remain until the coming of the Lord, will not precede those who have fallen asleep."
- *King James Version*: "For this we say unto you by the word of the Lord, that we which are alive and remain unto the coming of the Lord shall not prevent them which are asleep."

There is some scholarly debate as to whether the passages in verse 16 and 17 were part of the 'word of the Lord.' E.P. Sanders writes the following in respect to this question:

> "It is not clear that the 'word of the Lord' includes verses 16 and 17, but the conclusion in v. 18, 'comfort one another with these words,' makes it probable. In any case, the similarities between this passage and the synoptic depictions of the Son of man coming with angels, accompanied by the sound of a trumpet, while some are still alive (Matt. 24:30 and Matt. 16:27), are so close that it is difficult to avoid the conclusion that both reflect a tradition which, before Paul, was

already attributed to Jesus…Paul's expectation of the coming of the Lord (see also I Cor. 15:23) is not his own creation, but was doubtless held in common with other Christians."[7]

- Matthew 24:27 says, "The sign of the Son of Man will appear in heaven; and then all the tribes of earth will mourn, and they shall see the Son of Man coming on clouds of heaven with power and great glory. And he will send his angels with a trumpet of great voice, and they will gather his elect from the four winds, from one side of heaven to the other." This passage in the Gospel of Matthew follows a similar explanation to that of Paul with the dead being raised, Jesus coming in the clouds, the sound of a trumpet, and the gathering of the elect. When Paul had written the book of Thessalonians the Gospel of Matthew had not been written. As far as we know, Paul could not have taken his information from Matthew or any other written source for there were no Gospels when Paul wrote. Paul gives credence to his teaching to Jesus as his source. The teaching of Jesus to which Paul referred as the "word of the Lord" would have to have come to Paul post the resurrection. Matthew likewise didn't have Paul's epistle for it had not been circulated widely with no printing presses or email or Web services at the time. We have two different sources, Matthew's Gospel and Paul's epistle, testifying to Jesus telling the disciples that he would return in their lifetimes.

The above verses offer some of the most convincing scriptures telling us what Jesus believed about the future. Jesus was mistaken in his understanding of when the kingdom would occur and the New Testament gives evidence of that. He really did believe it was to occur in the generation of those people to whom he spoke and preached in his day. His predecessor, John the Baptist, was wrong about what

God was going to do in his day and when it was to be done. Paul was wrong.

Interpreters have offered all kinds of explanations to avoid the conclusion that Jesus believed the kingdom was imminent and going to occur in his day. Even John Dominic Crossan admits that the quibbling over terms doesn't change the fact that Jesus initially proclaimed the kingdom's arrival was right around the corner. He writes,

> "I myself cannot see much difference between phrases like 'imminent' or 'soon' or 'within this generation.' And, while 'imminent' or 'soon' may be a little vague 'within this generation' strikes me as clear enough. None of these phrases, at least, means two thousand years and counting. If 'the future, definitive, and imminent arrival of God's kingly rule was central to Jesus proclamation,' then Jesus' central proclamation was quite simply wrong and misguided. And neither special pleading nor semantic evasion can rectify that situation."[8]

Sanders states as a summary of what he believes were the thoughts of Jesus concerning the arrival of God's kingdom.

> "The best evidence in favor of the view that Jesus expected that God would very soon intervene in history is the context of the movement that began with John the Baptist. John expected the judgement to come soon. Jesus started his career by being baptized by John. After Jesus' death and resurrection, his followers thought that within their lifetimes he would return to establish his kingdom. After his conversion, Paul was of the very same view."[9]

John A. T. Robinson writes in his book *In The End God*, there is...

> "a very considerable body of evidence in the New Testament which, though it declines to place any date upon the coming of the end and the return of Christ, undoubtedly regards it as temporarily extremely near...the church, unlike scores of millenarian movements before or since, survived the non-fulfillment of this expectation, and survived it, with remarkable ease."[10]

After a lifetime of study of Jesus' life, Wolfhart Pannenberg writes,

> "There is no doubt that Jesus erred when he announced that God's Lordship would begin in his own generation (Matt. 23:36; 16:28; Mark 13:30 and parallels; cf. Matt. 10:23.) The end of the world did not begin in Jesus' generation and not in the generation of his disciples, the witnesses of his resurrection."[11]

11

What the Early Church Believed

"The question is the more pressing because early Christian literature testifies that believers were troubled by the failure of prophecies in the Jesus tradition to come true."

—Dale Allison, *Jesus of Nazareth Millenarian Prophet*

"To be sure, it is highly likely that the earliest circles of Jesus' followers expected him to return in eschatological glory to consummate God's redemptive purposes (as we shall see later in this book), and passages in the Gospels indicate that the scene in Daniel 7:13–14 where God gives dominion and vindication to 'one like a son of man' was interpreted as a prophecy of Jesus' eschatological victory" (Mark 14:62–24; Matt. 25:31).

—Larry Hurtado, *Lord Jesus Christ*

"That Jesus prophesied the imminent arrival of God's rule is beyond dispute."

—Edward Schillibeeckx, *Jesus— An Experiment in Christology*

I could begin this chapter by saying that very few Bible scholars and very few theologians would disbelieve the statement that the early church firmly believed that Jesus would return in their day. The only debate comes from whether they were taught this by Jesus. There are some groups as I pointed out which are making a major effort to change opinions on the subject. Most conservative Bible scholars and liberal Bible scholars teach and believe that the early church clung to the belief Jesus would return soon after his departure. The final book of Revelation in our New Testament is about the prophesied soon coming return of Jesus to this earth, as we have seen already.

It is evident that Jesus in his preaching and teaching before his death and after his resurrection, indicated it was just around the corner, much like John the Baptist did. Wright states within his vast study of Jesus, that any way we slice the pie afterward, we will find it is evident also from the Gospels that Jesus taught throughout his ministry that Yahweh was to come to this earth and arrive in the city of Jerusalem for that rule. Jesus expected to drink wine and banquet again in his own day with the twelve resulting from Yahweh's rule on earth and the establishment of his kingdom. It was Jesus' departing message to the twelve the evening of his death as pointed out and we will cover in the next chapters.

Verse 1 of the first chapter of Revelation says, "The revelation of Jesus Christ, which God gave him to show his servants what must soon take place" (Rev. 1:1).

John wrote that Jesus revealed to him that he was coming soon. The train schedule was set by Jesus for a soon coming arrival.

The clearest example of what the early New Testament church taught of course is Paul's writings in his address to one of his churches in Thessalonica. I have already quoted E. P. Sanders comments on this verse already.

In his letter to the church in Thessalonica written some thirty years or so after Jesus resurrection, Paul says,

> "Brothers, we do not want you to be ignorant
> about those who fall asleep, or to grieve like the
> rest of men, who have no hope. We believe that

Jesus died and rose again and so we believe that God will bring with Jesus those who have fallen asleep in him. According to the Lord's own word, we tell you that we who are still alive, who are left till the coming of the Lord, will certainly not precede those who have fallen asleep. For the Lord himself will come down from heaven, with a loud command, with the voice of the archangel and with the trumpet call of God, and the dead in Christ will rise first. After that, we who are still alive and are left will be caught up together with them in the air. And so we will ever be with the Lord forever. Therefore, encourage each other with these words" (1 Thess. 4:13–18).

What is very interesting about Paul's information we obtain from him about the resurrection is that the information he gives us, especially in Thessalonians, is discussed by Paul solely resulting from individuals in his churches dying before Jesus had returned. Many exegetes point this out. John A. T. Robinson explains it most clearly in his book *In the End—God*. He says,

"The doctrine of the resurrection is formulated by St. Paul almost as an afterthought to meet the problem raised by that minority of Christians who had already died prior to the Parousia. Indeed, the resurrection hope is one of those subjects which gains even the limited space accorded it in the New Testament writings because it had not had a central place in the original preaching and had since become a matter of controversy."[1]

Church members began to die. It became a controversy or subject of concern by early Christians because Jesus hadn't returned and people were dying. We see this emphasis in looking closely at the passages above where Paul answers the questions about those few people in Thessalonica that had died before the second coming.

This same theme is picked up in another chapter of the New Testament in one of Paul's books addressed to another one of his churches. Scholars say the books were written about five years apart from each other. In 1 Corinthians 15, Paul is discussing the resurrection from another issue based on members of his church in Corinth stating the resurrection was already past. "Now if Christ is preached as raised from the dead, how can some of you say that there is no resurrection of the dead?" (1 Cor. 15:12). Paul was attempting to clarify several points concerning what he believed and counter what he considers false teaching about the resurrection.

Paul begins to reveal his beliefs about the resurrection, resurrected bodies, mortality versus immortality, and when all this takes place. What is most important in all the verses covered (verses 12–58); it turns out to be the longest discussion by a Christian writer on the resurrection and what is believed to take place than any other section of the New Testament. My point now is to reference Paul's thinking concerning *when* that all takes place. Paul makes clear that he believes the resurrection or the second coming, which precedes the resurrection, will be in the lifetime of members of the church at Corinth. Specifically, he makes a statement to show that.

"Lo, I tell you a mystery. We shall not all sleep, but we shall all be changed."

The phrase "we shall not all sleep" is a phrase conveying they would not all die before his coming. Again, it shows that Paul believed Jesus return was imminent.

Death was spoken of as a sleep or state of sleeping for early Christians. He tells the Corinthian church obviously, that not all of them will die, but they will be changed in the twinkling of an eye. This adds to his comments to the Church in Thessalonica where he referenced that the first event would be the dead in Christ being activated and rising to meet Jesus as he returns to earth, and then in the twinkling of an eye he expected to be changed, along with all his congregants. Even though he doesn't state it, Paul expected everything to take place on earth, not in heaven.

Paul wrote and spoke to all his congregations of the soon coming of Jesus. All his instructions to them concerning how to live and wait and fulfill a Christian life was tempered with preparing for Jesus coming. He says to the church in Thessalonica "may your spirit and soul and body be kept sound and blameless at the coming of our Lord Jesus Christ" (I Thessalonians. 5:23). He saw that coming impacting those to whom he wrote then.

In the first chapter of 1 Thessalonians, Paul wrote, "we wait for his son from heaven, whom he raised from the dead, Jesus who delivers us from the wrath to come" (1 Thess. 1:10). Deliverance from the wrath to come is a continuation of the message of John the Baptist to whom Jesus came to be baptized and whose message Jesus fully endorsed. John's bold sermons included condemning statements warning that generation of the imminence of the wrath of God to be poured out upon Israel with "the axe being laid to the tree" already and the need for repentance to escape God's soon coming fiery judgment upon the nation when the "chaff would be burned up."

Paul continued throughout his life to teach and preach and speak of the immanency of the return of Jesus. His thoughts expressed in his last book in Romans ends with calling attention to the fact that everything he had preached about was right around the corner and soon to be approaching for his converts. He says,

> "Beside this you know what hour it is, how it is full time now for you to wake from sleep. For salvation is nearer to us now than when we first believed; the night is far gone. The day is at hand" (Rom. 13:11–12).

There can be no doubt, from the context, that the day being at hand, refers to the wrapping up of the plan of God and finishing of his work of preaching and educating and preparing people for arrival of Jesus Christ upon earth.

Sanders says in his highly acclaimed book *Paul and Palestinian Judaism* that

> "no two elements of Paul's thought are more certain, or more consistently expressed, than his conviction that the full salvation of believers and the destruction of the wicked lay in the near future...."[2]

In his book titled *What Saint Paul Really Said*, N. T. Wright states

> "Jesus believed himself called to be the one through whom God's strange purposes for Israel would reach their ordained climax."[3]

Jesus believed the wrapping up of God's plan was right around the corner, as did Paul who taught that to all his churches.

In his book titled *Jesus, A New Biography*, Shirley Jackson Case summarizes Paul's thoughts in respect to the future.

> "Believing that the end of the 'present evil age' was near, he looked for the early coming of the Son of God from heaven (I Thess.1:10; 3:13; 4:15-18). On various occasions his readers were warned of this impending 'day of our Lord Jesus Christ' (1 Cor.1:8, 5:5; 2 Cor. 1:14; 1 Thess. 5:2; Phil. 1:6, 10, 2:16). Present earthly activities were of minor importance since only a short time would elapse until, "the fashion of this world passes away" (1 Cor. 7:29–31).[4]

How did this all come about? Why was the early church faced with disappointment? It is because from the time Jesus appeared on the scene in all the Gospel accounts he constantly spoke of the imminent arrival of God and of his reign. John Meier writes concerning the beginning of Jesus ministry the following:

> "Somewhere around ad 28, Jesus broke with his honorable though modest socioeconomic status, his settled life in Nazareth, and his close family ties to undertake the unusual role of an itinerant celibate layman proclaiming the imminent arrival of the kingdom of God. Being about thirty-four years old at the time he began his ministry, Jesus would have already seemed unusually socially marginal in the eyes of his fellow Jews by his conscious choice of a celibate state. He now made himself even more unusual or marginal by his consciously chosen ministry of an itinerant prophet of the end time."[5]

We have already quoted the direct words of Jesus from the book of Revelation where Jesus is quoted by John as saying: "I am coming soon." These statements allegedly came from Christ, thirty or so years after the statements made in Acts by Jesus. Jesus is still announcing his coming soon.

Most third quest scholars, with obvious exception of the Jesus Seminar, freely admit that Jesus believed the kingdom was to be in the lifetimes of his audience of the day. Schillibeeckx, that I have quoted, went further and said regarding the belief of the reign of God being imminent it was "beyond dispute." Jesus' words, stating he didn't know the end, were a confession, most likely. He didn't. The fact that the early church believed they were taught by Jesus that the kingdom would be in their lifetimes is evident if we take the New Testament scriptures at face value. In the next chapter, we will review what C. S. Lewis called Jesus most embarrassing statement in the Gospels.

12

DID JESUS NOT KNOW WHEN THE END WOULD BE?

"Understandably there is a desire to know what Jesus himself said, thought, and did in the final hours of his life. Yet Jesus did not write an account of his passion; nor did anyone who had been present write an eyewitness account. Available to us are four different accounts written some thirty to seventy years later in the Gospels of Mark, Matthew, Luke, and John, all of which were dependent on tradition that had come down from an intervening generation or generations."
—Raymond Brown, *Death of the Messiah*

I wrote earlier of scholars speaking of Jesus' "self-awareness." How can we know what was going on in the mind of Christ or what his "self-awareness" contained? In that way, we would really know what Jesus believed and thought.

James D. G. Dunn explains our difficulties to know the thinking and thoughts of Jesus and his "self-consciousness" or inner thoughts when he says that it is highly unlikely that we can know and that it is most likely an…

> "impossibility of uncovering a historical individual's self-consciousness—how can we at 2,000 years removed in time and culture put ourselves in the shoes of, enter into the mind of one from whom we have nothing direct and most of whose sayings are uncertain as to original context and form?"[1]

Scholars at best can surmise or imagine what Jesus might have been feeling or thinking about his life on earth while a human being. We have just a few accounts where we find a Gospel writer telling us what was on the mind of Jesus or what he was thinking in each situation. But, as we have covered, we are reading a script or literary story, like Hamlet, when we read the Gospel snippets of Jesus' life.

As an example, we have a Gospel account of the woman with the issue of blood, who said to herself (according to the writer), that if she could just touch him, she would be healed. Our storytellers tell us that she did touch him and she was healed. We can imagine how she stood in the crowds along the street and thought to herself about what to do as he walked by, then dramatically reached out quickly and touched Jesus. It is a moving account and one we can picture happening.

When it happened, the Gospel accounts portray Jesus turning around and considering the crowd and asking, "Who touched me?" (Luke 8:45–46). It is humorous in one of the Gospel accounts that the writer also had thoughts of his own, when writing the passage. One of the Gospel writers says someone said to Jesus, "Lord, there are thousands around you and you asked us who touched you?" Luke records that Peter reacted to Jesus question by telling Jesus, "'Master, the multitudes surround you and press upon you!" Peter was vexed that Jesus would ask and the verse seems to show, that at least Peter, didn't see him as God and expect him to know who in the crowd had touched him. They saw Jesus as any ordinary human being, unable to know, with the size of the crowd, who it was that had touched Jesus.

In that instance, we see clearly the thoughts of Jesus in a moment of time in his life, if we have a truly accurate account of what Jesus said. That is an example of what we would call "self-talk" within Jesus when we perceive his thoughts occurring in the stories of his life. Scholars seek to understand what Jesus inwardly thought about himself but didn't necessarily tell others. In this way, we would know the aims and purposes and mission of life as Jesus felt and believed it.

C. S. Lewis wrote about this verse:

> "It would be difficult, and, to me, repellent, to suppose that Jesus never asked a genuine question, that is, a question to which he did not know the answer. That would make of his humanity something so unlike ours as scarcely to deserve the name. I find it easier to believe that when he said, 'Who touched me?' (Luke 7:45) he really wanted to know."[2]

Out of this one Gospel account, numerous debates have occurred resulting from how we all have viewed Jesus and his capabilities. The issue again, is why Jesus, being God. would need to ask, "who touched me?" Indeed, this doesn't make sense if Jesus is God, for, he would have known who touched him, for God knows everything, including our unknown future.

This scripture and others, seeming to indicate that Jesus was very human, are found throughout the Gospels. In one account in the Gospels during Jesus' travels and ministry, it says that he preached in one city and couldn't do many mighty works in the city:

> "And he could do no mighty works there, except that he laid his hands upon a few sick people and healed them" (Mark 6:5).

The World's Last Night, written by Lewis, was a long essay about Jesus, and particularly the second coming. In it Lewis covers the debated passage in Mark 13:32 where it is stated of Jesus that of the time of the end or final cataclysm to come, that even Jesus didn't know when it would occur:

> "But of that day or that hour no one knows, not
> even the angels in heaven, nor the Son, but only
> the Father" (Mark 13:32).

Lewis wrote of this verse: "It is certainly the most embarrassing verse in the Bible." Lewis explains the reasons why, the embarrassment to the early church. It was that, as we have seen, what Jesus believed and taught. The conclusion that any one of us would reach is that Jesus

> "shared, and indeed created, their delusion. He
> said in so many words, 'this generation shall not
> pass till all these things be done.' And he was
> wrong. He clearly knew no more about the end
> of the world than anyone else."[3]

Considering that one has gotten past clinging to plenary inspiration of the Bible, we must ask ourselves if this is truly a statement of Christ or something similar. Or is it an addition or afterthought by the author of the book and was created as didactic fiction to teach what someone felt hadn't been taught about Jesus.

There probably is no passage written in the New Testament that there is a greater consensus by Bible scholars from the extreme left to the extreme right that something like these words were uttered by Jesus rather than placed in the Bible in an editorial comment by a writer.

Regarding whether these were the words spoken directly by Jesus, Raymond Brown quotes in his book *Jesus God and Man* the *Encyclopedia Biblica* which states that this verse is one "among the five 'credible' general statements of the Gospel about Jesus."[4]

The "criteria of embarrassment" becomes one of the rules of engagement that Bible scholars use in reaching conclusions of what statements we have in the Gospels that were actual statements of Jesus rather than something put in the mouth of Jesus by authors and writers that were not actually spoken by Jesus. There are others which scholars use. Dale Allison has an excellent accounting in his book *Constructing Jesus.*

Lewis is pointing out that this statement would have been embarrassing to the early church because Jesus was in error about the end of the age. This scripture would make him out to be ignorant and not possess the characteristics of God. Jesus would have possessed, being God, omniscience. Writers would not have left this embarrassing statement in their tradition about Jesus unless it was a historically accurate statement. This may make sense to some people. To others it may not. But the criteria of embarrassment is used by theologians and scholars to try to decide if we are reading the actual words of Jesus or those made up by writers of our Gospels. Lewis addresses the aspect of embarrassment of the editors of the Gospels when he states,

> "Unless the reporter were perfectly honest he would never have recorded the confession of ignorance at all; he could have no motive for doing so except a desire to tell the whole truth. And unless later copyists were equally honest they would never have preserved the (apparently) mistaken prediction about 'this generation' after the passage of time had shown the (apparent) mistake."[5]

Raymond Brown states regarding the issue Lewis raises as to its authenticity. He writes in *Jesus God and Man*

> "One is certain, however, that it ran against the grain of the Church to attribute ignorance to Jesus, and most authors would accept the say-

ing as authentic…Many Catholics are willing to accept this today, but on this very basis they explain away the statements that attribute to Jesus the expectation of an immediate Parousia or of one within the lifetime of his disciples."[6]

The portrayal in this verse of Jesus being ignorant of when the end would come is supported by Wright's comments that Jesus didn't truly know when the end was going to come and Yahweh was to take over rulership of the kingdoms of the world. Jesus was always warning them to be ready for an event that he didn't know when was going to take place.

Wright argues in *Jesus and the Victory of God* that all the passages we find throughout the New Testament of Jesus repeatedly warning in different ways about the future, and especially for them to be on guard, alert, wide awake, observant, and ready, is because even Jesus himself, as this verse indicates, didn't know when the end would come. If he did know everything and when it was to occur, Wright says it makes no sense to constantly be using terms to be alert and on guard, for you know not when things will explode.

In Wright's book, in support of his thinking, he quotes Caird:

"It is hardly credible that [Jesus] should have required his disciples during his lifetime to be on guard night and day for an emergency which, to say the least of it, could not happen until sometime after his death. If, however, he did not know when to expect the final and fatal outbreak of official hostility to his ministry, it was inevitable that he should repeatedly and earnestly warn his friends to be ready…"[7]

We will leave this statement of Jesus stating that he didn't know when the end would come by going to Acts 1:6 where, after the resurrection, the disciples are seen asking Jesus about the establishment of the kingdom and when it would come. Jesus tells them again it is in the hands of the father.

> "So, when they had come together, they asked him, 'Lord, will you at this time restore the kingdom to Israel?'" (Acts 1:6).

Jesus says to them:

> "He said to them, 'It is not for you to know times or seasons which the Father has fixed by his own authority'" (Acts 1:7).

During the forty days and nights Jesus spent on earth with the disciples, he failed to give them any information to dispel their beliefs the arrival of the kingdom was not imminent. During his lifetime, Jesus taught the restoration and intervention of God was right around the corner and could come at any time. He gave constant warnings. The Gospels are filled with them.

13

JESUS GOD AND MAN

"Jesus did not, in other words, 'know that he was God' in the same way that one knows one is male or female, hungry or thirsty, or that one ate an orange an hour ago."

—N. T. Wright, *Jesus and the Victory of God*

"To put it starkly; whereas God is bent on showing himself in human form, we on our side slip past this human aspect as quickly as we can in order to admire a 'divine Ikon' from which every trait of the critical prophet has been smoothed away...A one sided apotheosis of Jesus that restricts him exclusively to the divine side actually has the effect of removing from our history a nuisance-figure who would challenge our self indulgence, and the dangerous memory of some provocative and vital prophesying—is also a way of silencing Jesus the prophet!"

—Edward Schillibeeckx,
Jesus—An Experiment in Christology

The issues we face in accepting that Jesus erred lies solely with our beliefs about Jesus. He was supposed to be God. We think of God as being omnipotent, omniscient, and omnipresent, as a few of his characteristics. As Schillibeeckx points out above, Jesus would not have been human and made any mistakes in his preaching and teaching. Individuals have snuffed out the messages of Jesus of the kingdom being imminent, to avoid the issue of his being mistaken. The historical Jesus is a nuisance-figure with his provocative prophesying.

Jesus, being God would know the future. In the introduction, I quoted Richard Friedman who wrote a book about who wrote the Bible. Friedman was quoted as having said that when in Genesis, it states that Yahweh repented or regretted making man, and for that reason destroyed the world with water, that this was an unusual statement about God. He said that, after all, with God being God, why wouldn't he have known how his human experiment was going to turn out? Friedman's phrase was in the second edition of his book that

> "If God is all knowing, how could he possibly regret any past action? Did he not know when he did it what the results would be?"

We all think of Jesus in the same way. He was the son of God. He was incarnated. He had prior existence with God. He came down to the earth and lived among us. He would be then omniscient and possess the powers of God. We believed this despite all the accounts we covered in the introduction showing that the father of Jesus repented, regretted, grew impatient, changed his mind, and evidenced all kinds of very human qualities in his behavior—all too human as Harold Bloom states.

Even though I was a part of a group with very sectarian beliefs, I think I believed what are typical protestant and catholic outlooks about Jesus.

Essentially what Christianity has taught us is that Mary was the first surrogate mother. The God or Gods of heaven and earth decided to procreate a son through choosing Mary to be a mother of a child.

God supernaturally took matter from outside her body and placed supernaturally physical particles into her womb to unite and begin the process to form a child. Or somehow, in some way, God formed a child within her womb. Jesus changed water into wine. God, having all power, could have formed the child Jesus through any choice. This is what is called the virgin birth. God fathered or manufactured a human child. Matthew says, "What is conceived in her is from the Holy Spirit" (Matt. 1:20).

How God chose for Jesus to be procreated other than what nature teaches us about all human births from time immemorial we simply don't know. Human birth only results from the uniting of a sperm with an egg within the womb of a female, unless done artificially.

A significant part also, depending upon emphasis or slant of groups within Christianity, is the belief that within that sperm cell or womb of Mary in the zygote that formed was encapsulated the second member of the God family. This was done through what scholars and theologians call the "kenotic" theory. This is the belief that somehow the second member of the God family (the one who became Jesus Christ the Son of God) was squeezed or condensed into the life formed in Mary's womb and became the human child Jesus. The doctrinal term used for it is "incarnation." God was united with all the blood and liquid and muscles and ligaments and bone and tissues of human flesh and lived in the matter of the brain attached in some way to the synapses and other particles that create human mind. God somehow cloned himself in the process. We have in this process what is called in theological jargon the "hypostatic union." From a cosmos of planets and galaxies and matter which expands for light-years and apparently has no end, and with an infinite period of time preceding the event, God reduced himself to skin and bones and through the birth of a child within Mary, made an appearance on our planet.

Under the kenotic theory, in some mysterious way for some Christians (not all), the second member of the God family gave up all his powers and incapability of death. He gave up omnipresence, omnipotence, and omniscience, all of which are characteristics of God by our definitions of God, which classical theological language has given to us. A God was born in human flesh and thereby could become the sacrifice that was needed to atone for the sins of all human beings from the time of Adam. A large sacrifice needed to be made to be able to cover all the sins for every man, woman, and child that has ever lived and those who will yet live. The second member of the God family could be a sufficient sacrifice.

The Jewish belief taught in the sacrificial system of Israel is

> "indeed, under the law almost everything is puri-
> fied with blood, and without the shedding of
> blood there is no forgiveness of sins" (Heb. 9:22).

Christianity is based upon the principle of atonement theology which requires a blood sacrifice for sin. The only being capable of that to cover the sins of all people that have ever lived or will yet live was the blood sacrifice of a God. In a nutshell, we have our Judeo-Christian heritage, a term we use commonly in referring to our country's philosophic religious commonality to the Jewish race.

Much of mainline Christian belief is that Jesus was 100 percent God. I believed Jesus to be very God in the flesh with full powers we attribute to God for I learned that from the time I sat in church basements in Sunday school. I believed Jesus to be God for I grew up being taught that. I also felt I saw it right out of the Bible.

Church creeds also tell us this. Jesus was, the creed says, very God. The direct words from the creed are

> "the properties of each Nature being preserved,
> and [both] concurring into One Person and One
> Hypostasis; not as though He were parted or
> divided into Two Persons, but One and the Self-
> same Son and Only-begotten God, Word, Lord,
> Jesus Christ."

From this we all assume that Jesus had all the characteristics we attribute to God. He was no less than God the father. They were as the creed states "coequal," "wholly God and wholly man."

Ed Sanders says of this creed that he doesn't understand it. None of us do. Sanders says concerning this hand me down creed:

> "It is beyond my meager abilities as an interpreter of dogmatic theology to explain how it is possible for one person to be 100% human and 100% divine, without either interfering with the other."[1]

Pannenberg explains our difficulties post all the church conferences of Jesus being both God and man, when he states, "The Antiochene theologians left unexplained how man and God could be united in the one person of Jesus."[2]

Because I believed Jesus was God in the flesh and truly God, I felt that Jesus could read minds and thoughts of others. He had x-ray like vision so that he could see from afar. He could see angels and demons and the spirit world around him when others had no clue. He rebuked Peter on an occasion for allowing Satan present in his mind. Somehow in the atmosphere Jesus knew Satan had appeared and was present in some way among them when Jesus spoke of him. Demons cried out when being exorcised that he was the Son of God. I felt that Jesus could flit off anywhere in the universe, take a trip to mars, or Saturn, or fly into the face of the sun if he should choose for he was God and nothing could hurt him.

Because he was God while waiting for the resurrection of his body, some feel by quoting 2 Peter 3:18 he went into the burning fires of hell and preached to the spirits in prison while waiting for the conclusion of three days and nights and a resurrection of his body.

I believed Jesus knew the future for he was, as God, omniscient. If he chose, he could have looked forward and see me right now typing on the keyboard of my HP laptop, for space and time didn't limit him. Jesus would have known when alive in Jerusalem on earth both your birth and your death and your fate. As Jesus hung on the cross, he allegedly knew all this and encompassed it as God as part of his hard drive and knowledge database. If you just look at the theology of Calvin and Luther, both believed this to be the capabilities of God. He knew each of you, and your fate, before you were born.

I believed Jesus remembered the day of creation, the day of the flood, and his visit and meal with Abraham and everything he did in the Old Testament accounts of him. He at some time had a battle with Satan and saw him fall from heaven. The man Jesus lived with all this as his "second consciousness" even as he lived a human life on earth. Jesus, I believed, was conscious as God and conscious as man. That's what I believed and I think a whole bunch more Christians do currently as well.

In John Hick's book *The Metaphor of God Incarnate*, he explains the view most Christians have about the person, Jesus, when he quotes A. T. Hanson, who says,

> "It seems probable that this account of two consciousnesses will become the accepted method today for those who wish to defend the Chalcedonian Christology in such a way as to make it intelligible to modern minds."[3]

I believed with all those powers of God, Jesus still could experience humanity and human thoughts resulting from his existing in the body and mind of Jesus. He was connected to the neurons and synapses and nerve cells of his physical body. He was tempted in all ways we are tempted. But like Clark Kent, he could take off his clothes and don the uniform of superman anytime he chose. He was superman before superman. Wolfhart Pannenberg wrote in his book *Jesus—God and Man*,

> "Accordingly, Jesus as an individual was never a man, but from the very beginning was a superman, the God-man. This is the tendency of Alexandrian Christology."[4]

Concerning his being actual God and having "preexisted," I relied upon all the standard scriptures used by Protestants and Catholics alike in the New Testament. Here are a few of them:

- "Have I been with you so long and yet you do not know me, Phillip. He who has seen me has seen the Father; how can you say, 'Show us the father'?" (John 14:9).
- "'Your father Abraham rejoiced that he was to see my day; he saw it and was glad.' The Jews then said to him, 'You are not yet fifty years old, and have you seen Abraham?'" (John 8:36–37)
- "Truly, truly, I say to you, before Abraham was I am" (John 8:38).
- "And now, Father, glorify thou me in my own presence with the glory which I had with thee before the world was made" (John 17:5).

From all these passages, I reached, as millions more individuals reach, the same conclusions Raymond Brown reached, in that he wrote,

> "In the Fourth Gospel Jesus speaks openly as a
> pre-existent divine figure."[5]

Wright and other current scholars of the historical Jesus tell us this wasn't on Jesus' mind in the way it has been given to Christianity through indoctrination. We should forget that Jesus lived as God and was God with all his recall of prior existence and with memory of eternity past as a prior occupant in heaven as a second member of the God family.

The reason at this point of going through all this and detailing how Christendom has viewed Jesus is to get to what third quest scholars tell us about Jesus. We should instead focus on a young Jewish prophet proclaiming the return of his father Yahweh to Jerusalem and taking over rulership of the kingdoms of the world. Jesus hoped to return Israel from exile and preached a message of hope, change, and a new age to soon come. He promised change to come in the kingdoms of the world of his day. He never saw the future. He didn't know of you and me.

Dale Allison writes of the struggle he had after his studies of the historical Jesus to accept Jesus as fully human as Wright and many others have described him. Allison says that for him to admit that Jesus believed that the kingdom of God was to be in his day would mean he could only reach one conclusion—Jesus, the Son of God, was in error.

> "Although I wanted Jesus to be right about every-thing, I concluded that he had not been."[6]

When I first began to read statements of Allison, Schweitzer, Wright, Meyer, Meier, Weiss, Sanders, Pannenberg, Schillibeeckx, and other theologians and scholars telling me that Jesus preached about the arrival of the kingdom of God in his day, it shattered my concepts from a child. My thoughts, as Mark Twain wrote, had been "trained" into me. How could Jesus be God with qualities of omnip-otence and omniscience and be in error on anything? The biggest clash I had was that if I accept him in error on the arrival of the kingdom, I must ask myself in what other ways might he have been in error and have mistaken ideas and beliefs? Did he believe things he was taught by his Jewish race that were mistaken?

Johannes Weiss explained two hundred years ago the mental agony he experienced from his detailed studies of Jesus life when he reached the point that he believed the Gospels taught that Jesus expected the arrival of the kingdom of God in his day. There were no other theologians who believed as he did. His father was an estab-lished theologian and scholar in the university he attended. Weiss said that he experienced "distressing personal conflict."

I began to experience the distressing personal conflict of Johanne Weiss in having my beliefs of Jesus challenged. Again, my gyroscope moved out of kilter. A defense mechanism within all of us as human beings prevented me from admitting that Jesus was wrong. For years, I refused to admit that Jesus had been mistaken on the arrival of the kingdom.

Finally, in asking myself why it was that Paul, Peter, and all the early church also expected the kingdom to come in their day, I had to admit that the most likely conclusion was that they got that from Jesus himself who believed it and taught it to others.

Sanders writes,

> "If Jesus expected God to change the world, he was wrong—is by no means novel. It arose very early in Christianity. This is the most substantial issue in the earliest surviving Christian documents...The fact that this expectation was difficult for Christians in the first century helps prove that Jesus held it himself. We also note that Christianity survived this early discovery that Jesus had made a mistake very well."[7]

I believe this is a little of an understatement somewhat on Sanders' part as to the broad church having no problem with Jesus being mistaken and capable of error. We don't have any literature expressing doubts and misgivings of those who died disappointed. We will get to the death of Jesus in the next chapters that indicate his life and thoughts were shattered in shreds before he died, and he cried out in disbelief that he had been forsaken by his God in all he set out to do and what Jesus believed was going to occur in his day.

In the foreword to Schweitzer's book which was republished in 2001, *The Quest of the Historical Jesus*, Dennis Nineham writes,

> "The findings of historians and critical scholars are simply being ignored by the churches and most of their members. It is true that some congregations have been taught to recognize that the Christmas stories are largely legendary, and that the same is true of parts at least of the resurrection narratives; but there is little practical awareness that the churches are faced with a radically new situation, one clearly set out by Schweitzer,

in which Christian belief has to take account of
the Jesus revealed by the historians as well as the
Jesus of the orthodox tradition."[8]

Mainline churches are not pointing out that Jesus was mistaken
in his understanding of the arrival of the kingdom of God. Our theologies are built, and our beliefs of a second coming and a rapture,
around a Jesus that knew when the end of the age was going to occur.
Everyone waiting believes we have, in the Bible, a list of items to be
fulfilled, before Jesus' return. It is believed that Jesus gave those to
us and the Olivet prophecies were for our day today. It was just the
opposite. He addressed only those of his day.

Allison writes that when he began to accept from his reading of
the historical accounts we have of Jesus that Jesus believed the kingdom was to arrive in his day, that he had no friends in his church that
believed the same. I don't know how many pew sitters would be in
church the following week after any minister would get up and tell
his congregation Jesus missed the arrival of the kingdom by two thousand years. I would think any minister could empty his church by
doing so. That would be especially the case of churches that contain
126,000,000 Americans on a countdown to Jesus return in 2050.

Accepting a fully human Jesus, wholly capable of error and
being in error, is a major fork in the road for anyone who studies
the historical Jesus. For years, I read various books written by Bible
scholars telling me that Jesus was wrong and misunderstood the
times and seasons of his day. Again and again, over a period of years,
I would put a book back on my closet shelf of books on the subject
for I could not bring myself to believe that Jesus was wrong. I did
this for a quarter century of study. It totally contradicted my mental
images etched in stone over my lifetime. I vacillated fifty-fifty for
years and then woke up one day at least on the 60 percentile range
that Jesus had been in error about what he believed God was going
to do in his life and the nation of Israel. Before the day was over, the
pendulum had swung back the other way to my childhood beliefs,
for they were so ingrained. It was comfortable to stay with what I
believed about Jesus.

14

READING THE GOSPELS
AS LITERATURE

"We have seen how the whole message of Jesus
flowed from an awareness that God was about to
break into history, an awareness of the approaching crisis, the coming judgment; and we have
seen the significance of the fact that it was against
this background that he proclaimed the present
in-breaking in his own ministry of the kingdom
of God."

—Joachim Jeremias,
Problem of the Historical Jesus

Scholars have focused on events in the last week of Jesus' life more
than any other section to search for meaning of his life and Jesus
"self-understanding." In this chapter, we will look at specific verses
and then begin to ask questions following the lead of scholars of the
historical Jesus who have sought after what is called Jesus self-understanding or conceptions. They obtain their concepts of what
they feel Jesus believed about himself from the literature we have of
him in the four Gospels. All this is to give background to what Jesus

believed about the end of the age and a second coming and whether he believed in Tim LaHaye's end of the world, or the end of the age described by the one we know as John the Divine, the alleged author of the book of Revelation.

Jeremias is quoted above. You will not read a book on the historical Jesus where a background is given of the endeavors of scholars in the past and not see his name. He is quoted in the quest for he was one of the first theologian writers to point out Jesus' limitations and the fact that Jesus believed the kingdom was to come in his day. He says concerning the many pictures of Jesus that are presented by scholars that in efforts to understand him, Jesus' message and proclamations help us identify his thoughts. Jesus wasn't a wandering sage with no specific thrust in his addresses to audiences. His words all carried a theme of a soon coming event which he spoke constantly.

Here is one of the very emotional statements Jesus makes in the Gospels:

> "O Jerusalem, Jerusalem, killing the prophets and stoning those who are sent to you! How often would I have gathered your children together as a hen gathers her brood under her wings, and you would not!" (Luke 13:34).

We can ask ourselves at this point what Jesus was thinking when he uttered this statement. What was his "self-awareness"? The words would tell us he was at an emotional highpoint in his life over events occurring in his interaction with the citizens of Jerusalem Israel in and around 30 AD. In looking at the verse and those verses surrounding it, Luke, in his storytelling, has placed emotional scenes in Jesus' life right before the words are uttered. In verse 31,

> "At that time some Pharisees came to Jesus and said to him— 'Leave this place and go somewhere else, Herod wants to kill you.'"

Jesus responds back to them and says,

> "Go tell that fox, I will drive out demons and heal
> people today and tomorrow, and on the third day
> I will reach my goal. In any case, I must keep
> going today and tomorrow and the next day—
> for surely no prophet can die outside Jerusalem"
> (Luke 13:32–33).

Scholars point out that it would be totally reasonable to draw from this that Jesus is thinking of his possibly being killed by Herod, similarly maybe to the way he had just seen John the Baptist killed. Our account shows he feels frustrated that the whole city of Jerusalem has not responded to his message. Everything he set out to do has been defeated. He has received nothing but rejection. Besides the expression of disappointment and frustration and vexation the story teller (Luke) tells us that Jesus ends the conversation with disgust and anger in telling them:

> "Look, your house is left to you desolate. I tell
> you, you will not see me again until you say,
> 'Blessed is he who comes in the name of the
> Lord'" (Luke 13:35).

How do we reach those conclusions? We get them from the words of the literary character that Matthew, Mark, Luke, or John have put on paper in three languages removed from what we are reading if we are reading the Bible in English.

From reading the literature, we can begin to get a feel of what we think the Jesus character is feeling and thinking. This is called Jesus "self-awareness" in scholarly works. We feel also that when we reach this point we are discovering the "real" Jesus or the "historical" Jesus. We obtain our mental pictures of Jesus from a literary character of four different authors.

This will sound highly offensive to ultra conservative folks who haven't thought through how it is that we come to know Jesus. It was offensive to me for years. After years of study, I finally had to accept that Jesus comes to us from the Gospels as a character of literature. We form our mental pictures of him through its pages. Other mental pictures we all form come through childhood Sunday school classes, Hollywood movies, sermons, Bible studies, meditation and prayers, and books we have read. From all this, we all manufacture our mental images and thoughts of Jesus. They are made and formed by each individual believer or nonbeliever.

Having been married for fifty plus years, I occasionally say to my wife, "I will look forward to meeting you one day." I am of course telling my wife that it is a hope that I will have one day in the resurrection to see all the experiences of her life from the time she was a child and everything she has gone through mentally in thought to become the person she is. There is no way I could see that or know that for it is all those private thoughts in our life that make us the people we are. She could never know my thoughts that have made me the mental construct which I am. No one knows them but God and there are scriptures that speak of our very thoughts being known in some way to God. I would imagine, to him, it is a simple procedure to look inside us. John Polkinghorne tells us that all our thoughts are most likely stored in our hard drive. All of them can be recalled.

Albert Schweitzer commented on the difficulties we have to know the real Jesus of the Bible by saying:

> "Of that which constitutes our inner life we can impart even to those who know us most intimate only fragments; the whole of it, we cannot give, nor would they be able to comprehend it. We wander through life together in a semi-darkness in which none of us can distinguish exactly the features of his neighbor."[1]

We have only fragments of stories about Jesus' life written years and years afterward created from oral traditions and stories passed along verbally to others about him. How difficult it is for us to know Jesus for we only study him off pages of paper and ink of things people have written about him. As Schweitzer has just stated, it is difficult to even know often those we love.

We see in the Gospels that people who allegedly knew him and spent time with him eating and drinking and walking with him daily didn't understand him as Raymond Brown points out. That is also the basis of Raymond Brown's comments that it would be utterly impossible for someone writing a thousand years before Christ and saying anything of knowledge about Jesus before he was born.

Peter and several disciples returned to their homes and went back to their professions of being fishermen after his death, we are told (John 21:3). The hopes and message they felt they heard didn't turn out the way they thought it was to turn out. They didn't know Jesus even though they spent years with him. The disciples who lived and worked with Jesus didn't understand or have any insight to who he was.

Regarding the account in John 21, Raymond Brown writes of the story we get from this passage the following:

> "The whole atmosphere of 21, where Peter and the others have returned to their native region and have resumed their previous occupation, suggests that the risen Jesus had not yet appeared to them and that they are still in the state of confusion caused by his death."[2]

How much less can we understand Jesus from diverse accounts of his life written by very fallible human non-eyewitnesses of events in his life thirty to sixty years after they had occurred?

When the Gospels were written, there were a lot of omissions, revisions, alterations, or retelling of the oral stories in respect to Jesus' life that the Gospel writers worked with. Ben Meyer points out that we must focus upon, relative to our stories, that "folklore and Midrashic motifs"[3] went into the Gospel traditions given to us.

Meyer says we must read past all the editorial comments and the theology of the writers and points they were trying to make about Jesus, obviously some of them different from the others, as we have seen in account examples that have been referenced. There was a lot of creativity or editorial activity on the part of writers over time.

What people don't reflect upon relative to Jesus' "self-understanding" is that Jesus could "speak" something in literature (a Gospel story) and have an opposite thought going through his mind if we could go back in history and be told, at any given moment, what Jesus was thinking when Mark, Matthew, Luke, or John wrote an account of events in his life thirty to sixty years after they are reported to have occurred. There is no way on earth we could ever know the actual thoughts of Jesus just as you could never know my actual thoughts from what you are reading right now that I am putting on paper.

As I was typing this in a backroom of our home, my actual thoughts were that my wife who is in our living room has the TV blaring loudly. It is distracting. Also, our little Yorkie who is at my feet is shaking one of her toys and wants to play. Knowing the thoughts of Jesus when we read literature about him written thirty to sixty years after his life over two thousand years ago is utterly impossible!

Occasionally I will rent a DVD of a movie and watch what is called the "directors cut" after I have watched a movie. A recent example is the movie of JFK by director Oliver Stone. I recently watched it again after buying a DVD with a director's cut on it. My grandson in college was studying American history and wanted to see it. We watched it together.

It was fascinating and interesting. In the director's cut which was part of the DVD, Oliver Stone, as director takes the time to tell the viewer exactly what was going on in his mind when he filmed every scene in the movie. I suddenly found myself seeing nuances within the movie I never saw while watching it. I especially found by watching it and listening to Stone exactly what he thought about the death and assassination of President Kennedy. By watching a director's cut, I found sometimes from what the director said he was doing in a scene, I had totally missed the point of a movie.

Someone other than the director is doing the director's cut in preaching and sermons we are hearing today about Jesus, his message, his purpose, his coming, and the stories in the Gospels about Jesus.

I am sure if we had Jesus to sit in a broadcast studio and do a "director's cut" of the Gospels, while reading the New Testament aloud on camera for a worldwide audience, we would all find it very interesting. I would imagine he also would find it interesting. I am sure that he would have to stop frequently in his reading to clarify scenes. As he did so, he would tell us often "that's not quite the way it was." From time to time he would say—"that wasn't even close." Occasionally he would say, "I don't know how Matthew, Mark, Luke, or John came up with this." Wouldn't we all like to get a director's cut on the Gospels?

Raymond Brown, a catholic Bible scholar and theologian, wrote what I call two crushing books on the life of Jesus, titled *The Birth of Christ* and *The Death of the Messiah*. Years ago, I wouldn't have opened his books because he was part of the great spiritual whore. When I use the term crushing, I mean that the depth and scope of research and analysis of his books, smothers lesser works on the life of Christ.

Brown says that when we read the Gospels we often assume that when reading the New Testament that we are reading "historical biographies." We assume also that "everything related in the NT about Jesus has to be historical."[4] Instead we are reading letters written to specific people with specific backgrounds and interests who were told stories themselves of Jesus which the writers take and then put into their own words as they understand and perceive Jesus.

As an example, we don't really know who wrote each of the Gospels. There were no names put on any of them. Names, by individuals guessing years later, were added to the Gospels as they circulated among the Christian community. Ed Sanders points out that

> "Matthew, Mark, Luke, and John—really lived, but we do not know that they wrote gospels. Present evidence indicates that the gospels remained untitled until the second half of the second century...Names suddenly appear on them about the year 180."[5]

Most of the stories and accounts of Jesus for years were just oral stories or what we might call campfire stories or folklore legends, for clear use of language, repeated about him. Traditions or story accounts which varied between groups were shared with others about Jesus after his death simply by word of mouth and it wasn't always in formal settings. Gregory Boyd, a conservative evangelical pastor and author, wrote in his book *The Jesus Legend* that

> "most scholars acknowledge that the gospel material primarily, was entirely transmitted orally within the Christian communities for decades prior to the writing of the canonical gospels."[6]

Boyd went on to say concerning the various traditions of Jesus' life and sayings that even those over time, since they were oral traditions, were lost or disappeared. His purpose in stating the obvious is that there are scholars who appeal to those unknown sources as if they existed somewhere in a document. Boyd says,

> "It is frustrating for some to have to admit that this oral world is now largely lost to us and that we are forced to imaginatively speculate about it to make sense of the texts before us."[7]

Some try to conjecture that memories were better in those days. This appears to be a defense by conservatives to try to support factualness or truthfulness of the content of accuracy when we must acknowledge that Gospel tradition was transmitted orally for almost a generation or two of the day.

The difficulties human beings have in retaining facts and accuracy in their memories is magnificently covered by Dale Allison in his book *Constructing Jesus*. It highlights all the difficulties we have in obtaining or having true historical accounts of anything from human memory. The human mind can be very tricky and deceptive, even to itself, in recalling truth accurately.

There can be no clearer illustration of this reality than an account of recall of history by two of our nation's founding fathers—John Adams and Thomas Jefferson. Both men worked around the clock for days to write and create our nations Declaration of Independence. They worked in fear of their lives and were soon threatened, by King George, of treason. You would think the circumstances would have given both crystal clear memory recall.

We all are familiar with that celebrated day, July 4, 1776. What is most interesting about it is that the two men most involved in its creation and writing, later in life in their old age, screwed up the accurate historical day of signing of the document by all its historical participants. David McCullough, in his biography *John Adams*, points out that both men in their old age swore that the document was signed by all signatories on July 4. Historical accounts of those involved document that it wasn't signed until August 2, 1776, by most of the original signers and a new representative from Delaware, Thomas McKean, did not sign the document until January 1777. Both Adams and Jefferson lived until the fiftieth anniversary of the creation of the document and both men strangely died on the fiftieth anniversary of its creation. Both missed the historical fact it was not signed by all those present on July 4, 1776, as they both believed. My point is to simply illustrate that the verbal transmissions of events in the life of Jesus, written by non-eyewitnesses thirty to sixty years after events in Jesus' life, would have no way of knowing what went on and was said on many occasions in the life of Jesus and the disciples. It is a guess sometimes when we compare the contradictory Gospel documents.

There is some claim that John's Gospel was written by the disciple Jesus loved and that he was an eyewitness to some degree. This is disputed by scholars. His accounts seriously contradict all the others. These contradictions illustrate the difficulties we have to know exactly what Christ said and did. All the Gospels, including John's Gospel, tell us Jesus was forsaken by the disciples. Yet John shows up at the cross in his own account even though John wrote in another place that "all" would desert Jesus. He contradicts his own accounts. We will get to that account.

The stories the Gospel writers tell or relate are different. They give or paint totally contrasting pictures of Jesus. Their words are small snap shots of scenes in Jesus' life, much like a movie script or the film we are so familiar of the death of President Kennedy. Jesus will be observed in the snippets they give us in totally different frames of mind in different scenes and say totally different words in each of them than others reported.

Brown says that each Gospel writer had various traditions and information that were passed down to them, years and years after the events, and they wove a story to their individual audiences "to communicate to their audiences an interpretation of Jesus that would nourish faith and life as John 20:31 states explicitly."[8]

By 1960, the official position of the Roman Catholic Church was that the Gospels were not necessarily the literal words and deeds of Jesus. There is a term used in theological parlance of "ipissima vox Jesu." The "original voice of Jesus" is a good translation of the Latin term. It is a simple statement to simply say that we never really hear that voice in the pages of the Bible. Without recorders at the time, it is utterly an impossibility. One may argue endlessly over just how accurate any statement is, that we read in the Gospels, where Jesus is allegedly quoted verbatim.

When I speak of Jesus being a literary character, this is what is meant. All we have of him are the words put down on paper in print in whatever version of what we call the Bible, which we are reading. Jesus spoke what is called today Aramaic, scholars believe. It is only in the last one hundred years that a consensus of agreement has been reached among Bible scholars that this was the native language of Jesus. We don't have any original texts in Aramaic of the Gospels.

The legendary stories of Jesus that were all passed down through generations of people were originally placed in Greek. The Greek has been translated as best it can be translated into English. We are three or four languages away from the original speech of Jesus. From this factoid of life, we individually construct our mental pictures of the one we know as Jesus. One can see why the pope would say that we never hear the original voice of Jesus in the Gospels. It is just impossible to have a word for word translation for we never have the actual words Jesus spoke in the first place. Richard Hiers writes in *Jesus and the Future*:

> "Often it is impossible to determine with any assurance whether a particular saying can be considered a reasonably accurate recollection and rendition of Jesus' own words."

Concerning the different stories of what Jesus said and did, Raymond Brown finally says the obvious—they can't all be right. We find the truth in understanding what is written in the Gospels. The writers tell different stories about Jesus and they tell us their story. They are not the same and totally different in many cases from what the other writers wrote about Jesus and his life, words, and actions. This explains the difficulties we have in finding Jesus and what he thought and believed. This is what third questers of Jesus hope to achieve. They tell us we must learn to read the Gospels differently. We must see past the theology of the authors to get to the theology, or beliefs, of Jesus. Wright says,

> "It is perfectly true that the New Testament presents us with Paul, Mark's, Luke's, etc. theology 'about' Jesus, so that Jesus theological beliefs cannot be read off the surface of the text."[9]

We also find writers made up stories or accounts about Jesus to try to get across a theological point they were trying to make about Jesus. We will see that as we go along. We don't find what Jesus believed from the theology created about him 30 or more years after his death. What we don't focus upon is, that when we read the Gospels, that we are reading the theology of the authors. All I saw was my own church interpretation of the accounts of Jesus.

In our individual efforts to find what Jesus said and did, little support is given by the religious world in which we lived to be open minded in our search for answers. We find that true believers and those who have settled and locked in beliefs strive to protect a position or view, usually theirs.

Here is a quote from one of the most respected evangelical scholars in the twentieth century. His name is George Eldon Ladd and he wrote an outstanding book titled a *Theology of the New Testament*. It is probably used in some way in every seminary in the country. As to whether anything that a gospel writer tells us is historically accurate or true or whether an event he has written about did or did not occur, Ladd says it really doesn't matter.

> "If Matthew has paraphrased and interpreted the words of Jesus, then that interpretation comes to us with all the authority of canonical Scripture... This recognition of the Evangelists' role as pastor and preachers rather than mere annalists is endorsed by all modern study of the Gospels and it in no way impugns the veracity of their accounts or their aim and ability to provide us with the historical records of what Jesus did and said...The evangelists clearly exercised a certain measure of freedom in reporting both the words and deeds of Jesus that violates the technical norms of modern history. Matthew and Luke feel free to rearrange Markan material, and to report Jesus words with some variation from their Markan source, in a way that modern historians would not do."[10]

It is Ladd's statement that all this editorial freedom to create stories or imaginary scenes in Jesus' life that presents difficulties. It has everything to do with whether we have the "historical records of what Jesus did and said." He speaks of Matthew and Luke altering Mark's account, as if Mark even knew what Jesus said and did in the first place. Jesus either did say something or do actual things or he didn't. This sounds like Jack in the Beanstalk story telling as a basis of our theology and Christian beliefs of Jesus.

If Matthew has told a tale concerning the birth scene of Jesus used in our Christmas stories, it is a tale, and it isn't what occurred in history. It should be recognized as a tale. If Matthew says that Jesus said something, and Jesus really didn't say it, doesn't make it truth or history or fact because Matthew said it. The fact that Gospel writers have added an embellished story that didn't happen and occur doesn't make it the truth or inspired scripture containing historically accurate facts concerning the life of Jesus. You can't get there from here to reach historical facts about Jesus' life. Some go so far as to say if it is in the Bible it is inspired of God and therefore can't be questioned. I would have expected that within my circle of friends in my prior life but not from a serious mainstream highly respected and quoted scholar of the New Testament. This reasoning can be found in both protestant and catholic approaches in study of the Bible.

Raymond Brown, in his book *Death of the Messiah*, says God doesn't have to communicate in historical accounts in the Bible and could use "imaginative poetry, parables, and didactic fiction"[11] as a means of communicating to human beings.

A classic example to illustrate both Ladd's and Brown's comments about tales or didactic fiction which most all Bible scholars freely acknowledge, are the opposing accounts in the gospels of Jesus birthplace. We commonly hear the phrase "Jesus of Nazareth." In Peter's great sermon in Acts, he calls him Jesus of Nazareth, not Jesus of Bethlehem. That's where he grew up and was from.

But despite that, a didactic fictionalized story is created of Jesus in the Bible to show that Jesus was born in Bethlehem. The reason for the fictional writing or story is to place Jesus' birth in that city because Jesus was to be a descendent of the kingly line of David and must come from that city for it was David's birthplace.

Sanders says,

> "It was a 'mere' fact that Jesus was a Galilean and
> that he came from Nazareth. Yet, Matthew, Luke
> and the other early Christians regarded him as
> the fulfillment of the biblical prophecies that
> Israel would be restored by a scion of the house

of David…To reconcile these two 'facts', one derived from history, the other from prophecy, they chose different ways of locating Jesus' birth in Bethlehem, though he was known to have grown up in Nazareth."[12]

Sanders also points out that a story was created in the Gospels of Joseph and Mary and a journey into Egypt to fulfill the Old Testament scripture that God's son was brought out of Egypt, which followed the story line in the Old Testament of Israel having been brought out of Egypt by Moses. There probably was no journey into Egypt by his parents. Brown acknowledges the didactic fiction of the account in Matthew's work and states in his studies of Matthew's Gospel that Matthew was more prone to a "tale" in the writing of his Gospel than other writers.

In the next chapter, we will show how all the contradictory stories and accounts can't be harmonized.

15

THE GOSPELS CAN'T
BE HARMONIZED

"Even more clear-eyed was Origen, who in the
third century anticipated modern criticism by
candidly observing that at 'many points' the
four gospels 'do not agree.' He inferred that
their truth cannot reside in 'the material letter.'
The Evangelists 'sometimes altered things which,
from the eye of history, occurred otherwise.' They
'could speak of something that happened in one
place as if it had happened in another'...they
introduced 'into what was spoken in a certain way
some changes of their own'...'The spiritual truth
was often preserved in the material falsehood.'"
—Dale Allison, *The Historical
Christ and the Theological Jesus*

One's eyes don't open until recognition is made that the Gospels can't
be harmonized. It is key to a study of Jesus' life.

When I first began to read statements of Bible scholars telling
me the Gospels can't be harmonized, it was offensive. All my life,

of course, I believed they could. One of my first Bible classes in my freshman year of college was titled "Harmony of the Gospels." I had an instructor that started off the course by writing John 10:35 on a chalkboard in front of the room. It says, "Scripture cannot be broken." That started the class off into a study of the Gospels. The basis of the instructor's point was that Jesus spoke and said and did everything spoken of him in the Gospels. It just had to be determined what order he said what he said. I believed in plenary inerrancy of the Bible which is the same outlook most conservative evangelicals hold. They are all factually accurate and true.

One of the first people in history to recognize the disharmony of the Gospels was Origen, one of the early catholic fathers of the third century. Allison quotes him in his book *The Historical Christ and the Theological Jesus.* Origen's statements about the difficulties we find in the Gospels in getting a straight story are not too different from George Eldon Ladd. It is okay to fudge stories and accounts, if it serves formulating the theology of the church which is declared to be the truth.

The official position of the catholic church relative to historical content of the Gospels is explained by Raymond Brown when he says that…

> "these memories, Catholics are told, underwent years of development through apostolic preaching and rewriting by individual evangelists, so that the end products, the Gospels, 'relate the words and deeds of the Lord in a different order and express his sayings not literally but differently.'"[1]

With what we covered in the previous chapter, this statement and others like it by Bible scholars and theologians is why we can't read theology and find what Jesus thought, believed, and did. We must probe past the product of the evangelists.

Why go into a harmony of the Gospels relative to Jesus' beliefs of a second coming? The purpose is to show what Jesus believed about his day and time and the future for his age. It is important because, as Bible scholars tell us, you can't find out what Jesus believed in reading the theology of Gospel writers. You don't find it in the book of Revelation either, a total mythical creation of one seeking an explanation of why Jesus hadn't returned. Revelation was an effort to cover for the fact Jesus hadn't returned just as much as we will see in the next two chapters that the Gospel of John, tries to cover for or conceal the humanity of Jesus. History has proven Revelation to be devoid of understanding of future events in the world. The author's first-person quotes of Jesus are no different than dozens of proclamations in the prophetic books which began with "thus sayeth the Lord." The fact that their prophecies went unfulfilled tells us with what authority the author of Revelation spoke and with what capability the prophet of old knew or understood the future. Revelation duplicates the same mythology upon which Jesus relied to establish his beliefs about what God was going to do through him.

As we go forward, we will see that that Jesus didn't believe in the end of the age as Revelation portrays. His mind was on the nation of Israel and what he had tried to do and accomplish in his life. He wasn't thinking two thousand years into the future to our day but solely living in his day with his mind on all those around him. His theology was restoration theology—making things right between Yahweh and Israel under what Christians term the old covenant.

We will go through what we can discover of Jesus' own thoughts about his death and the end of the age and whether he believed in the end of the age as the *Left Behind* series pictures. We will cover what third quest scholars tell us Jesus most likely believed was going to happen in his life and the way he saw and envisioned his future. We will look at what he hoped to achieve as best it can be known.

Bible scholars feel Mark wrote first and that whoever wrote Luke and Matthew had a copy of Mark's Gospel when they wrote theirs. This is based upon the fact that in the Gospel of Matthew and Luke, there are many verses that are identical in wording to that of Mark. It is assumed that for Matthew and Luke to write exact words that Mark has written in his Gospel that Matthew and Luke must have had a copy of Mark when they wrote their Gospel. Most Bible scholars believe this is probably a correct assumption. When we read

Luke and Matthew, we find they have chosen to add or embellish and tell stories about Jesus that Mark did not relay as Origen points out above. Or they leave off and don't quote some things Mark wrote or they change a word or two here and there in their quotes from Mark.

As much as it may be a surprise, scholars for a century or more have believed generally that the authors of the Gospels used also what is called a "Q" source of information.

The "Q" source is explained in A. T. Robertson's book *Harmony of the Gospels.*

> "But another thing is equally clear and that is that both Matthew and Luke had another source in common because they each give practically identical matter for much that is not in Mark at all. This second common source for Matthew and Luke has been called Logia because it is chiefly discourses. It is sometimes referred to as "Q," the first letter of the German word Quelle (source)."[2]

That Q existed and is important in what is contained in the Gospels is detailed in Larry Hurtado's exhaustive work in his book *Lord Jesus Christ*. Hurtado writes about the source scholars call "Q":

> "In the main it probably includes a number of authentic sayings of Jesus (howbeit translated and likely adapted in the process of transmission), and it represents the most substantial body of sayings of Jesus that can make a plausible claim to authenticity."[3]

There are no extant copies of the "Q" document, but it is believed by scholars and theologians they once existed and were used by those who wrote the Gospels.

Matthew and Mark present a Jesus who is deserted by his cowardly disciples. Matthew's account shows all the disciples forsaking Jesus including Peter who went at least, it appears, to one of the trial scenes but finally even Peter leaves him after being questioned by a lady while warming himself outside the trial proceedings. In her asking him if he was a part of the group, Peter declared affirmatively three times he didn't know the Galilean Jesus.

All this abandonment by every one of his disciples was to be a fulfillment of Jesus' own words recorded in Mark's account where on the night of the last supper, Jesus and the disciples had sung a song and prepared to depart. Before doing so, Jesus said,

> "You will all fall away...for it is written: 'I will strike the shepherd, and the sheep will be scattered'" (Mark 14:27).

Mark connects the prophecy of Jesus to a scripture in Zechariah 13:7. Therefore, the fleeing and scattering of all the disciples were foretold by God and part of the divine plan.

The author of the Gospel of John also tells us that Jesus said they would all forsake him:

> "The hour is coming, indeed it has come, when you all will be scattered, every man to his home, and will leave me alone; yet, I am not alone for the father is with me" (John 16:32).

John also has a totally different accounting of scenes at the cross which we will cover in the next few paragraphs. What is interesting about the account in John, is that he states that the disciples all flee with Jesus expressing permission for them to flee (John 16:32).

John also has an account of the passion narratives peculiar only to him where...

> "Jesus himself begs the soldiers to let his disciples go; it contains no reference at all to the disciples falling asleep at the time of Jesus' agony in Gethsemane, or indeed to the agony itself. This tendency to exonerate is very likely a sign of the

authentic nature of the tradition about the disciples' turning tail."[4]

Luke has a contrasting account of significant difference when
he says that "all" of Jesus acquaintances were at the cross with the
women. We would assume Luke's statement is an all-inclusive statement meant to include all the apostles and disciples. If Luke wrote
Acts, he referenced that there were approximately 120 original followers of Jesus including the women (Acts 1:15). Luke says *all of
them* stood a distance from the cross. What is obvious is that they
would not be in hearing distance of what Jesus spoke on the cross.
Luke seems to tell us they saw what happened, but he doesn't use the
term they heard these things. It was Luke's intent, he says, to give an
account of history as he says in opening statements in Acts. Luke's
statement would lead us to believe 120 or so individuals stood from
a distance and watched.

Luke writes,

> "And all his acquaintances and the women who
> had followed him from Galilee stood at a dis-
> tance and saw these things" (Luke 24:49).

John Meier, in volume 3 of the life of Jesus, points out that this
description was "a phrase probably meant to include Peter and the
rest of the Eleven as eyewitnesses of the passion."[5]

Luke presents a different Jesus in mood and spirit from that of
Matthew. Luke's Jesus is much closer in state of mind to the Jesus
described in John. Matthew has Jesus terribly distraught and "near
death."

In Luke's scenes of Jesus in the garden of Gethsemane, Jesus is
shown as relatively calm and his prayer to God receives or brings the
presence of an angel to the garden to strengthen Jesus (Luke 22:43).
In Luke's account, Jesus doesn't pray three separate times he might
be spared his trial as he did in Matthew's Gospel. He humbly asks
one time in Luke and says, "Not my will but yours be done" (Luke
22:42). Luke says Jesus was so earnest that "his sweat became like

drops of blood falling down upon the ground" (Luke 22:44), which is an account no other writer has referenced.

In Luke's scenes of the cross, he portrays Christ to be at peace with God and in communion in spirit with him throughout the ordeal, and he records Jesus' final words to be the tranquil and peaceful departure from this life as being: "Father, into your hands I commend my spirit" (Luke 23:46). Luke also does not portray the disciples in a negative way as being cowards and fleeing as Matthew and Mark write of them all fleeing Jesus. Luke records that Jesus congratulated them by Luke's recording that Jesus said to them: "You are those who have stood by me in my trials" (Luke 22:28). Raymond Brown probably rightly says regarding Luke's portrayal at this point of the disciples that only a discreet silence about them after Jesus' arrest gives evidence that Luke knows they fled.

Luke also records word's none of the others do while Jesus is on the cross. I think they are the most beautiful words placed on the lips of Jesus in the entire Bible:

> "And Jesus said, 'Father, forgive them; for they know not what they do.' And they cast lots to divide his garments" (Luke 23:33).

Matthew gives a totally different portrayal of Jesus starting in the garden of Gethsemane and ending with his death on the cross.

For a sharp contrast, we can start with the death of Jesus on the cross according to Matthew. Matthew has Jesus cry out and scream aloud to God questioning why he has been forsaken. Most of us are familiar with his words. It is sometimes called the cry of dereliction.

> "And about the ninth hour Jesus cried with a loud voice, 'Eli, Eli, la-ma sa-bach-tha-ni' that is, 'My God, my God, why hast thou forsaken me?' And one of them at once ran and took a sponge, filled it with vinegar, and put it on a reed and gave it to him to drink" (Matt. 27:45–48).

Matthew says he screamed out again and said the same thing and he died. From the time that Jesus is seen in Matthew's account of leaving the meal of the last supper, Matthew portrays Jesus as agitated, sorrowful, distraught, and fearful, to the point of his possible death. Jesus says,

> "'Sit here, while I go yonder and pray,' And taking with him Peter and the two sons of Zebedee, he began to be sorrowful and troubled. Then he said to them, 'My soul is very sorrowful, even to death; remain here, and watch with me.' And going a little farther he fell on his face and prayed, 'My Father, if it be possible, let this cup pass from me, nevertheless, not as I will, but as thou wilt.'" (Matt. 26:36–39)

Matthew shows Jesus as praying for a way out three different times. The second time his words in Matthew are "'My father, if this cannot pass unless I drink it, thy will be done" (Matt. 26:42). In scenes in Matthew's and Mark's accounts, Jesus goads his disciples constantly to stick with him and join him in his agony. They collapse into sleep according to Matthew, Mark, and Luke. Luke still writes they stood by him.

Brown writes concerning Jesus thoughts:

> "In Mark he has been plunged into the traumatic knowledge of the weakness of his own flesh; out of his anguish prayers have been wrung from his lips begging the Father that he be delivered from the hour and the cup that he once so bravely anticipated; those prayers have not been granted; rather God has given him over to sinners that he himself once predicted would happen to the Son of Man...but overall God's lack of assistance and the eventual scattering of the disciples have not changed."[6]

Edward Schillibeeckx says concerning all these contradictory accounts,

> "From this varied picture which the gospels present of Jesus' close disciples, especially of Peter, we must conclude that there is no uniform tradition indicating what these men actually did at the time of Jesus' arrest."[7]

The contrasting stories in the Gospels one must face. They contrast and they are different. You can't harmonize them as I did and others try to do to whitewash or do away with the obvious differences. Bart Erhman explains our problems well when he says in his book *Misquoting Jesus* the following:

> "The point is that Luke changed the tradition he inherited. Readers completely misinterpret Luke if they fail to realize this—as happens, for example, when they assume that Mark and Luke are in fact saying the same thing about Jesus. If they are not saying the same thing, it is not legitimate to assume they are—for example, by taking what Mark says, and taking what Luke says, then taking what Matthew and John say and melding them all together, so that Jesus says and does all the things that each of the Gospel writers indicates."[8]

There are literally hundreds of different accounts or statements throughout the New Testament that contradict each other or tell a divergent account. Allison writes at one point in his book *Constructing Jesus* the following:

> "Beyond that, however, the discrepancies are notorious. The textual disparity, no matter what the historical facts, should not surprise."[9]

16

John—A Totally Different Gospel

"Thus, even if one were to grant the possibility of God becoming incarnate, on the Fourth Gospel model, as a physical human being who is (always or sometimes) conscious of being divine, and thus eternal, omnipotent and omniscient, this would not be the Jesus whom historical research has glimpsed through the Synoptic traditions."
—John Hick, *The Metaphor of God Incarnate*

"To recognize that Jesus was mistaken in his belief that the eschatological events were soon to occur would present some problems for traditionalist faith. Such faith, which is grounded substantially in the Fourth Gospel, commonly ascribes to Jesus all the attributes of deity, including omniscience. Since, in the view of traditionalist interpreters, Jesus could not have been mistaken, his sayings about the coming Kingdom must have referred to something that did soon occur, such as his resurrection, Pentecost, or the establishment of the church."

—Richard Hiers, *Jesus and the Future*

John's account of the passion week stories radically differs from all three Gospels. From the time that Jesus was arrested in Gethsemane, John gives an account of events, words, and actions of Jesus that contrast sharply and contradict the other three Gospel accounts. When I use the term *contradict*, that is meant to say is that the author just tells or gives an altogether different version or story of events from the other Gospels. The solution to understand them is not to take all the contradictory stories and arrive at the conclusion Jesus said and did them all. Each author was telling a different story.

Briefly we find Jesus in the Gospel of John as being all powerful. Raymond Brown writes,

> "All this is part of the Johannine tendency to picture Jesus without any element of human weakness or dependence."[1]

We covered in chapter 13 the issues of Jesus' limitations. Was he God? Did he know everything? The author of the Gospel of John goes way out of his way to write about Jesus to keep people from believing or thinking he was human. Brown says,

> "In response, the evangelist defended the divinity of Jesus so massively that the Fourth Gospel scarcely allows for human limitation."[2]

In the Gospel of John when Jesus asks a question, John makes note that Jesus was testing those in his audience or that Jesus already knew the answer. When he chose a bad egg in Judas, John makes a point to say that Jesus knew he was going to betray him from the beginning. When he prays aloud and asks God for anything, it isn't that he needed to ask God, but it was done as an example or to educate his audience. He doesn't ask for help in his final hours but explains that all that he is doing is intentional and planned from the beginning of time. He is never at the mercy of his captors but always orchestrating events around himself. All three gospels except John's gospel, shows that Jesus grew weak and struggled to carry his cross. Roman soldiers, each gospel says, upon seeing Jesus unable to carry his cross, compelled Simon from Cyrene to carry his cross for him. John references nothing of the sort happening to his Jesus. John's Jesus didn't need help carrying the cross. Jesus was, as Brown states, all powerful.

Jesus is shown in John's Gospel to be totally in control of his life in all that happens to him from the time of his arrest in the garden to the last words he speaks on the cross. Starting in the garden with the account of Judas leading a band of soldiers to point out Jesus and betray him in the process, the scenes of John are all his own. Instead of Judas having to walk up to Jesus and kiss him on the cheek to point him out, there is no kiss in John's account. Instead Jesus is shown assertively walking toward and confronting the band of soldiers and asking them whom they seek. After being told they seek Jesus, he boldly says, "I am he" (John 18:5).

John records a dramatic scene peculiar only to him where the soldiers and band who come to seize Jesus, all dramatically fall to the ground after Jesus speaks to them. It is as if Jesus spoke as the great "I AM," which was a name for God in the Old Testament and they fall to the ground in fear (John 18:6).

Jesus is not shown to falter, ask for a way out, being weak in the flesh, sweating blood, nor doubting God in any way as the other authors show him in his last hour. Jesus is nowhere near portrayed as reaching a point of being "near death" as Matthew states.

We have no accounts of John from the garden. Instead, John gives some long discourses that none of the other Gospels mention even with Jesus praying that God would "glorify me in your presence with the glory I had with you before the world began" (John 17:5). This shows Christ asking that he might return home like the small character in the movie *E.T.* It is a proof text for some of Jesus' preexistence as a member of the God family. It was that for me.

The author of Hebrews writes,

> "In the days of his flesh, Jesus offered up prayers and supplications, with loud cries and tears, to him who was able to save him from death, and he was heard for his godly fear" (Heb. 5:7).

The Jesus of Hebrews isn't the same Jesus of John. John shows Jesus to be calm, cool, collected, and unshakeable in his thoughts and demeanor while facing death.

At the trial scenes in John's Gospel, Jesus isn't shown as reserved and meek as in the other Gospels where he rarely utters a word. John has Jesus speaking boldly to both Pilate and to the high priest. He tells Pilate that "you would have no power over me if it were not given to you from above" (John 19:11). He spoke back to the solider who struck him when he appeared before the high priest. In all the other accounts, each writer emphasizes that Jesus basically says nothing to those who addressed him, neither the high priest or the soldiers.

In John's Gospel, Jesus is shown to be thinking about his mother that he sees at his feet and asks his friend John (a disciple) to take care of her. He tells his mother to go with John into his home. All this, of course, contradicts all the other Gospel accounts of Jesus being forsaken and an earlier quote which I gave even in John's own Gospel that Jesus was to be deserted by all his immediate disciples.

> "When Jesus saw his mother, and the disciple whom he loved standing near, he said to his mother, 'Woman, behold your son!' Then he said to the disciple, 'Behold, your mother!' And from that hour the disciple took her to his own home" (John 19:2–27).

All this beautiful account of John starkly contrasts even John's own words already quoted stating that they all would forsake Jesus.

Adding to the confusion as to what happened, we have an account in Mark which is the more traditional source that says the following:

> "There were also women looking on from afar, among them were Mary Magdalene, and Mary the mother of James the younger and of Joses and Salome, who, when he was in Galilee, followed him, and ministered to him; and also many other women who came up with him to Jerusalem" (Mark 15:40–41).

Mark, strangely, doesn't even detail that Jesus own mother, Mary, was even at the cross. John, again, seems to have manufactured a story differently for some teaching purpose for his audience.

What do we make of all the contradictions of the state of mind of Jesus during his ordeal leading up to the cross and during the crucifixion? Somewhere along the line, we must make choices of really what is history or fact according to our best judgment.

After reading them all over again several times and trying to take off my distorted spectacles, I lean to the comment of Schweitzer who says about the accounts we have in John. It is an "idealized" portrayal of Jesus through the eyes of John. Bible scholars call them Christian meditations post Jesus death. It would be another way of saying didactic fiction.

Schweitzer says the same thing Dunn has previously stated,

> "The dilemma is finally resolved in the farewell discourses and in the absence of all mention of the spiritual struggle in Gethsemane. The intention here is to show that Jesus not only had foreknowledge of his death, but had long also overcome it in anticipation, and went to meet his tragic fate with perfect inward serenity. That, however, is no historical narrative, but the final state of reverent idealization."[3]

John sees Jesus with prior existence as God, bringing into Jesus' thought "ditheistic" concepts in Jesus' speech, when Jewish tradition of Jesus' own day was strict monotheism. John presented a binatarian God family, not a trinity, in his Gospel. He shows Jesus to be God, having prior existence, being a coequal with God and creating the world. That is exactly what I believed and the images in my mind of Jesus residually remain the same.

One of the most thorough and exhaustive works done on the issues involved in a search for understanding John's gospel, is made by James D. G. Dunn. Dunn says concerning the portrayal of Jesus in John's Gospel the following:

> "John does seem to present Jesus as 'a being self-consciously distinct' from his Father and to that extent is in danger of stretching the 'nascent binitarianism' of Jesus monotheism into some form of unacceptable ditheism (two gods)."[4]

Dunn is saying that Jesus didn't present himself, while walking the earth, as one of two Gods of the Jewish race. A significant majority of Bible scholars don't believe Jesus went about telling people he was God, nor did he believe he was actual God. Jesus is presented in the Gospels, other than John whose historicity is in doubt, as a very human being.

To show Jesus as being weak, tempted, crying out to God for help and strength would not fit John's theological message in his Gospel which was to show Jesus as God, the creator of heaven and earth, and the preexistent one. John begins his Gospel in what is called the prologue by giving a picture of Jesus as being actual God. He was with God from the beginning (John 1:1). Jesus is shown to be the one through whom God created the world. John presents a Jesus in what is called by scholars a "higher Christology." The first chapter of John's Gospel forms the source of the creed which has already been quoted showing that Jesus was actual God, composed of the same substance.

Richard Hiers states in his book, *Jesus and the Future*, concerning the Gospel of John and what is contained in it, the following:

> "New Testament scholars have recognized for the greater part of the past hundred years that the Fourth Gospel is best understood as the faith statement of a particular individual or community which was written down near the end of the first century A.D. Periodic efforts to discover historical tradition in the Forth Gospel have not yielded any substantial results. The impetus for such efforts largely derives from interpreters' desire to find an historical Jesus more congruent with the faith-understanding of traditional Christianity than the Jesus portrayed in the synoptic gospels."[5]

Sanders says something similar when he writes in his often-quoted book about Jesus titled *The Historical Figure of Jesus* the following:

> "Consequently, for the last 150 years or so scholars have had to choose. They have almost unanimously, and I think entirely correctly, concluded that the teaching of the historical Jesus is to be sought in the synoptic gospels and that John represents an advanced theological development, in which the meditations on the person and work of Christ are presented in the first person, as if Jesus said them."[6]

Christology is based upon stories and statements and speeches in Jesus' life taken from the words of the Gospel of John that Bible scholars believe Jesus didn't make. The position that readers of the Bible are asked to take is to accept all these as factual representations of Jesus' words and deeds while at the same time recognizing they were not really said or spoken by Jesus. Dunn writes,

> "Rather than assume that the Fourth Evangelist intended to record the very words of Jesus, the implication is that John's gospel is the Evangelists meditation on Jesus ministry and its significance for his own day, intended as a portrait rather than a photograph, as a statement of conviction concerning Jesus unique role and its importance as seen with the benefit of hindsight of faith (cf. e.g. 2:22; 12:16; 20:9), rather than 'a historical commentary.'"[7]

Dunn notes in his book *Jesus Remembered,*

> "The inference is inescapable in that the style is that of the Evangelist rather than that of Jesus... On the whole, then, the position is unchanged: John's gospel cannot be regarded as a source for the life and teaching of Jesus in the same order as the Synoptics."[8]

Albert Schweitzer and other Bible scholars recognized the difficulties with the historicity of John years ago. Schweitzer, concerning whether the stories in John are factual says the following:

> "John represents a more advanced state of the formation of myth, as much as he has substituted the Greek metaphysical conception of divine sonship for the Jewish messianic conception and, since his acquaintance with the Alexandrian Logos doctrine, even makes Jesus apply to himself the Greek speculative notion of pre-existence."[9]

This approach to Biblical interpretation of Jesus' life is like what we covered earlier in respect to Yahweh's life. As Walter Brueggemann wrote regarding our acceptance of the God of the Old Testament that ("Of course, beyond Israel's insistence, we have no evidence that Yahweh has uttered these words") we find ourselves in the same quandary in interpreting Jesus' life.

We can't have made-up stories about Jesus and read imaginary speeches and fiction and have historical information at the same time about Jesus which forms the basis of our beliefs about him. We can't use the mythical accounts of John in Revelation to determine what Jesus believed about the future. He didn't see the future ahead of the world the way John portrays it in Revelation. He expected a whole different world for himself and for Israel and the disciples. Jesus expected Yahweh to come to earth, reconstitute the lost tribes, and rule the world from Jerusalem.

Jesus did not see himself as God, existing previously in heaven as God, or think he was God. Christendom, in its beliefs of Christology, is banking on the feuding pontificates of Chalcedon to know more of Jesus than he knew of himself. The creeds are beginning to leak water.

As covered previously, interpreters take the position that the exaggerations and hyperbole and didactic fiction, for preaching and teaching, are permissible. George Ladd's viewpoint is typical in what is contained in the gospel of John. It is considered okay for John to teach his readers that Jesus spoke as if he was preexistent God. John makes exaggerated statements and created imaginary stories and a dialogue that didn't exist to preach and teach to impart a truth— Jesus was a member of the triune family of God.

John uses statements like—"*before Abraham, I AM.*" More than likely, Jesus never spoke those words nor gave anyone the impression he was the I AM of the Old Testament (a name for God) or that his mind contained memories of his life in the Old Testament as God. Neither did he have any awareness of having preexisted as God in a two minds theory of Chalcedon and the creed we have covered already. N.T. Wright says that Christians should "forget the pseudo-orthodox attempts to make Jesus of Nazareth conscious of being the second person of the Trinity."[10]

For years, I conducted what were called Passover services in my church. It was an evening when bread and real wine was used in what is commonly called the Lords Supper. Before that service commemorating Jesus death, we had a foot washing service, trying to duplicate his last evening with his disciples.

After the meal was over, as a part of the service, I would read aloud to the congregation passages from John's gospel which contained those very emotional scenes in Jesus' life given to us only in John. We tried to duplicate the emotional moment shown in John's accounts. One passage was John's statements in chapter seventeen.

> "When Jesus had spoken these words, he lifted up his eyes to heaven and said, 'Father, the hour has come; glorify thy son that the Son may glorify thee since thou hast given him power over all flesh, to give eternal life to all whom thou hast given him. And this is eternal life, that they know thee the only true God, and Jesus Christ whom thou hast sent. I have glorified thee on earth, having accomplished the work which thou gavest me to do, and now, Father, glorify thou me in thy own presence with the glory which I had with thee before the world was made.'" (John 17:1–5)

When I read the statement (*glorify thou me in thy own presence with the glory which I had with thee before the world was made*), I visualized for a quarter century that Jesus, in this statement, was speaking to God and an infinite past of memories as the second member of a God family. I believed that it reflected recall and memory of the bursting forth of our universe in a flash and his creating suddenly, as it were, Yellowstone, the Grand Canyon, mountain peaks of the Himalayas, the oceans, giant whales, porpoises, lions, elephants, tigers, and all we know of our planet. Jesus created it with God and brought it into the world. He now upholds and sustains it all and keeps it going. Those mental images formed through all my beliefs about Jesus are etched in marble in my mind to this day. Jesus wasn't there to do all that.

Wright states when we read the gospels we must scrutinize the materials. In many cases, they are created by the author. He says in reading the gospels we must ask ourselves this question about what is written:

> "Was it perhaps, created out of nothing to meet needs which remained unmet by actual sayings of Jesus?"[11] Wright says this particularly might have been the case in needs for the "highlighting of Jesus divine sonship." We find this commonly in the gospel of John.

Marcus Borg writes of his frustration in seminary at Oxford when he learned what Wright has stated, that when it comes to the divinity of Jesus, much of the content of the gospel of John is manufactured out of thin air. Borg says in his book *Meeting Jesus Again for the First Time*, that when he learned that the Jesus of history never spoke of himself as the Son of God, as one with God, as the light of the world, and that he didn't even speak the words of John 3:16 and other passages where Jesus is directly quoted, and that some writer of the gospel made up those alleged words of Jesus 50 years after Jesus had lived, that,

> "I remember becoming angry at John when I became aware that its' account was largely non-historical."

Borg said he wanted to excise the gospel of John from the New Testament.

When that is observed, and seen when reading a text, we are not reading history or actual accounts or real words or actions of Jesus in most cases. Those moments of imaginary creating writing or didactic fiction within the gospels stories, don't contain history of what really went on in Christ's life or what he thought about himself or spoke. Meyer, Dunn, and others point out, we don't get Jesus theology and outlook and worldview from these passages. That also was the purpose of Dunn's statement where he said we don't find in the gospels any information that tells us Jesus thought or spoke of his "preexisting" with God as a member of the God family, prior to his appearance on earth.

Jesus didn't say some of the things John said he said. The conversations and scenes are created ones and they are fictitious. John portrays a Jesus that does show that Jesus did have conscious awareness of existing in the Old Testament; being with God in heaven; speaking and interacting with Abraham; coming down from heaven and desiring to return to heaven from where he came. When Wright tells us to forget that Jesus had conscious memory on earth of being with God, his being God, or the I AM of the Old Testament, Wright is telling us to do exactly the opposite of what John asks us to believe about Jesus in his prologue and much of what he writes in the gospel of John.

James D.G. Dunn summarizes it in *Christology in the Making*, when he states:

> "The best explanation still remains that the Johannine discourses are meditation or sermons on individual sayings or episodes from Jesus' life, but elaborated in the language and theology of subsequent Christian reflection."[12]

The author or writers of the gospel of John, 30-40 years after the gospels of Matthew, Mark, and Luke were written, completely rewrite history of what we have of Jesus life in the synoptic gospels and Hebrews, where Jesus is shown to be very human, weak in the flesh, crying out with loud cries and tears for God to save Him from his plight. Instead of Jesus being human with human weaknesses, one needing help and strength form God, John's gospel shows Jesus to be all powerful, never crying out and asking for help, having no thoughts of fear or dismay, and needing no help to carry his cross.

He is presented as preexixtent God and having and possessing the powers of God. As Raymond Brown was quoted earlier,

> "the evangelist defended the divinity of Jesus so
> massively that the Fourth Gospel scarcely allows
> for human limitation."

James D.G. Dunn was quoted to say, resulting from all the contradiction of Jesus' life and words in John's gospel, compared to what we have in Matthew, Mark, and Luke that

> "John's gospel cannot be regarded as a source for
> the life and teaching of Jesus in the same order as
> the Synoptics".

Richard Hiers was quoted in his comment that bible scholars have simply not been able to find much history in the gospel of John. He said:

> "Periodic efforts to discover historical tradition
> in the Fourth Gospel have not yielded any sub-
> stantial results. The impetus for such efforts
> largely derives from interpreters' desire to find an
> historical Jesus more congruent with the faith-
> understanding of traditional Christianity than
> the Jesus portrayed in the synoptic gospels."

We must keep on believing about Jesus what we have been told about him. Dennis Nineham was quoted earlier, and he stated that no effort is made by church bodies to detail in any way the life of the historical Jesus, by pointing out the differences we have in gospels of his life, and particularly how that contrasts to doctrines and beliefs which have been developed about him.

Raymond Brown is noted for, in biblical scholarship, his extensive studies of the gospel of John and what was known as the Johannine community of disciples which bible scholars believe were responsible for the creation of the gospel of John. It reflected their theological beliefs.

He states that they found themselves thrown out of the synagogues and not able to worship in them due to the fact they were stating that Jesus was God. He says they were seen by the Jews as

> "proclaiming a second God and thus violating the basic principle of Israelite identity: 'Hear O Israel, the Lord our God, is One' (Deut. 6:4). No wonder then that the Jewish authorities thought that such people should be expelled from the synagogues and even exterminated for their blasphemy."[13]

What is puzzling about honesty in interpretations of the Bible and what George Ladd said regarding accepting fictive imagination in our gospel accounts, in another section of his book, he says:

> "The decision to accept Jesus as Lord cannot be made without historical evidence—yes, historical—about Jesus. If it were a decision without any historical evidence it would not be about Jesus, a historical person, but about an ideology or an ideal."[14]

Ben Meyer states in his book *The Aims of Jesus*:

> "From the beginning Christianity has been a confession of events in human history."[15]

Theologians, by making comments like those of Meyer and Ladd, seem to overlook how lay people view their telling us that didactic fiction can be equal to, or the same as, an historical event and that we should accept them as actual spoken words to develop church theology, as is the case of John's gospel. We deny those statements of Ladd and Meyer when we take gospel accounts that contain created fiction that allegedly describe to us real events and real conversations of Jesus that didn't occur and use them to hang or pin our theology. This is exactly what has gone on in the formation of doctrine in respect to Christology.

Brown points out that John, in his gospel, changes history for other characters in his stories and accounts. One of them is John the Baptist.

We all know the stories and accounts of John the Baptist that tell us, while John was in prison before his death, he doubted exactly who Jesus was and he sent emissaries to ask Jesus questions about who Jesus was. The author of John shows John the Baptist having no question. He knew Jesus and his significance, and he has John the Baptist speak of his being aware of Jesus preexistence (John 1:15,30).

Brown writes:

> "Already in the first chapter of John there are remarkable differences from the Synoptic picture of Jesus' ministry. All four Gospels show respect for John the Baptist (henceforth JBap), but the Fourth Gospel attributes to him a knowledge of Jesus' preexistence (1:15,30)! Since the exalted Christology of pre-existence never appears even on Jesus' lips in the other Gospels, its appearance in JBap's proclamation is surely the product of Johannine theology."[16]

Of all we have viewed in these last chapters, the contradictory accounts and stories, the different pictures of Jesus saying and doing different things, one has to draw the line somewhere to separate fact from fiction. Bible scholars for years have been telling us that there is little history in the gospel of John, but rather an interpretation of his life after the fact. We can't harmonize all the accounts. They differ, and we must face it. We have traditions about Jesus. They are not the same.

Wright states regarding evangelicals and Catholics that take the approach that all is well with the conflicting Bible stories and contradictions and didactic fiction and inaccuracies.

> "Negatively, it has been said time and time again that the picture of Jesus in the gospels is historically incredible and that Christianity is, therefore based on a mistake: Theologians from Martin Kahler to Luke Timothy Johnson have denied the inference, saying that Christianity is unaffected by the gospels inaccuracy and unreliability. Most, myself included, accept that the inference is valid: if the gospels got it wrong, Christianity is indeed ill-founded."[17]

I could not agree more. In the remaining chapters we will come back to Jesus beliefs of the end of the age and how it is that we come up with all the wild stories we have about the end of the age, Armageddon, and the second coming.

17

WHY DO 126,000,000 PEOPLE BELIEVE JESUS WILL RETURN BY 2050?

"Jesus was not publishing time tables to inform some later generation when the end was near. Instead, he was summoning his own generation to repentance because he believed the end of the age already was near. Popular theories to the effect that modern events constitute 'signs of the times' are at best naïve attempts to clothe dubious human speculations with biblical authority. They also involve the arrogant assumption that history hitherto has had little or no meaning, since the 'Bible prophecies' refer only to our time. Jesus did not proclaim that the Kingdom of God would come at some point in the then distant future."

—Richard Hiers, *Jesus and the Future*

"As we ponder the question of its meaning today, candor requires that we acknowledge that the early Christians (and Jesus himself, if he had an apocalyptic eschatology) were wrong about the end being near. Are we to say, 'They got the belief right—Jesus really will come again; but their timing was off?' To use a specific example, does Christian faithfulness entail retaining the expectation of the author of Revelation and transferring it to our time or to some distant future, even though he expected it in his time and was mistaken? Or do we say that his expectation was mistaken not only in its timing, but also in its content? His symbolic language refers to the Roman Empire in his own time; why should we think it refers to some still future scenario?"

—Marcus Borg, *Meaning of Jesus*

Borg's comments above contain the question of the hour. The timing has been adjusted and not the content. All prophecies, since they weren't fulfilled, have been moved forward. E. P. Sanders was quoted earlier when he said that the early church changed its expectations again and again. We also have seen it in our day for over two hundred years in American history from those groups that have arisen, from Seventh Day Adventists, Mormons, Jehovah's Witnesses, the Worldwide Church of God, and dozens of other churches. I assume Hal Lindsey has made a few adjustments.

With events in the middle east rising to a crisis point, an imminent arrival of Jesus is again being anticipated by evangelical Christian groups. Muslims look for the last Imam. Sunday morning sermons on TV have that air of urgency just as I lived for twenty-five years of my life.

How have we ended up with 126,000,000 people believing Jesus is to return in 2050 if the Son of God himself believed the kingdom was to arrive in his day?

If you have ever bought a car, of any brand, it is amazing how you begin to notice all the cars of the same make and model of yours running down the road. You even notice the number of cars of the same color as yours. Prophecy works upon the human mind in much the same way. It sees what it wants to see. It creates the world it becomes programmed to find.

The major reason that people believe the second coming is approaching is that religious exegetes and interpreters have taught them that. All the prophecies of Jesus in respect to the end of the age are for our time today. Jesus wasn't speaking to his generation when he talked of the end of the age and the arrival of the kingdom of God. He was addressing ours.

I believed, as I am sure many people do also who hold the belief of everything being in the future, that Jesus knowingly spoke "above the heads" of his audience. That's how we end up with 126,000,000 Americans that believe Jesus will return by the year 2050. The blood moon spoken in Joel to occur in Joel's day was later believed to occur in Jesus' day. Since the end did not come then, individuals are proclaiming Jesus' arrival in the next blood moons. They will go on forever if the earth stays in its current orbit.

One of my favorite scriptures to quote telling individuals Jesus' return was right around the corner was Daniel 12. It reads,

> "At that time shall Michael stand up, the great prince which standeth for the children of thy people; and there shall be a time of trouble, such as never was since there was a nation even to that same time; and at that time thy people shall be delivered, everyone that shall be found written in the book. And many of them that sleep in the dust of the earth shall awake, some to everlasting life, and some to shame and everlasting contempt...But thou, O Daniel, shut up the words and seal the book, even to the time of the end; many shall run to and fro, and knowledge shall be increased" (Dan. 12:1–3).

Here we have condensed Daniel foretelling the resurrection of the dead, the great tribulation, a judgement day, and obviously the end of the age with God finally stepping in to take over rulership of the kingdoms of the world. Jesus quoted it as we will see and Jesus saw all this occurring in his day. I saw all this occurring in 1975. One hundred twenty-six million Americans see it occurring in 2050.

I lived biblically, applying scriptures to events in the world. From this ancient scripture in Daniel, I extrapolated events occurring in the world from the phrases—"many shall run to and fro" and "knowledge shall be increased."

Humankind "running to and fro" was a metaphor that symbolized jet travel, sputnik, astronauts, and the fairly sudden ability to move about on our planet faster than the speed of a horse with the arrival of trains, automobiles, and airplanes. In 1962, John Glenn circled the globe three times in four hours and fifty-six minutes.

Just 101 years prior, Abraham Lincoln was elected president. News was carried by Pony Express from St. Joseph Missouri to Sacramento, California, a distance of over 1,800 miles. It took ten days to deliver the mail. Today we effortlessly send email messages over the globe.

Knowledge being increased had do to prophetically with the introduction in our world of scientific information never known before in human history that has changed our world so dramatically that it is difficult to keep up with it all. Overnight, it did appear that God had somehow allowed or brought about all the events and circumstances in a rapidly changing world to expand information exponentially. It continues on at a dizzying pace as Elon Musk and Richard Branson race to put us into cozy aircraft to cruise around the globe on a Sunday afternoon flight in craft heretofore reserved for NASA personnel. Stephen Hawking keeps telling us that in order to save humanity we must leave the earth and travel to other planets in order to survive. Putin keeps making speeches about the blending of machines and man that will create a weapon system that whoever does it first will rule the world.

When Dr. Chris Barnard performed the first human heart transplant in 1967, it stunned the world. I remember we had to find answers for this in the Bible, and it was found right in Revelation 18:13 where it says that when Babylon falls at the end of the age, there will be a massive business enterprise being carried on around the world in selling organs and body parts. The NIV reads that one of the commodities being traded by this worldly system would be "bodies and souls," perhaps for the mending of Putin's superhumans after galactic battles. Today there is a shortage of eyes, livers, kidneys, and body parts due to the huge demand in a changing world where operations to replace body parts occur on a daily basis in our hospitals. On my driver's license, I am an organ donor. I don't think that is what John in Revelation was trying to address in his book. I believed at one time that John foretold organ transplants and individuals dealing in body parts.

The church of which I was a part went so far as to take the passage in Matthew 10:23 where it says that "you will not finish going through the cities of Israel before the son of Man comes," as applying to ourselves. This speaks to how churches and groups live when believing God has marked or chosen them for special tasks. You read yourself into the pages of the Bible.

This scripture interpretation was a variation of Albert Schweitzer's basis of establishing his belief that Jesus felt the kingdom would come before the seventy had finished covering the geographical space of a ministry to Israelites located in ancient Palestine. Schweitzer had believed that Jesus felt the end would come before the disciples finished preaching to the nation of Israel.

My church would send out urgent letters prodding members for money by making an appeal to that passage by applying it to the work that had to be gotten done in the preaching and teaching of the church's message because Jesus was soon returning. We believed we were the only voice of God getting out the true message of the end of the age and a soon coming World Tomorrow. The statement in Matthew applied specifically to us: "And this good news of the kingdom will be proclaimed throughout the world, as a testimony to all the nations, and then the end will come" (Matt. 24:14).

When 1975 rolled around and Jesus hadn't returned, church elders found scriptures showing the "delay" of the Lord's return. God was postponing or delaying Jesus return because the Gospel had not been sufficiently spread around the world, which was the mission of the church. It was our fault as a church. We were slack in doing the work of God.

To get yourself to this kind of reasoning in interpretation of scripture, you follow the standard assumptions and mental gyrations that prophecy is "dual." That would be a term meant to say that when we read prophetic statements made to individuals in the Bible to audiences that some of the statements were for the "now," and others were for the "future." Or that some of the statements were "imminent" and others were "nonimminent."

We have academic names for it now like hermeneutics and a bunch of others, but when it is looked at closely, it is just one man's interpretation or exegesis, or explanation or theory of the future promulgated by what he or she reads in the Bible, just as it was in my church. We took all the passages instructing people to flee Jerusalem when armies surrounded the city as applying to the siege of Jerusalem by the Romans with the full belief that what happened then, was only a type of the big and important events to occur at the end of the age—a time that all human life could be destroyed by nuclear warfare. Armies were to again surround Jerusalem with tanks and planes and atomic weaponry. Millions believe that is exactly what is going on in the Middle East now.

The truth of prophesies and statements of prophets is more near what Allison states in *Constructing Jesus* when he writes,

> "'Neither Testament shows us prophets entertaining a compound, temporally disjoined perspective, both imminent and non-imminent.' Rather, in the words of Johnathan Goldstein, 'The authors of Israelite prophecy were seldom if ever interested in the remote future, and the audiences who preserved their words were chiefly interested in the present and in a future, that included little if more than their own lifetimes.' The rule in the ancient sources is this; if it is coming, it must be close."[1]

Individuals look today at the Middle East and see Russia in Syria and the whole political scene once again in disarray. We see Iran threatening to destroy Israel and believe they will ultimately obtain a nuclear bomb and undoubtedly try to destroy Israel. Millions interpret this to be the event spoken in the Gospels, where armies are again surrounding Jerusalem. People believe China will be brought into the caldron that is brewing. It all will lead up to millions of soldiers and weaponry gathering for the battle of Armageddon. Jesus will return to save the world. The stage is being set.

All those "prophecies," however, Jesus intended for his generation, not a time thousands of years into the future. When Jesus walked into the synagogue and was handed the book of Isaiah (Isa. 61:1–4) to read and spoke of his proclaiming the day of vengeance and the day of the Lord to occur, he said to the crowd concerning what he had just read,

> "Today this scripture is fulfilled in your hearing"
> (Luke 4:21).

Jesus was telling members of the congregation they were witnesses of what was occurring in his life and what would be the future of theirs. There could not be a clearer text in the Gospels to show that Jesus expected all the things about which he preached to occur in the lifetime of the audiences to whom he spoke. They took him out and tried to kill him for what he said.

Raymond Brown states regarding Jesus understanding of the future that...

> "The gospel evidence when critically examined would demand no more than that Jesus would have had firm general convictions about the unrolling of God's plan in a way that would lead to death and victory for him and to punishment for Jerusalem. This type of conviction is characteristic of the Old Testament prophets. Neither in their case nor in Jesus' do we have scientific

proof for a detailed foreknowledge of unpredictable future events, a foreknowledge that could be given by God alone."[2]

One of the prophecies of Christ about Jerusalem and what was to happen, Jesus was totally wrong. Jesus said that in the destruction of Jerusalem that "not one stone would be left upon another" (Mark 13:2). Brown says,

"If anyone would propose that this represented an exact foreknowledge of what would happen in A.D. 70, he need simply be reminded that the gigantic blocks of the Temple foundation are still standing firmly one upon the other in Jerusalem."[3]

Ed Sanders says regarding this same verse the following:

"The principle thing to note is that the prediction was not precisely fulfilled. When the Romans took the city in 70 CE, they left much of the Temple wall standing, indeed, most of it is still there, supporting the present Muslim holy area. Most of the stones in the surviving wall weigh between two and four tons, but some, especially those on the corners, are much larger. One is 12 meters (39 feet) long and weighs almost 400 tons. Jesus said that not one would be left on another."[4]

James Tabor, regarding these alleged prophecies of Jesus says:

"There is though, another text, Luke 19:41–44 when Jesus weeps over the city and there he speaks of the entire ancient city being taken down and not one stone on another…of course we have huge remains all around the ancient wall, at the foundations, and Titus left the Tower of David area as a witness to how great the city was, according to Josephus."

I have referred several times to Jesus' statement "except those days would be shortened no flesh would be saved alive." Jesus also said at the same time according to Matthew,

> "Pray that your flight may be not in the winter or on a Sabbath. For then shall there be great tribulation, such as has not been from the beginning of the world until now, no, and never will be" (Matt. 24:20–21).

Jesus repeats in this verse most of the phrase in Daniel ('there shall be a time of trouble, such as never was since there was a nation even to that same time'). There is no doubt that Jesus had in mind in these verses the same time as the tearing down of the temple in Jerusalem and the destruction that was to come upon Jerusalem. Jesus also had in mind the tribulation and trial when that occurred that would come upon the city and its inhabitants.

What is insightful is that Jesus said that this time would be a time that has never been seen since the world began or ever would be observed in its history. Obviously, Jesus didn't reflect in that statement knowledge and awareness of the holocaust, World War I with over a million deaths with ugly trench warfare, nor World War II and its atrocities, napalm bombing of cities, or Nagasaki or Hiroshima. Jesus' statement that it would be the worst time ever in history appears to be a shortsighted human statement with total misunderstanding of the future of the world.

Jesus was not omniscient as God. He was fallible. He was human. Regarding predictions that I once believed that Jesus so divinely accurately made in his life, Tom Wright says this about Jesus' alleged predictions of the future:

> "This did not, actually, take a great deal of 'super-natural' insight, any more than it took much more than ordinary common sense to predict that, if Israel continued to attempt rebellion against Rome, Rome would eventually do to her as a nation what she was going to do to this strange would-be Messiah."[5]

Wright is saying that Jesus didn't have supernatural or God powers to predict or know exactly how the future would turn out. Jesus had a gut feeling, much like someone might have made comment when Hitler rose to power that Europe would go to war eventually. Or, as I recently took a college class on history, the professor digressed at one point in covering the middle east and made the statement, "Mark my words, we are going to get caught up in a war again as a nation in the middle east." Any observant person would have to agree. It would be common sense in surveying the political scene. NBC recently declared in a broadcast that an overwhelming majority of Americans—76 percent—are worried that the United States will become engaged in a major war in the next four years.

Some of the "prophecies" in the Gospels, Bible scholars feel were added after the fact by redactors of the Gospels. An example is the passage that says, "When you see Jerusalem surrounded by armies, then know that its desolation has come near" (Luke 21:20).

Ed Sanders writes concerning this text in his book *The Historical Figure of Jesus,*

> "Scholars generally maintain that it is Luke's own revision of a saying in Matthew and Mark, which he brings 'up to date.' This seems to me to be correct. Luke, that is, wrote after the Roman armies had in fact surrounded and destroyed Jerusalem,

and his knowledge of what happened in the year 70 influenced his revision of Mark."[6]

If we are going to take the position of plenary inspiration of the Bible, Jesus was wrong about no stone being left standing. He was woefully wrong in predicting the worst time in the world's history would be the fall of Jerusalem in 69–70 AD. In a study of the historical Jesus, I found I had to apply the wisdom of Dallas Willard in examination of all my beliefs. I quote it again at this point in the book:

> "You are quite certainly, as I am the student of a few crucial people, living and dead, who have been there in crucial time and periods to form your standard responses in thought, feeling, and action. Thankfully the process is an ongoing one and is to some extent self-correcting."

For two thousand years since Jesus' announcement of a soon coming kingdom, we live in a world that goes on as it always has. Two thousand years ago, the writer of the book of Peter tells us there were scoffers doubting the return of Christ due to a delay at that time.

The author wrote that "scoffers will come" asking, "Where is this coming he promised?" (2 Pet. 3:3–4). That was a favorite scripture quoted from the pulpit to bolster the faith of congregants when Jesus didn't arrive in 1975. They were scoffing.

Anyone who questioned why Jesus hadn't returned in that early generation of Christians of Peter's day was classified as a scoffer. Whoever wrote 2 Peter was deriding those two thousand years ago who were simply asking the same question: "Where is he?"

The reason is simple, as Marcus Borg writes, "Jesus did not return as many had expected."[7]

18

Summary of Quest for Jesus

"So if we are to do something with the historical Jesus, it will have to be someone's historical Jesus—Wright's Jesus or Crossan's Jesus or Sanders' Jesus; it can no longer be the Jesus of the guild or the Jesus of the scholars, because they, in their writings and at their academic conferences, argue with each other over almost everything."
                    —Dale Allison, *The Historical*
                    Christ and the Theological Jesus

"Did Jesus have determinate knowledge of what God intended by the symbolic scheme of things which Jesus himself was commissioned to announce? The answer again, would seem to be no."
                    —Ben Meyer, *The Aims of Jesus*

"Since the synoptic evidence indicates that Jesus was looking for the new age within the lifetime of at least some of his contemporaries, it seems that John Knox is more nearly correct when he

insists that Jesus 'was not thinking of us or of the centuries which separate our time from his.'"
—Richard Hiers, *Jesus and the Future*

From everything we have covered by those who have dominated studies in the third quest, there are six points that stand out about Jesus that are not commonly taught about him.

- Despite didactical fictional comments made in John's Gospel, Jesus never proclaimed himself to be a second God, preexistent, divine figure, come down to earth, who had been the maker and creator of the universe.
- Jesus saw himself as a prophet, in a long line of Jewish prophets.
- His message was the imminent end of the age as he knew it, the arrival of the rule of Yahweh, one whom he addresses in an intimate way as his father.
- Jesus spoke to those we know as Jews of Israel. His message was narrow and limited only to the nation of Israel and pertained to a proclaimed renewal of the covenant Jesus believed had been made between Israel and Yahweh.
- Jesus did not declare himself to be a sacrifice for the sins of all the world for time immemorial.
- Jesus was wholly man, capable of error, and did not achieve in his lifetime what he believed he was to accomplish and bring about. His life ended for him in disappointment because he didn't see come about what he believed God was going to do in and through him.

After a quarter century of studying the life of Jesus of Nazareth who walked this earth during the days of Pontius Pilate, I finally gave up my efforts to be able to retain the Jesus of my youth. I grew as convicted of heart as Edward Schillebeeckx and James D. G. Dunn that Jesus believed the kingdom was to arrive in his day.

Schillebeeckx wrote, "That Jesus prophesied the imminent arrival of God's rule is beyond dispute."[1]

James D.G. Dunn says, "Putting it bluntly, Jesus was proved wrong by the course of events." Dunn's quote, from his book, follows below in its entirety.

I became convicted of Jesus being in error after reading all N. T. Wright's books, E. P. Sanders' books, Raymond Brown's books, John Meier's books, Ben Meyer's books, Dale Allison's books, Schillibeeckx, Schweitzer's books, Dunn's books, Pannenberg's books, Hiers' books, and dozens of other Bible scholars' books. After reading all these books, I was finally able to admit the apostle Paul stated (1 Thess. 4:16) that he learned from Jesus of his imminent return. From that evidence, with all the other accounts of the Gospels, I accepted Jesus Christ to be, as the creed says, wholly human, capable of error, and error-filled in his beliefs of the end of the age. I had always been taught, as most of Christendom has been taught, that Jesus' students got it wrong. In respect to the source of the beliefs of the early church, C. S. Lewis explained it right in chapter 12 when he stated,

> "And, worse still, they had a reason, and one which you will find very embarrassing. Their Master had told them so." It was Jesus who was mistaken, not the disciples nor the apostle Paul.

Allison states regarding Jesus life,

> "Jesus' generation, however, passed away. They all tasted death. And it is not the kingdom of God that has come but the scoffers who ask, where is the promise of his coming? For all things continue as they were from the beginning of creation. Jesus the millenarian prophet, like all millenarian prophets, was wrong: reality has taken no notice of his imagination. Was it not all a myth, an unfounded fantasy—a myth, in the derogatory sense of the word?"[2]

Those words almost sound cruel to characterize Jesus' beliefs. Jesus obtained his beliefs from the books of Zechariah, Hosea, Joel, Amos, Isaiah, and dozens of Old Testament passages describing Yahweh and his kingdom to come. One might choose to call it instead of mythology, didactic fiction or Hebrew folklore, but that hardly fits how Christendom has viewed the Old Testament. God allegedly used holy men of old to give us those prophetic scriptures upon which Jesus relied and who applied them specifically to himself. Jesus read himself into the words of Isaiah and all the prophets. Allison says that Jesus construed Old Testament scriptures as "literally" being fulfilled in his lifetime.

I find it saddening to dwell upon the reality of what Allison has put in words and to absorb what he has stated. One hurts for the human being, Jesus, in realizing his own tremendous disappointment he must have experienced after the passion he had expended in his life in his day for his cause. The crucifixion, for me, takes on even greater tragedy when one accepts that Jesus misunderstood what he thought God was going to do in and through him and his work. He really did feel deserted and forsaken and it is expressed in his final words.

For Jesus, it was not God's time to act. Jesus believed God was going to act decisively in his day and age and that God was going to bring in the kingdom of God imminently. When Jesus intellectually grasped it wasn't going to go the way he thought life was going to go, no one knows, of course. Some point to specific sections in the Gospels where they feel they see Jesus grasping things were falling apart. We can't know the thoughts of Jesus. All we can theorize is, that while hanging on the cross, he cried out to God asking why he had been forsaken in what he set out to do. On that last fateful day of his life, his intent was to make things right between God and Israel. It was his aim to restore the broken relationship between Israel and God. He went to the cross as Wright has proposed, to take upon himself the "messianic woes."

I had read all my life the words—"my god, my god, why have you forsaken me?" One thing I got out of it was that Jesus really wasn't hurting. He was God. He knew it would be just a couple of days until he would be rising glorified just like he had been for eons of time before coming down to the earth to take on human flesh. He had asked God in the Gospel of John to glorify him with the glory he had before the world was created. He would be soon sitting on the throne beside his coequal God partner. Some religious groups believe that Jesus never died. He didn't experience death, for he was God. All this is confusing in the world of Christian groups all because Alexandrian Christology is confusing.

My theological understanding of this passage in the Gospels of Jesus screaming out was that Jesus suffered the impact emotionally of God placing all the sins of humanity upon his shoulders. His father turned his back on him. His cry expressed his shock of being cut off from God in some way, whatever way that could be, if Jesus was God.

The cry of dereliction as it has been called, most likely didn't have anything to do with atonement theology as we know it in our Jesus' stories. Jesus' cry had to do with something else. Those words were meant to express a tradition of our Jesus' character that cried out in frustration and bitter disappointment. Some group thought he died disappointed and saved his words for posterity. It may be the more accurate tradition of Jesus' last words.

Relative to whether Jesus said this on the cross, James D.G. Dunn wrote that of the seven sayings on the cross of Jesus, this one stands to be the more logical choice, considering how Jesus evaluated his life's accomplishments. The criteria of embarrassment takes the high ground on this choice for Jesus final words. C. S. Lewis explained how it works in chapter 12.

James D.G. Dunn is quoted for a source in Wikipedia about the sayings of Jesus on the cross and he...

> "considers the seven sayings weakly rooted in tradition and sees them as a part of the elaborations in the diverse retellings of Jesus' final hours. Dunn, however, argues in favor of the authenticity of the Mark/Matthew saying in that by presenting Jesus as seeing himself 'forsaken' it would have been an embarrassment to the

early Church, and hence would not have been invented" (Wikipedia, Sayings of Jesus).

Ben Meyer quoted Reimarus earlier in this book as a source of interpretation as to what Jesus meant when he cried on the cross, "my god, my god, why have you forsaken me?" Reimarus, who wrote in 1768, has this to say about Jesus plea to God.

> "He ended his life with the words, 'Eli Eli lama sabachthani?' 'My God, my God, why hast thou forsaken me?'—a confession which can hardly be otherwise interpreted than that God had not helped him to carry out his intention and attain his object as he had hoped he would have done. It was then clearly not the object of Jesus to suffer and die but to build up a worldly kingdom, and to deliver the Israelites from bondage. It was in this that God had forsaken him, and it was in this his hopes had been frustrated."[3]

Ben Meyer's own comments in respect to the Gospel account and Meyer's evaluation of the validity of Reimarus comment was stated in his book in *The Aims of Jesus*. He writes,

> "He closed his life with the words 'Eli Eli lama asaphtani: My God! My God! Why have you forsaken me?' A confession—no other interpretation is possible without obvious violence to the sense—that God had not helped him compass his aim and object as he had hoped."[4]

John Meier has spent his lifetime studying the historical Jesus in microscopic detail. He has now finished his fifth volume. The evening before the crucifixion, in Mark 14:22–25, John Meier says that when Jesus sat down with the apostles at the last supper that...

"Instead of saving anyone from death Jesus needs to be saved out of death himself, and only God can do that. The death itself is spoken of indirectly (Jesus will never enjoy another festive meal in this world). Its nearness, while intimated, remains indistinct; no timetable is given. Neither is any cause-and-effect relation created between Jesus death and the coming of the kingdom; indeed, the only relation between the two events is that the kingdom's arrival will somehow bring Jesus out of death. There is no hint of Jesus' death as atoning sacrifice, to say nothing of an explicit affirmation of his resurrection, exaltation, or parousia. In all this there is something disconcerting to Christian expectations. Not only does Jesus not mediate access to the eschatological banquet for others; there is no indication in the saying that he will enjoy any special place in the banquet, even as host. He is simply placed at the banquet table drinking wine; he is one of the saved, no more, no less."[5]

By putting together all the other Gospel accounts we have of Jesus, his original teaching and preaching, his following John, Paul's statement that he learned from Jesus of his imminent return—all the proclamations made—it is not a challenging thought process to reach the conclusion of Reimarus. Jesus ended his life in bitter disappointment. We can see that from our character in the literature of the New Testament without having Reimarus' words available to us or even Mark's words of Jesus on the cross.

That Yahweh was going to step into the world, appear on earth, and establish the kingdom in his day, was a mistaken belief Jesus had of his world. He misinterpreted the Jewish scriptures of a coming kingdom and read himself into their fulfillment and its arrival, as did John the Baptist, as did the apostle Paul, and the early church. History has shown they were all mistaken. They all relied on the scriptures of the Old Testament for their beliefs. Jesus' cry on the cross reflected his frustration that Yahweh had let him down. It wasn't supposed to turn out this way. One can draw their own conclusions.

Jesus looked for and expected God to rule Palestine in his day. Allison says,

> "That Jesus was baptized by an eschatological prophet and had among his followers people who proclaimed a near end, that certain followers of Jesus proclaimed his resurrection soon after the crucifixion, that his passion and vindication were associated with eschatological motifs, that many first-century Jews expected an apocalyptic scenario to unfold in their near future, and that our sources compare Jesus with others who believed in such a scenario or at least expected God soon to rule Palestine—these indisputable facts together tell us that Jesus held hopes close to those attributed to him by Weiss and Schweitzer."[6]

Ed Sanders expressed it clearly when he states in *Jesus and Judaism* that Jesus believed "the kingdom would come soon and that God was at work in his ministry in a special way in his own ministry."[7] He says further in his book that "within that thought world, Jesus saw himself as God's last messenger before the establishment of the kingdom."[8]

Sanders goes on to say about Jesus' views and how he saw the future that,

> "He looked for a new order, created by a mighty act of God. In the new order the twelve tribes would be reassembled, there would be a new temple, force of arms would not be needed, divorce would be neither necessary or permitted, outcasts, even the wicked, would have a place,

and Jesus and his disciples—the poor, meek and lowly—would have the leading role."[9]

John Hick summarizes the conclusions of third quest scholars in a statement of Jesus' life when he writes in *Metaphor of God Incarnate*,

> "'He was fulfilling the unique role of the final prophet, come to proclaim a new age, the divine kingdom that God was shortly to inaugurate....' Jesus, the eschatological prophet was transformed within Christian thought into God the Son come down from heaven to live a human life and save us by his atoning death."[10]

As to the church or that group of disciples or believers that Jesus left behind and what they believed about him, Sanders says the historical facts

> "show that he fits into the general framework of Jewish restoration eschatology, and they identify him as the founder of a group which adhered to the expectations of that theology."[11]

Jesus taught that God was soon to come. The kingdom was imminent. He followed John the Baptist; he was baptized by him; Jesus fully endorsed his message which was the imminent arrival of Yahweh to earth and a judgment day. Jesus believed and taught the apostles that they would all have a part and rule on thrones over Israel.

Ben Meyer has been quoted as a source for both Sanders and Wright for their views of the historical Jesus. Concerning what Jesus expected and viewed to be the future for Jerusalem and its citizens, Meyer's writes,

> "The disciples would be enthroned, the tribes of Israel restored (Matt.19:28 par.), the temple

rebuilt (Mark 14:48 par.; 15:29.; cf. John 2:19); and just as the rejection of Jesus would launch the ordeal, so his vindication would signal its reversal."[12]

Concerning what Jesus believed, Allison writes,

> "Specifically, if Jesus hoped for the ingathering of scattered Israel, if he expected the resurrection of the patriarchs and if he anticipated that the saints would gain angelic natures, then his expectations, like the other eschatological expectations of Judaism, have not yet met fulfillment. To this extent, we may speak of his 'unrealized eschatology.'"[13]

Jesus' message wasn't one of atonement theology as commonly taught and believed, according to Wright and Sanders and dozens of other Bible scholars and theologians. Accepting this shines a whole new light on Jesus of Nazareth. His purpose was restoration theology. His aim was to unite God and Israel once again under the same covenant which had been broken and was in disrepair. Jesus looked for his father to arrive on earth and rule in Jerusalem with Israel being the center and focus of the nations of the Gentile world that would come to the city to extol and praise the lord God of creation. Israel was to merge from exile by the death of Jesus on the cross.

Wright says that Jesus saw his death as occurring for the nation of Israel. It was Jesus intent to take upon himself the suffering of the nation of Israel. He was to endure the messianic woes or tribulation to come upon the nation for sin. Wright says in his book *Simply Jesus*,

> "Jesus seems to have believed that this would occur, uniquely and decidedly, in and through his own suffering and death. He would take upon himself the 'messianic woes' on behalf of Israel...
> This, in other words, was how he would win the

victory that would establish him as Israel's true messiah and transform the kingdom from its current present-and-future state into a fully present reality."[14]

As quoted previously, Alister McGrath says of Wright's beliefs that

"the death of Christ can indeed be thought of as being 'for others', but it is to be understood as having corporate significance for the people of Israel, not individual significance for sinners."[15]

In respect to this comment of Wright that Jesus saw his death in this manner, Alister McGrath wrote,

"If Sanders or Wright is correct, Martin Luther is wrong."[16]

Wright, whom we have quoted throughout this book, said,

"If Jesus was as Reimarus, or Schweitzer, or Sanders, have portrayed him, then the church needs at the very least to revise its faith quite substantially."[17]

It doesn't take a rocket scientist to figure out the so-called third quest—we have a problem. These statements of a need for change present a challenge to the guild and the entire group of the third quest, whoever they may be. That is—which Jesus will emerge from all the fog after it clears, and we move to the fourth or fifth quest?

Each of the three men Wright references shook up the age in which they produced their work on the historical Jesus. It included the first, second, and third quests which Wright feel's, each in his own way, led in their respective time. Each of them firmly believed that Jesus believed the kingdom was to come in his day. Each believed that Jesus saw himself as a prophet of the end of the ages announcing the imminent arrival of Yahweh on earth. Jesus was the source of the disciples' beliefs and those of Paul concerning the second coming, which we have covered in detail. As Paul wrote, he got what he got about the second coming "from the Lord."

In his book *Simply Jesus*, Wright says,

> "I have deliberately set out these passages at some length to show just how strong, just how deep-rooted in scripture, is the idea of YHWH himself coming to rule and reign as Israel's king."[18]

Wright details what he believes is the way Jesus viewed his world in *Jesus and the Restoration of Israel*, when he states,

> "My view was, and remains, that Jesus shared the belief of many of his contemporaries: Israel's god would act decisively within history to fulfill his promises, to liberate Israel and thereby to set the whole world to rights."[19]

Jesus' father didn't enter the world. Israel was not restored. The kingdom was not established. The resurrection did not occur. Political situations went on as normal in the world with Rome victorious over all. Evil wasn't vanquished. The apostles didn't sit on twelve thrones judging a reconstituted Israel. The exile did not come to an end.

Regarding Jesus' beliefs, Richard Hiers writes,

> "It must be admitted without reservation that Jesus was mistaken. The kingdom of God simply did not come, certainly not in the form that he expected and announced that it would. Even if it could be shown, exegetically, that Jesus did think that the Kingdom had come, we would still have to conclude that he was mistaken, for there is no

evidence that it did come, either in or during his ministry, or subsequently."[20]

Theologians who recognize the problems Christianity faces in its interpretation of Jesus have tried to devise numerous theories to remove human error from Jesus beliefs. Wright's interpretation of all of Jesus' prophecies being for events of 70 AD with the destruction of Jerusalem, and has nothing to do with a prophesied second coming, is the latest in a number throughout history. In respect to efforts of theologians to cover for Jesus' error or mistaken beliefs, James D.G. Dunn writes,

> "Jesus' kingdom preaching cannot be disentangled from imminent expectation, with or without 'apocalyptic' features. Which also means that Jesus had entertained hopes which were not fulfilled. There were 'final' elements in his expectation which were not realized. Putting it bluntly, Jesus was proved wrong by the course of events."[21]

Hiers says something like Dunn when he states in his book *Jesus and the Future* that interpreters try to cover for Jesus being shown as being wrong in the Gospels.

> "Since, in the view of traditionalist interpreters, Jesus could not have been mistaken, his sayings about the coming Kingdom must have referred to something that did soon occur, such as his resurrection, Pentecost, or the establishment of the church."[22]

Dale Allison says of Jesus' beliefs and expectations:

> "A Jesus who expected a radical transformation of nature and the last judgment, especially if he spoke as though those things might come soon, is

not very congenial to either orthodox or modern thought; he raises disturbing questions."[23]

In the same book in a critique of Wright's view, Marcus Borg writes,

> "If Jesus did believe that his death would bring about the defeat of the final enemy and the real return from exile, Jesus was wrong. It didn't happen. The real return from exile did not occur. The final enemy was not defeated. The conditions of life for Israel (and the world) remained unchanged."[24]

Whether we choose Wright's view, Weiss', Schweitzer's, Meyer's, Meier's, Sanders', Reimarus', Dunn's, Hiers', or Allison's, Jesus was wrong about the future of Israel and what was to occur. He was terribly wrong. All that Jesus reportedly believed and proclaimed God was going to do in his day didn't happen.

The third quest presents inconvenient truths about Jesus. The churches theology needs to be changed about Jesus relative to what he believed and proclaimed if there is a shred of truth in the Jesus of the third quest. Wright says it needs to be substantially changed if Sanders is correct. It would mean that Jesus' whole life would have to be reinterpreted. It involves incarnation theology, Christology, eternal judgment, and what Jesus really believed about future events in his world. We can rest assured he didn't visualize arriving on the earth in 2050 or anytime thereafter.

Dale Allison says that those who cling to concepts of Chalcedon for their interpretation of Jesus "should be anxious, for the historical Jesus did not think of himself what they think of him."[25] Most individuals in traditional church congregations have all believed that Jesus acted and spoke as God and was God, as I did. Allison writes regarding modern Bible scholarship in the twenty first century "modern criticism has, in the judgment of many of us, exterminated this possibility."[26] Tom Wright tell us we should forget Jesus being omniscient or his having any concepts of being God or speaking as God.

Apparently, as he faltered in the garden, he faltered on the cross, and while spending his last moments of life, it appears Jesus felt he had been utterly forsaken of God and that all had failed in what he had tried to do for the citizens of his country. That's what we see from the character of our literature.

Allison writes of what we have in the Gospel accounts, "His end is physical torment and mental anguish, loss of life and loss of meaning."[27]

Richard Hiers explains why interpreters struggle with accepting Jesus being in error in *Jesus and the Future:*

> "It simply does not occur to traditionalist interpreters who subscribe to the high Christology of the Fourth Gospel that Jesus might have been mistaken about anything, particularly anything so important as the coming of the kingdom of God. How could Jesus, who was one with God—indeed, was God—be in error?"[28]

19

New Horizons of the Apostle Paul

"I am speaking the truth in Christ, I am not lying; my conscience bears me witness in the Holy Spirit, that I have great sorrow and unceasing anguish in my heart, For I could wish that I myself were accursed and cut off from Christ for the sake of my brethren, my kinsmen by race."
—Romans 9:1–3

Thirty or so years after the death of Jesus, Paul began to wonder about the eternal fate of the bulk of the Jewish race and the citizens of the known world at the time. Jerusalem Jews had not responded to the message of Jesus when he was crucified, and as the New Testament shows, a crucified Messiah became a *stumbling* block to them. Even though Paul's work was to the Gentiles, in Romans, we see him worrying about the salvation of the whole world. If things went on as they had to that point in Paul's life and the life of the church, he saw few people being saved. This is not too different from major mainline Christian groups that teach "broad is the way" to destruction and "narrow is the gate" for those who make it into heaven. It wasn't too different from my cultic background that taught only those who were called and became members of the church were part of God's elect and chosen ones. The inclusion of only the few bothered Paul.

Paul became so moved by the agony he experienced from the viewpoint that only an elect few would make it, he made the famous statement that he would exchange his own salvation if God would just choose to elect all of Israel and reject him. It is quoted at the beginning of this chapter.

We have three chapters in the book of Romans that Paul devotes to the subject of salvation of the Jews and salvation of the world and the ultimate plan of God in respect to all. Those chapters are Romans 9–11.

Paul was experiencing the winding down of his work and ministry before Christ returned. Those three chapters are well-known to theologians, and it is from them that Luther and Calvin and Augustine all manufactured the concepts of predetermination of God and predestination of souls. In the introduction, we read of the statements made by Calvin and others about God pertaining to predestination, eternal judgement, and an ever-burning hellfire for the unrighteous. Calvin wrote, "Some are born destined for certain death from the womb, who glorify his name by their own destruction."

We have in these three chapters, Romans 9–11, Paul's ruminations on questions in his own mind as to what God was doing and what God ultimately was going to do. Paul saw the Jews losing out in the plan of God and the special place the Jewish race has with God in his plan.

Ed Sanders believes we have in these three chapters a complete change of Paul's mind relative to the plan and intentions of God and what God was doing and ultimately going to do. We have covered in detail the thoughts and speech of Jesus as much as we can know it during his public ministry to Israel. Jesus warned of judgment to come. He upbraided whole cities and spoke of them going down to destruction. He warned of Gehenna fire to face his adversaries and those who rejected him. Darrel Bock was quoted in the preface in his statement that Jesus saw hellfire and eternal punishment for those who turned their back on him. He told the apostles in going out to address the known world at the time to restrict their preaching to Israel. They were told not to go to the Samaritans nor to any Gentile cities. The instructions to the seventy were the same. We see that all this brought poor response to the message of Jesus.

We have already quoted Hurtado who wrote in respect to what Paul believed.

> "Paul held together fiercely two things that most of Christianity subsequently came to regard as incompatible: (1) He confirmed the continuing ethnic identity of Jews and the continuing special significance of 'Israel' (by which Paul always refers to a group made up of Jews): and (2) he affirmed the necessity for all people to obey the gospel and, through faith in Jesus, to receive God's eschatological salvation."

Sanders writes that as Paul labored over the conundrum of trying to figure out God's plan for mankind that,

> "Romans 9–11 begins with these two questions, the fate of the Jews, and God's fairness, and they lead on to a third; the fate of the universe."

The Bible tells us that God is not willing that any should perish (God willeth that all men should be saved and come to a knowledge of the truth [1 Timothy 2:4]). God is to be fair. And, at the same time, it is abundantly clear in many verses that it shows that God had *blinded* eyes so that they might not see and understand Jesus and his message. How could God be fair in the process of salvation if that is the case?

Sanders says on his effort to cover Paul's thought:

> "In Rom. 9–11 one finds seven major assertions; (1) Despite appearances, God is just; (2) Israel

was elect and remains so; (3) The election was always selective and never covered every descendent of Abraham; (4) Israel, at least at present, has 'stumbled'; (5) God will save only those who have faith in Christ; (6) All Israel will be saved; (7) Everyone and everything will be saved."[2]

Sanders believes that Paul's answers for the conflicting questions he faced was that God changed his plan. God changed by changing the timing of who would be first. The gospel, for Paul, was to go to the Jew first and then to the Greek. God was getting the gospels to the Gentiles to make the Jews jealous, and they thereby would be turned to God.

Salvation, Paul says, has come to the Gentiles first so as to make Israel jealous. It was a way God was going to bring about an eventual response to the gospel of Jews who had been declining the message of Peter and Paul. Paul makes the statement that his work with the Gentiles and their accepting Jesus was "so that I may make my kin jealous, and I will save some of them" (Romans 11:11–14). Paul believes the plan of God relative to the order of who will be first has been reversed.

In Romans 11:11, he asks of his race.

"I say then, have they stumbled that they should fall? God forbid; but rather through their fall salvation is come unto the Gentiles to provoke them to jealousy."

Paul goes on to exhort the Gentile members of the Roman church for them to not be arrogant in the way God was dealing with the Jews. God had hardened the minds of the Jews toward Christ for a purpose. God was using the Gentiles to provoke the Jews to turn to Jesus as their savior. He then states:

"For I would not, brethren, that ye should be ignorant of this mystery, lest ye should be wise in your own conceits; that blindness in part is happened to Israel, until the fullness of the Gentiles be come in. And so all Israel shall be saved; as it is written, There shall come out of Zion the Deliverer, and shall turn away ungodliness from Jacob: For this is my covenant unto them, when I shall take away their sins. As concerning the gospel, they are enemies for your sakes; but as touching the election, they are beloved for the fathers' sakes. For the gifts and the calling of God are without repentance. For as you in times past have not believed God yet have now obtained mercy they also may obtain mercy. For God hath concluded them all in unbelief, that he might have mercy upon them all." (Romans 11:25–32)

Paul's exuberance over the thought of God saving all humanity carries forward in chapter 11 when he has just stated the future of mankind:

"O the depth of the riches both of the wisdom and knowledge of God! How unsearchable are his judgments, and his ways past finding out!"

This expression comes out of Paul's thought that God is eventually going to save all. Sanders points out that this isn't the only place in Paul's writings where universal salvation is reflected in his thinking. He references Romans 5:18 and 1 Corinthians 15:21–22.

"We meet it in Romans 5:18; 'Then as one man's trespass led to condemnation for all people, so one man's act of righteousness leads to acquittal and life for all people.' This sentence echoes I Corinthians 15:21-22. He does not say in Adam all die, but all those in Christ shall be made alive.

The two all's are directly parallel. All will live just as much as all die."[3]

Sanders goes on to say that in 1 Corinthians 15,

"We have a prediction of the return of the Lord and the end of the world, with no judgment and no condemnation. Christ wins and gives all things over to the father."[4]

Paul writes:

"Then the end will come, when he hands over the kingdom to God the Father after he has destroyed all dominion, authority and power. For he must reign until he has put all his enemies under his feet. The last enemy to be destroyed is death. For he has put everything under his feet. Now when it says that 'everything' has been put under him, it is clear that this does not include God himself, who put everything under Christ. When he has done this, then the Son himself will be made subject to him who put everything under him, so that God may be all in all." (1 Corinthians 15:24–28)

Paul ultimately says that everyone and everything will be saved. Sanders says:

"The third image is that of God as creator and omnipotent king. This is a God who gets his way. He created the world and he will save all that he created. We see this image very clearly in I Corinthians 15 and also in Romans 11:36 ('from him all things'). It is this image which takes control in the closing verses of Romans 11."[4]

This is a quantum leap from the Lord God of the Old Testament, the father of Jesus who saw human beings as incorrigible and destroyed them in a worldwide flood! It is a major revision of God's character from when Yahweh told Moses to step out of the way for he was going to destroy Israel and start all over by using Moses' progeny to produce a new Israel. It is light-years away from the stuff of Zephaniah, Haggai, of the pronouncements of Yahweh covered in the preface of this book that he proclaimed would befall the earth upon his arrival. It is a complete contradiction of the Jesus described by John in Revelation of a King of Kings showing up on a white horse with a sword in his hand wearing a garment dipped in blood pouring out death and destruction to earth's citizens and its entire ecosystem.

We have seen from Paul's statement in Romans that he saw the whole creation groaning and waiting, he felt, for this future day soon to arrive in his time and age upon Jesus's return (Romans 8:22). Paul sees the world's ecosystem saved by Jesus upon his return, not burned, scorched, and almost destroyed. He saw the whole natural world to be soon changed upon Jesus's coming, probably because of what he had read in the book of Isaiah and other places in the Old Testament.

> "The wolf shall dwell with the lamb, and the leopard shall lie down with the kid, and the calf and the lion and the fatling together, and a little child shall lead them. The cow and the bear shall feed; their young shall lie down together; and the lion shall eat straw like the ox. The sucking child shall play over the hole of the asp, and the weaned child shall put his hand on the adder's den. They shall not hurt or destroy in all my holy mountain; for the earth shall be full of the knowledge of the Lord as the waters cover the sea." (Isaiah 11)

Sanders's conclusions about Paul's final thoughts on salvation for the world are remarkable. I am sure that this interpretation of

Paul's thought is one of the reasons that Tom Wright said the church will have to change its doctrines "considerably" if Sanders is correct.

This interpretation of Paul's thoughts flies against Luther, Calvin, Aquinas, Augustine, and dozens of evangelical pastors' proclamations of wrath and judgment of God upon his arrival with death and destruction to be the fate of the world and the planet.

They are especially remarkable in that the author of the book of Acts concluded his book by effectively saying that it was Paul's belief, before Paul died (Luke gives us no information whatever about that event in history), that the Jews were finished and God was done with them.

The account is found in Acts 28, where we find that Paul rented a room at his own expense while imprisoned in Rome and preached to Jews in that city who came to him. The last chapter of Acts ends with an incident where Jews in his audience left the house, angered by what Paul told them. Luke writes:

> "So, as they disagreed among themselves, they departed, after Paul had made one statement: 'The Holy Spirit was right in saying to your fathers through Isaiah the prophet: Go to this people, and say, You shall indeed hear but never understand, and you shall indeed see but never perceive; For this people's heart has grown dull, and their ears are heavy of hearing, and their eyes they have closed; lest they should perceive with their eyes, and hear with their ears, and understand with their heart, and turn for me to heal them. Let it be known to you then that the salvation of God has been sent to the Gentiles; they will listen.' And he lived there two whole years at his own expense, and welcomed all who came to him, preaching the kingdom of God and teaching about the Lord Jesus Christ quite openly and unhindered." (Acts 28:25–31)

We don't see Paul's vision of the future that Sanders talks about in any of Luke's account. Luke had no idea that Paul wrote a single book of the New Testament or that he had read any of them, nor did he show any knowledge of them. Luke reflects no knowledge of either the book of Romans or of Corinthians.

That's one illustration of how we should approach every book of the Bible as being exactly what it is—a whole new book by a different author, under different circumstances, and a different story to tell in many cases. Luke had no clue Paul had changed his mind about the Jewish race and the fate of the cosmos. It is pitiful that Luke ended his book the way he did in his characterization of Paul, if Sanders is anywhere near close to interpreting what Paul meant in Romans and Corinthians. Luke's words probably reflect his own thoughts of the fate of the Jewish race.

Raymond Brown writes in his book, *The Churches the Apostles Left Behind*:

> "For the author of Acts (28:25–29), however, the very last words of Paul terminating the book indicates the Jews will never see, nor hear, nor understand; they are permanently closed from the gospel...Both attitudes are at a distance from that of the historical Paul in Romans who argues that the Gentiles were converted to make the Jews jealous, that ultimately the Jews themselves will be converted, and that the Gentiles are but a wild olive branch grafted onto the tree of Israel." (Romans11:11–26)[5]

Could God really have it all in control for Jews and Gentiles, male and female, young and old, throughout the ages? Could it turn out that God is truly a totally different personality than Yahweh of the Old Testament and the literary Jesus of Revelation, and Augustine's and Calvin's and Luther's god whom they believed predestined people before they were born to be punished and tortured forever in the lake of fire? Is there something beyond all the wrath and killing and anger and punishments in the Bible? One well-known Calvinist has gone so far as to say that the Bible is a book of a history of the wrath of God. Is there something optimistic for the world and humanity to look forward to in the arrival of God upon earth, if and when that might occur? I certainly hope so.

Universalism, or the belief that God will save all, has been a part of theology going back to Origen's day. Wright has stated that Sanders's understanding of Paul has *towered* over the field and has created a *Sanders' revolution* in interpreting Paul. Perhaps, Sanders is right. He says nothing more than what John A.T. Robinson concludes in his book *In the End God* and what dozens of other bible scholars and theologians have stated for years in respect to what God ultimately brings about. Wright was quoted earlier in stating that if Sanders is correct in interpreting Paul, Christendom is going to have to *substantially* change its beliefs. One would hope that it would be done without kicking and screaming.

I know some who reading this are probably sputtering now. For they have, in their own minds, thrown up a missile barrage of scriptures in both the Old and New Testament to tell them Sanders is wet and simply doesn't understand the Bible and other scriptures relative to the subject. I know. I did it. I had to cling to what I believed. Like the human mind with its synapses and dendrites where paths are formed habitually in our thought processes, we all have our set of wired scriptures to back our beliefs. That blocks new insights. One is a whole lot better to be open-minded and not so convicted of heart that they understand the future of the world when we study in detail the life of Jesus of Nazareth. We find he didn't understand God's future either.

20

CONCLUSION

"One can, after all, wait quite a time for a train that fails to come. But anyone who in this day and age has waited by the track for a scheduled train, not just for hours, but for days and weeks—what for us is for centuries—when the train simply fails to materialize, can no longer psychologically maintain or substantiate his 'train-expectancy'. Anyone will conclude soon enough that trains have ceased to run on this particular track."
—Edward Schillibeeckx,
Jesus—An Experiment in Christology

If Jesus was wrong about his future, how can we believe we have more understanding of ours than he had of his?

Today my wife and I had lunch near where we live at Marina Jacks, a beautiful waterfront restaurant on the bay in Sarasota, Florida. Individuals were garrulous and having fun enjoying life. They were stocking their boats, picking up mail after long trips on the high sea, and generally basking in the good life.

As my wife and I sat and visited over lunch and enjoyed the beautiful setting, I was thinking of a conclusion to this book. As I looked over the hundreds of faces of everyone while they were dining, I inwardly asked myself the question—just how many people out of all this group could I walk up to and tell them I am writing a book on the second coming of Jesus who would have a dime's worth of interest in hearing what I had to say? I began to laugh inwardly. I got no indication any one of them had a problem in the world. No one I observed gave me the slightest impression they were concerned about the historical Jesus or if he ever is to return.

That's good. No one should ever have to wade through all the books that brought me to this point in my life. Yahweh probably never intended that a human soul would take the journey I have taken in trying to understand his son. He is most likely confounded that it has been made so difficult with all the creeds and doctrines and thousands and thousands of books written about him and myriads of concepts formed and created about the resurrection, judgment, heaven, hell, eternal punishment, grace, and a dozen or more other doctrines spawning big thick books on each.

He made it so easy. After all, didn't he, starting with Genesis 3:15, prophesy through Old Testament scriptures, in over one hundred passages, details of the future arrival of the Messiah, his son? I believed that as well for years, until I began to read and understand that most of those prophecies of Jesus were stretched to the breaking point by New Testament writers retroactively creating messiah stories of Jesus.

Regarding Old Testament prophecies of Jesus, Raymond Brown writes in his seminal book *The Birth of the Messiah* the following:

> "However, this conception of prophecy as prediction of the distant future has disappeared from most serious scholarship today, and it is widely recognized that the NT 'fulfillment' of the OT involved much that the OT writers did not foresee at all. The OT prophets were primarily concerned with addressing God's challenge to

their own times. If they spoke about the future, it was in broad terms of what would happen if the challenge was accepted or rejected. While they sometimes preached a 'messianic' deliverance [i.e., deliverance through one anointed as God representative, thus a reigning king or even a priest], there is no evidence they foresaw with precision even a single detail in the life of Jesus of Nazareth."[1]

Walter Brueggemann goes further to state that the Old Testament does not lead comfortably into or point to Jesus in its pages because

"it is so clear that the Old Testament does not obviously, cleanly, or directly point to Jesus or to the New Testament."[2]

Brown goes on to give an example of trying to use Old Testament scripture to foretell the arrival of Jesus' life in advance:

"A prime example of this was Isa 7:14 where the reading 'virgin' seems to imply that, 700 years before Jesus, the prophet had predicted a virginal conception, something unparalleled in history that would have had to involve foreknowledge of Jesus conception. The OT prophecy and the NT event gave each other support. The NT fulfillment verified the conception of prophecy as prediction and proved that God had planned the whole history of salvation; the OT prophecy helped to establish the facticity of the NT event."[3]

The virgin birth story was, according to bible scholars, a late story, not an early one, and created to make Jesus fit into a theological mold. John is concerned in his Gospel only with preexistence and tells us Jesus had been around from the beginning of time. His Gospel was written later than any other Gospel. John doesn't even mention the virgin birth stories to prove that Jesus was preexistent. It would have been a perfect fit to add the detail of Jesus having no earthly father to the logos story he created and all those verses where he mentions "coming down" from above and living in another world. We have viewed the contradictions of Jesus' birth even in John's Gospel, where John's Gospel simply states that Jesus' father was Joseph (John 1:45).

In Luke's account, Mary speaks openly that Joseph is the father of Jesus. Mary makes the statement in Luke 2:48, when Jesus became separated from her and Joseph and lost for a couple of days in Jerusalem that "your father and I have been looking for you anxiously." To augment this account, we have the other information recorded both by Matthew and Mark that the community in which Jesus lived all knew him as being the son of Joseph. They knew of no miracles, virgin birth stories, or that Jesus was divinely created through conception by the Holy Spirit. Matthew states,

> "Is not this the son of the carpenter? Is not his mother called Mary and his brothers James, Joseph, Simon, and Judas?" (Matt. 13:35).

James D.G. Dunn writes of Matthew's account:

> "There is no real indication that Matthew had attained a concept of incarnation, had come to think of Christ as a pre-existent and who became incarnate in Mary's womb or in Christ's ministry [as incarnate Wisdom]."[4]

Even though Dunn states that Matthew didn't believe Jesus had been incarnated, Matthew, as does Luke, goes out of the way in their genealogies of Jesus to point out that Joseph was his father. There was a specific reason. It is stated clearly by Shirley Jackson in his book *Jesus—A New Biography*.

> "Each evangelist found a genealogy among the traditions at his disposal. But the same original incentive had prompted the construction of these two-family trees. By this means Christian missionaries had hoped to convince Jews Jesus by blood descent was entitled to rank as the Jewish Messiah. It goes without saying that originally this line of argument rested on the assumption that Joseph was the actual father of Jesus."[5]

For Jesus to be fully human, he had to have a human father. Instead, like Greek mythology, he would be a Perseus or demigod had he been fathered by the Holy Spirit or Yahweh of the Old Testament. James D.G. Dunn writes in his book *Jesus Remembered*:

> "For Jesus to be fully human he had, for both biological and theological reasons, to have a human father as well as a human mother and the weight of historical evidence strongly indicates that this was so—and that it was probably Joseph. Any theology for a scientific age which is concerned with the significance of Jesus of Nazareth now has to start at this point."[6]

Because of this clear distinction made in the New Testament Gospels, Wolfhart Pannenberg went on to say

> "In its content, the legend of Jesus' virgin birth stands in an irreconcilable contradiction to the Christology of the incarnation of the preexistent Son of God found in Paul and John. For according to this legend, Jesus first 'became' God's son through Mary's conception. According to Paul

and John, on the contrary, the Son of God was already preexistent and then as a preexistent being had bound himself to the man Jesus."[7]

Paul never mentions the virgin birth and most likely had never heard the story when his books were written. If he did, what is even more important about it is that he gives no credence to it. Perhaps it is because it is contradictory to his outlook that Jesus was preexistent as Pannenberg points out above.

In that inspired sermon of Peter on Pentecost, one of the twelve, Peter knew Jesus only as a man, not as God.

> "Men of Israel, hear these words; Jesus of Nazareth, a man attested to you by God with mighty works and wonders and signs which God did through him in your midst as you yourselves know" (Acts 2:22).

Despite considerable evidence from our sources, that the virgin birth stories have been didactic fictional accounts to proclaim the special identity of Jesus, little gets said about it by churches. Dennis Nineham writes in *The Quest for the Historical Jesus*:

> "Partly as a result, no doubt, official church decisions and pronouncements blandly ignore the findings of biblical scholars, without so much as a pretense of examining or refuting them. For example, many scholars of all persuasions now regard the virgin birth tradition as "unhistorical." Their views have been ignored by all the churches, for example in proposals put forward for liturgical reform; but there is no evidence whatever that this has been the result of a full consideration of the arguments and the identification of flaws in them."[8]

All this logical survey of Jesus' birth stories became the basis for Schweitzer's statement, which has been quoted already but fits so well at this place. He wrote,

> "John represents a more advanced state of the formation of myth, as much as he has substituted the Greek metaphysical conception of divine sonship for the Jewish messianic conception and, on the basis of his acquaintance with the Alexandrian Logos doctrine, even makes Jesus apply to himself the Greek speculative notion of pre-existence."

Schweitzer also points out the same thing Dennis Nineham does above, concerning how churches and theologians avoid disturbing our beliefs and stories of Jesus. He writes,

> "This retarding knowledge is the prerogative of theology, in which, down to the present day, a truly marvelous scholarship often serves only to blind the eyes to elementary truths, and to cause the artificial to be preferred to the natural."[9]

We must keep on believing about Jesus what we believe about him. He is a protected species.

Jesus' home and birthplace was Nazareth as Peter states, not Bethlehem, which was a later story to proclaim Jesus being from the same city where David resided and lived. We covered Ed Sanders' comments about the birthplace of Jesus and whether there ever was a trip into Egypt by Joseph and Mary. A story was created out of thin air to fulfill the Old Testament prophecy that God's son was called out of Egypt. It is called didactic fiction. That trip into Egypt by the family was to be a type of the Israelites leaving Egypt in the Exodus. That most likely didn't happen. Bible scholars admit that all the Christmas stories we know were probably fictive teaching materials and woven to create a narrative in Jesus life. The pope has admitted the same as an official position of the Catholic Church.

Jesus is reported by Luke to have grown up having to learn from those around him as any child would. We see him in the temple asking questions (Luke 3:3). Jesus grew up believing whatever beliefs were normal to the world around him and would have had no idea that the earth moved around the sun which Copernicus discovered 1500 years after Jesus existence on earth. Raymond Brown writes in *Introduction to NT Christology*,

> "But in the general gospel picture there is no indication that in the questions of demons and the medical causes of sickness, he saw the inadequacies of the popular views of his time."[10]

Jesus adopted the religious beliefs of his community and the nation. Dale Allison points out that the Gospel accounts don't show Jesus to have divergent beliefs from that of the Jewish world in general in which he lived. Tom Wright says that Jesus "went along" with the beliefs of the day concerning everlasting punishing for the wicked. Sanders says that the Jewish race adopted the beliefs of the Zoroastrians regarding eternal punishment late in Israel's history. It is evident that everlasting punishing wasn't part of Yahweh's beliefs in what he taught Moses or the Israelites in the Old Testament. Sanders writes in his book *Paul and Palestinian Judaism* that

> "it was the biblical view, and one that remained influential in Judaism, that God's justice is meted out within this life."[11]

Jesus adopted beliefs of his day concerning life after death for both the righteous and the wicked. In the Old Testament under Moses, when you are dead, you are dead. That belief is common to this day among Jewish individuals, as it was for Albert Einstein, who clung to beliefs, before he died, of his Jewish teaching in childhood, that life would be over for him upon his death. We find in Acts 23:7-

8, that Jewish Sadducees of Jesus' day, didn't believe in a resurrection or life after death.

Jesus is shown that he didn't know who touched him when the woman in the crowd reached up and touched his garment as he walked by. Jesus grew tired and became exhausted. He could not carry his cross due to human frailty. He would have dealt with the problems we all face with cleanliness and caring for our bodies. On one occasion, we see a woman in the Gospels cleaning his dirty feet, drying them with her own hair. He hungered and thirsted and got mad and angry, at a tree on one occasion. He wept. It is the shortest verse in the Bible. He adopted the beliefs of the day that the kingdom was near, recycling the message of John the Baptist in his own way in his own ministry.

Throughout this book, we have seen the Bible was put together by very human beings. Jesus himself is shown to be very human in the most original traditions, and in error in respect to his belief and teaching of the arrival of the kingdom of God. Bart Erhman writes in *Misquoting Jesus*,

> "The Bible, at the end of the day, is a very human book."[12]

We have journeyed a long way from the sectarian beliefs of the cultish church of which I was a part. We have come a very long way since the production of a letter warning all my family of possible punishment forever in the lake of fire for keeping the Sabbath day. We also have moved a long way from many of the main stream beliefs held about Jesus. In a great book, *Sanity, Insanity and Common Sense*, the authors write,

> "Most of us, as individuals and professionals, have unknowingly lived our lives wrapped up in the contents of our own thoughts, operating within the details of our own beliefs, theories, opinions, fears, and judgments. We have lived in this world of thought without realizing that we are the ones who have accepted and continue to

give life to these thoughts in the first place. The moment that we realize that we are living in a world of thought that is our own creation, we are on the road to easier, more satisfying lives."[13]

I came to believe that I can't go on with thinking what I have thought and felt about God and Jesus. This change came about, as you can see from this book, over years of time and study. My state of mind through the process of change was, many times, very much like that of Dale Allison, who again puts words into plain English relative to the issues of discovering a different Jesus than that which we have all inherited. Allison says,

> "They may, for instance, fret upon learning that many modern scholars do not believe that Matthew wrote Matthew or that Jesus spoke the discourses in John. They may also, depending on their background, find themselves vexed upon becoming persuaded that the old props—miracles, eyewitness origins, the proof from prophecy—have seemingly fallen to the ground and need being themselves propped up or maybe abandoned as everlasting ruins. Such individuals have awakened from their dogmatic slumber and cannot go back to sleep. I find myself among them. I do not long for that old-time religion, nor do I wish to believe in my own belief but, as quaint as this may sound to some, I want to know the truth, even if I cannot cheer it."[14]

Reaching the conclusion I reached didn't bring cheering. It did bring peace of mind and eradication of my thoughts, that in accepting Jesus as fully human, and mistaken in his beliefs of the arrival of the kingdom of God, that I was turning away from God, and denying the divinity of Jesus and his Godhead. Jesus really was fully human, capable of error, and error filled in what he believed God was going to do in his lifetime and those of the disciples.

My indoctrinated beliefs of Jesus and his capabilities and God-characteristics, had been handed down to me from mainstream Christianity going all the way back to the church council in Chalcedon in 451 A.D., and later in life from the cult of which I was a part. Christendom has been taught that Jesus was God, preexisted as God, and was of the same substance as God, having all the powers of God, and was co-equal with God. He could not have been mistaken. For, we are all told, he was God and

> "that our Lord Jesus Christ is to us One and the same Son, the Self-same Perfect in Godhead, the Self-same Perfect in Manhood; truly God and truly Man" (Wikipedia—Chalcedon Definitions).

In my search to understand the first, second, and third quest for Jesus, I came to understand the second part of the creedal statements concerning Jesus. He was 'truly man.'

If one is a true believer, one thinks they know and understand. True believers are the mental product of churches with dogmatic theologies. They manufacture true believers. For any true believer, it becomes mentally distressing to admit error and it makes the psyche uncomfortable. Allison wrote that he pushed forward with his theology to free himself from dogmatic slumber even though he found nothing to cheer about in changing his beliefs. When it comes to truth, we can't run from it, hide, or avoid it.

The Jesus of the third quest I didn't want to meet, nor did I want to discover. Finding Jesus of the third quest wasn't exhilarating. It brought less understanding of Jesus rather than more understanding of his life, mission, and purpose. I thought I knew the Jesus of the Bible in what I previously believed about him, what his mission was, and his purpose in preaching to the nation of Israel. It was that he came here to die for the sins of all humanity for time immemorial.

Richard Hiers writes in *Jesus and the Future*,

> "Fidelity to truth, including the truth of the historical Jesus, requires that the first question be considered as much as possible without regard to desirable or undesirable results."[15]

Socrates is reported to have exhorted his students—'follow the argument wherever it led them.' Throughout this book I have tried to do that. In this book I have also been guilty of writing to confront doubts that often smite us when we open the Bible and try to make sense of the characters within it. I wrote, in the whole project, from a position like that of Philip Yancey. He wrote in his book, *The Jesus I Never Knew,*

> "I tend to write as a means of confronting my own doubts. My book titles—*Where is God When it Hurts?, Disappointment with God*—betray me. I return again and again to the same questions as if fingering a festering wound that never heals. Does God care about the misery down here? Do we really matter to God?"

We must learn to live comfortably mentally with the realization that it is impossible for us to know and understand an infinite God that lives beyond and outside any writings any human being could create to tell us about him. God certainly can't be contained and boxed in the 783,137 words of the King James Bible. We would have no clue as to what he is going to do, especially after we learn that Jesus didn't know either, nor did others know who wrote our Bible, starting with the so-called Old Testament prophets up through the final failed prophecies of whoever created the book of Revelation.

I stood so many times with Bible in hand beside a grave, reading passages from it and telling others about the resurrection and the future and things to occur in the future. I quoted the same scriptures Jesus used, Paul used, and all the early church used, telling themselves of events that were supposed to occur back there in their day, not ours. They were wrong about what they believed God was going to do. For years I had misquoted Paul in all those speeches I had given. Jesus and Paul believed all that I said was in the future was to occur in their day, not a future time in my world.

If we honestly face the issues involved in the reasoning process, we have only one choice—we leave ourselves open to the future, for we don't know it, and there isn't anything in the world we can do to create it or change it or bring it about. We can't even claim it, for if we quote the same scriptures they used to support their beliefs, as Dunn writes, "Putting it bluntly, Jesus was proved wrong by the course of events." Rather than feeling I must know or that I know what is right or I that I know the truth and true plan of God, I have learned to live peacefully and quietly with simply acknowledging that I don't know what it is.

When one changes one set of beliefs in the Christian story, it puts pressure in other areas for it raises questions about other beliefs tied to it. A couple right off would be the incarnation, definitions of Jesus and God given to us from Chalcedon, inerrancy of scripture, and just who and what was Jesus. There can be no more succinct statement of the broad issues involved when Dale Allison quotes Howard Marshall in *Constructing Jesus*. He says,

> "It has always been a vital question in Christology to discover how far the impact made by the earthly life of Jesus and his own understanding of his person can sustain the weight of the Christological construction put upon them by the early church."[16]

That is exactly what Carey Newman, in *Jesus and the Restoration of Israel* says, regarding the Jesus that Wright and other third questers present to us. Newman believes a Jesus who is shown to be very human, a prophet to Israel, one who is limited in his capacities and capabilities, one *truly man and capable of error*, and who was mistaken in his life, clashes with our Chalcedonian definitions of Jesus and is unacceptable as the historical Jesus. His shoulders are not broad enough. He writes,

> "It is not at all clear how Jesus, the prophet to Israel, and Jesus, the Messiah of Israel, became Jesus, the Lord of the Church. The shoulders of Wright's Jesus do not appear sturdy enough to bear the Christological weight the church willingly placed upon them."

As Schillebeeckx wrote in chapter 13, Christendom has chosen instead a *"divine Ikon"* to worship rather than a provocative prophet limited in his understanding, totally human, capable of error, and mistaken about what God was going to do in his life. He becomes a *nuisance*, as Schillibeeckx wrote, for he isn't the superman needed to wear the boots that Chalcedon created for him.

When we take this approach (using Chalcedonian definitions of Jesus to find him in the gospels), the synoptic gospels show us, as Peter Berger stated in chapter 9, he will never be found in any quest, for

> "there is near-complete consensus among New Testament scholars (including most of those who would adhere to protestant or catholic orthodoxy) about one point:

> 'Neither Jesus himself, nor his immediate followers, nor the synoptic gospels thought of him in terms of the Church's later teaching—that is, as the being affirmed in the great historic creeds.'"

It seems logical the synoptic gospel accounts of Jesus should be used to reinterpret Chalcedon, rather than looking for the superman who never lived among us. It appears also that Bible scholars and theologians on both continents know that too, but no one can start the wave in *Christendom Stadium* to bring it about.

Throughout the process of my journey to keep on stretching and reaching and seeking beyond my narrow cultic beliefs, I found inward courage from Daniel Taylor's book *The Myth of Certainty*. When doubting myself and where my journey would end up, several things he wrote kept me moving forward instead of frozen in thought or just calling it a day and saying there is no way to reach any conclusion. In his book, he writes,

> "The reflective Christian does well in my view, to freely admit this possibility of being wrong. All I believe may in fact may be false. God may only be wish fulfillment. The sense of his presence I sometimes get in worship and prayer may simply drive from chemicals in my brain. Those occasions where he seems to have guided my life may only be coincidence or reflect my human desire to find a pattern of events…And as I reach a point of potential paralysis, as I have before and I will again, I remind myself of the facts as I know them and the commitments I have made. I am willing to begin once more at the beginning to rethink and rebelieve from square one, even knowing that this time I may end up not believing at all. God is not afraid or offended by this—he who heard a wail of desperate questioning even from his own son."[17]

Once beliefs are set, it is difficult to change them. I still find it difficult for me to erase the mental pictures I gained from a child from the last book of the Bible, assisted by artist Basil Wolverton, who created some of the most grotesque and terrifying religious apocalyptic art, depicting scenes of the great tribulation, since the 1450 Dutch painter, Hieronymus Bosch. Wolverton parlayed his artistic talents after winning a 1946 nationwide contest in drawing the world's ugliest woman, *Lena the Hyena*, into creating imaginary scenes from the great tribulation. My church literature pamphlets and booklets were filled with his frightening futuristic drawings of the end of the age. When one reads

Dante's *Inferno* and views some of the illustrations in Dante's book and Wolverton's classics, it remains mentally imbedded forever, like the movie scene from *Jaws*, as Captain Quint is gobbled by the great white shark, or when Gregory Peck as Captain Ahab gets pulled under by the leviathan whale in the movie portrayal of *Moby Dick*.

I discovered also and came to realize my beliefs of the future were a form of superstition of God and Jesus based upon mythology from both the old and new testaments. The personal distress I experienced and occasional worries or concerns that I was denying God and Jesus' divinity and God-head, were unfounded. The anxiety I experienced diminished. I realized, as stated above from *Sanity, Insanity, and Common Sense*, that I was the one who gave life to my thought world and my concepts of God and beliefs I had about Jesus. They were self-created. All my visual images of the apocalyptic end of the world out of Revelation were of my own creation. I had gained them through projections of others that I accepted as a youth from countless sermons and from reading descriptions of God's behavior in the pages of the Old Testament, where it seems, one can hear the ominous music from *The Godfather*, playing in the background. Those wild story tellers of the Hebrew Bible show us, as Brueggemann writes,

> "an ominous dimension" of the father of Jesus "that falls outside any rule of law, outside vengeance as legitimate sanction."

Concerning those wild stories and threats made throughout the Old Testament by Yahweh, Brueggemann states that Christianity hasn't dealt with the protagonist of the Old Testament who doesn't quite fit (an understatement) into our concepts of the way Christians are supposed to operate in this world. Brueggemann went on to point out that the problem in explaining the actions of Yahweh, that the dilemma for Christians,

> "is the very God uttered in these texts and who lies behind the problems of perspective and method" in attempts to explain and interpret him.

In the choices I faced, there was no being to reject in changing my beliefs. My God and my Jesus and their alleged plans existed only in my head, given to me by those who had no better understanding of God and his plans and future than the next prophet who wrote after the last. The historical Jesus, and what he believed about the future of his world was very different from what I had believed. I was a product of Jewish apocalyptic revised and rerun in my day.

Millions of Americans find themselves today waiting for Jesus with the same mental images imbedded of how the future is supposed to turn out. They have gained those through their churches, movies, books, Bible studies, and sermons. The *Left Behind* series of books has been the basis of the views of millions. Right now, over two hundred million Americans look for the second coming, most of them as John describes it in Revelation. That's where we get our stories of the apocalyptic end of the world. We live in a world that is daily marinated with the apocalyptic. Mythology has risen again in our society as Rudolph Bultmann foretold years ago. It is predicated on the same old mythology upon which Jesus relied and believed that he thought was to occur in his day.

I slowly can work on discarding my end of the world beliefs as described in the book of Revelation. I would hope all those individuals in the past that I instilled the same mental pictures of the future will find intellectual escape as well, some of them, perhaps through this book.

The third quest will accomplish nothing and just be an exercise in intellectual theories of Jesus life, unless theologians make changes in what is taught about Jesus, as Wright states. I see little hope for any changes soon, as Allison states the difficulties of changes in chapter 18, when he says that in meetings and seminars and discussions, no one of the third quest can agree upon the same Jesus. Robert Funk spells out the results of this log jam that Allison references, when Funk writes,

> "This movement will be subject to repeated reformations born of repeated quests for the historical Jesus."[18]

That most likely will be the case. Maybe when 126,000,000 Americans wake up in 2050, and find the earth isn't a smoking mess at the hand of Jesus, society will force theologians to make some revisions about what is taught about what Jesus really believed. It will come from without, not within, no doubt.

If we take all the Bible story of what we have learned about what Jesus believed about himself, we can reasonably say that Jesus' return will never occur in the way it is portrayed in stories of the rapture and the *Left Behind* series and as it is described in the introduction of this book. We can go to bed tonight without worry or fear that the horrors of Revelation will one day be our future as a citizen of this planet. There will not be tomorrow pilotless commercial aircraft plummeting from the sky or driverless semi-tractor trucks careening down our interstates. We don't have to concern ourselves whether Barack Obama or the pope is the antichrist. We don't have to stay up late at night looking to identify the beast along with ten kings and the nations they are to rule. No search has to be conducted for the perfect red heifer to be used to cleanse a future Jewish temple, wherein animal sacrifices will again be offered before the return of Christ. We can stop looking for the next blood moon. This is mythology, rerun in our day, proven to be wrong from the day it was written by history of the world thereafter.

Those statements are made based on the reality that we have living witness and testimony from the Bible those individuals who wrote it, got it wrong. To put it bluntly, as Dunn stated, the history of the world even proved Jesus wrong about what he believed. If Jesus was wrong about his future, how can we believe we have more understanding of ours than he had of his?

We also see clearly once we understand the message of the historical Jesus, that Jesus, in his preaching and teaching of the future, didn't believe nor proclaim all those scenes from Revelation in his lifetime. He expected Yahweh to come to rule in his day. Those scary tales of Revelation are more mythological than the stories of the Old Testament prophets upon which Jesus relied.

At the end of World War II, Pacific islanders for years discovered occasionally Japanese holdouts still living on islands not realizing the war was over. John, the alleged author of the book of Revelation, is shown by history to be that last surviving new testament holdout on the isle of Patmos, still clinging to the belief the end of the age and the belief that Jesus second coming was to occur in his lifetime and telling his readers it was imminently to arrive. All those things John described of bowls of wrath, trumpet plagues, and vials of wrath, with Jesus coming back on a white horse, John believed were to occur in his day and age.

Ben Meyer has stated clearly the challenge to sit and wait in a countdown to the end of the world as described in Revelation.

> "We should not imagine that any prophet ever had before his inner eye the kind of scenario that history, on cue, and according to schedule, might literally follow."[19]

No prophet ever did. Revelation is filled with the same mythological concepts upon which Jesus based his thought world upon for what he believed God was going to do in and through him. As Allison writes, Jesus believed in "a myth, in the derogatory sense of the word."

Malcolm Muggeridge wrote in 1975 that today's calamitous newspaper stories adumbrating signs of Jesus' return for many become paper for the wrapping of fish by some event of greater Olympian significance which immediately follows. How true that is for the world in which we live. There will be, by the time this book will ever be printed, dozens and dozens of news events which prophecy watchers will consider to be bone-jarring indications of Jesus second coming approaching and the great tribulation about to come upon the world. We will see them day after day after day into the future.

Yahweh stories of Israel are the sources of Christian apocalypticism birthed from the Old Testament and form the basis for the wild apocalyptic stories of John in Revelation which tell us that Jesus is coming back to almost destroy the planet. The two protagonists of the Bible are merged together like twins, in character and demeanor, in that final book of the Bible where we have described the wrath of God to come upon the world. I can understand why someone wrote that the Bible is a story of the wrath of God. It begins with accounts of God's anger and frustration and destructive outbursts and ends with the same in the book of Revelation. By the time we get to the last book of the Bible, Yahweh is shown to have made no progress in working with his human subjects.

The quixotic and irascible character Yahweh can't be archived by Christendom, for he is used to form all the story card for the arrival of his son upon earth, through Old Testament prophecies that allegedly show Jesus came to give his life as a sacrifice for sin for all humanity. He is bound to be preserved as the father of our Lord Jesus Christ, for it is believed that the resurrection confirms the truth that God foretold Jesus throughout the pages of the Old Testament and that it leads automatically to the arrival of the Son of God.

Ben Meyer explains Christian reasoning when he writes in *Critical Realism and the New Testament*:

> "By the resurrection of Christ Christianity was bound to the scriptures of Israel, for the resurrection vindicated Jesus election-historical mission, which supposed and climaxed the election history of Biblical Israel."[20]

In our Christian waiting for God, we must ask which God or God's are going to show up? Will it be the cranky Yahweh, short tempered, capriciously irascible, emotionally challenged in working with his human subjects, and who has spoken in numerous minor prophet passages of his proclamations, that when he arrives, he intends to use a scorched earth policy in dealing with humanity? Will we have a continuation of what we see in the Old Testament of an emotionally bipolar Yahweh?

Which Jesus will show up with him? Will it be the one who said, "Father forgive them for they know not what they do?" Or will it be the literary character who cursed fig trees, one who promises from his hand upon arrival, in Revelation, plague after plague upon humanity and the earths eco-system, which we have detailed, or will the returning Jesus be a kindlier-gentler Jesus than the one who spoke of eternal punishing for those individuals that turned their back upon him—the beatings will continue until the morale improves?

Or is there a loving and merciful and all-powerful God outside the pages of the Hebrew Tanak and our New Testament scriptures, who will in the end save all, as Sanders' describes of what he feels are Paul's final beliefs of the plan of God, detailed in chapter 19? I remain open to all of that. I see it as a beautiful picture of what God, one day, is going to do.

In my journey, when I found one thing I didn't believe, this prompted me to examine other kindred beliefs I held which were directly tied to that outlook or belief. This has been an on-going process of 36 years. When I meet friends, who knew me years ago, they often ask what is it that I believe now about God and his plan. I tell them it is still under reconstruction. I could repeat what sociologist Peter Berger has said about himself for I feel that it is applicable to my own state of mind. He said:

> "I also consider myself a Christian, though I have not yet found the heresy into which my theological views would comfortably fit."[21]

A few years after reading Berger's comment, I discovered that Thomas Jefferson had made a very similar statement and most likely Berger had borrowed it. I have reached the point that I believe we all make a mistake to lock ourselves into dogmatism about the surety of our religious beliefs. We are all frail human beings living in a cosmos of planets with lots of surprises ahead for what exists in our universe and we could have no idea what is going to occur in it after our demise.

If one wants to cling to what they have, to what they understand about Jesus and Yahweh, Walter Brueggemann points out the conundrum of doing that. He writes,

> "Even if one intended to trust the established teaching of the church as the truth, the problem was that there was now more than one established teaching of more than one church. Obviously,

these teachings differed, disagreed, and contradicted each other in important ways."[22]

Paul, before disappearing off the scene in the literature of the New Testament, is shown in Acts speaking to King Agrippa regarding the kingdom of God. He says to him,

> "And now I stand here on trial for hope in the promise made by God to our fathers, to which our twelve tribes hope to attain, as they earnestly worship night and day. And for this hope I am accused by Jews, O king!" (Acts 26:6).

Paul, the putative founder of the Christian religion, says he was waiting for the fulfillment of the promises of Yahweh in the Old Testament—the coming of the kingdom of God spoken of throughout the pages of the Old Testament. He lived in the hope of its arrival in his day and time. The entire New Testament church was waiting for the same thing. Sanders says of Paul's beliefs about Jesus and the future of the world:

> "To an appreciable degree, what Paul concretely thought cannot be directly appropriated by Christians today. The form of the present world did not pass away, the end did not come and believers were not caught up to meet the Lord in the heavens."[23]

Not only what Paul thought can't be appropriated but also what Paul taught about the future can't be appropriated. It did not come to pass.

The hope of which Luke wrote was predicated upon the dreams of Paul's Jewish forefathers expressed in the mythological concepts of that kingdom scattered throughout the literature of the Old Testament. It was the same hope of Jesus Christ of the arrival of Yahweh's kingdom. They go back, if we take them to Abraham, nearly four thousand years. Those hopes included the end of Gentile rule over the kingdoms of the world, racial particularism, the hope for arrival of Yahweh to Jerusalem, the hope for resurrection of the dead, the hope for the earth ceasing to groan and travail, a hope in a change in the natural state of the world's ecosystem, and the hope of the arrival of Jesus a second time by Paul.

If Sanders' is correct, for Paul it included a discarding of the covenants and pluralistic thoughts of inclusion of others beyond Israel and God becoming "all in all," with God ultimately saving both Jew and Gentile, male and female, young and old, and all citizens of the universe from the beginning of time. If so, our two protagonists of the Christian Bible will turn out to be two totally different characters from those detailed in the pages of the Bible. Yahweh will fade off the scene forever. The same would be true of the angry Lamb of God who almost destroys the planet before he sets foot on the Mount of Olives and afterward stokes the furnaces of hell with millions of new bodies which he casts into it upon his return. The stories of a wrathful God will be tales of old. Racial particularism and the scandal of particularity or election selection departs the universe. God loves alike. Like the scene in *The Wizard of Oz*, the curtain will be pulled back and there will be someone beyond or behind the text, not within it.

Paul's views of universal salvation would involve a major change in heart and character of the two protagonists of our Bible. Whether Paul made this quantum leap in thought and beliefs of God and his plan will never be known in this lifetime. We are looking to one day waking up after having been transferred into a whole new dimension in time and space to ever know the future and whether Sanders' has correctly interpreted Paul. All I can say is, would to God, Sanders' interpretation of Paul is correct! We must admit, as history has shown, and Sanders states above, Paul didn't show himself in his writings to the Thessalonians to have any more understanding of the future than Jesus had in his day.

If Paul were somehow resurrected and revived and placed in our world today, he most likely would need psychiatric help to adjust to reality.

Obviously he would have to admit he was wrong about the second coming of Jesus. It is more than likely he would have to admit that his concepts of Yahweh and his plans and the way he thought the world was to turn out were wrong. He would have to admit a lot of things he wrote were simply misguided, including 2 Timothy 3:16 where he wrote that "all scripture is given by inspiration of God." Paul would have to rebuild, rethink, and change his whole worldview and explanations of the future upon being moved forward in time and living in ours.

All Christians can do is naturally what they have done—keep on pushing the second coming forward to a future time and keep looking for the train, for it obviously has not shown up. Pannenberg is quoted in the beginning of this book. For the significance of what he wrote relative to the second coming, I will quote him again in concluding this book.

> "Hence the reference of Jesus message to God's future, which has not yet definitely appeared, must have consequences for understanding his claim to authority in the sense that Jesus remains dependent upon the confirmation of his mission through the full Parousia of God's future."[24]

We all wait, as Jesus waited, as Paul waited, and the early church waited. History has shown, no one knows the future, especially the mildly hallucinated author of the book of Revelation.

Paul also wrote about life and its experiences and the unknown future:

> "Now abides faith, hope, and charity. The greatest of these is charity" (1 Cor. 13:1).

In respect to the contents of this book, the greatest of these three for Christian expectations is eternal hope. We can only live in hope that there is a good God who is going to bring good things to this earth one day, for he cares for each one of us individually. We wait for the time there will be no more pain nor tears and sorrows and a time that eyes have not seen, nor minds imagined, the things to come in that world. Christendom has a thousand versions of beliefs of the end of age and the second coming. A lot of people have wishes and dreams. Perhaps some of us should prepare ourselves to be wrong, for we can't all be right.

Postscript

In my efforts to write and publish this book, my greatest and most unexpected surprise came from Dale Allison who took the time to read the original manuscript and respond back to me. It follows:

(G-Mail notes)

August 12, 2018

Jack Pyle to Dale Allison:

I am sending you a copy of a book that will be produced shortly and on Amazon and distributed by Ingram. The ms you read had to be changed, as you pointed out due to the volume of quotations. I have my first test copy runs and CFP is in the process of setting up e-book capability.

Your note was included in the book. I hope that the content in no way is disappointing to you with use of the note you had forwarded to me.

In appreciation,
Jack Pyle

August 14, 2018
To: Jack Pyle
From Dale Allison

Jack

Congratulations on getting your book out. It looks good.

All the best,
Dale Allison

To: Dale Allison

I have spent twenty-five years trying to come to conclusions about what it is that I believe about Jesus. Of all the books I have read on the subject, yours have made the greatest impact in my life. It has been an emotional journey, for I viscerally lived for years believing the second coming of Jesus was imminent. I spent nearly a quarter century proclaiming the return of Jesus by 1975. Of all your books, I liked the honesty you portrayed in your book, *The Historical Christ and the Theological Jesus.*

I don't know to what extent you make an effort to understand lay people and their struggles to sort out what we read from the guild, but for what it is worth, I am sending you this manuscript which reveals an agonizing journey to sort and sift what is being put out there about Jesus. You will see your works have influenced my life greatly.

Sincerely,
Jack Pyle

September 18, 2017

Dear Jack

Thanks for your kind words. It's always heartening to know that something I have written had been of use.

I have looked at your manuscript with interest. You have read a lot, understand what you've read, and wrestled with difficult questions. Looks like we see eye to eye on most things.

Like me, it appears that your most helpful companions on your journey have been books. I appreciate that, although find it sad that so many of us find so little honest help in the churches.

I wish you the best as you continue on your journey.

Dale Allison

September 21, 2017

I would like your permission to share the note you sent me. I am trying to find a publisher. In doing this, I find questions like "—What other books have you written?" —or, "What individuals have reviewed your work?" May I use the note from you to provide to a potential publisher?

Jack Pyle

September 21, 2017

Jack, of course, you can use my note.

Dale Allison

Epilogue

The previous title of this book, *Was Jesus Potty-Trained?*, was intended to be provocative and cause one to think about a thoroughly *human* Jesus. Although this book is certainly about Jesus as a gifted but ordinary man, it is much more than that. Several people I respect, with publishing experience, urged me to reissue the book under a more comprehensive title that would convey my own personal experience as a minister in the Worldwide Church of God, a late 20th century apocalyptic sect, as well as what I have learned through assiduous study of books and materials from the academic Quest for the historical Jesus after exiting the church and having to change my beliefs of the end of the age.

Since writing the book, I have continued to deepen my understanding of the message of the early church, Paul's beliefs concerning the end of the age, what Jesus believed and taught, and what the early church anticipated in their day and time relative to a second coming and the establishment of the kingdom of God in their day. This process has involved my questioning everything that I wrote and asking myself about my conclusions. This has led me to other books on the subject.

In a few cases, Dale Allison of Princeton being one of them, and Philip Yancey and Paula Fredriksen and James Tabor being others, I received notes of encouragement. James Tabor's support in this title change and new publication, I could hardly put in words. The book would never have come about except for Robert Kuhn's encouragement upon reading the original ms. His words were: "I think you have something of value to say, and if I didn't feel that way, I would tell you." I hope it will be of value to others. I am deeply grateful for their help and support in subjects that involve a great deal of controversy in the evangelical world and even among members of my own family and friends.

I set in this book all of my newly discovered understanding and research alongside my own personal story of one person's very real experience in spending decades living and believing a very similar apocalyptic message to what we find in the writing of the New Testament period detailing the end of time or the end of the age. Where they believed they were living in the end times, my beliefs of the end time were reshaped to apply to the late 20th century—1975 to be exact—as the date for the return of Jesus. Apparently 126,000,000 American citizens are doing the same thing in expecting Jesus' return in 2050. They see themselves living in the end times and end of the age.

Since publishing the book, I discovered the works of James D. Tabor, of UNC Charlotte, who in turn led me to read the books of Paula Fredriksen of Boston University. I have read other books which she sourced in her books and have others on order.

Four of these books I would particularly recommend as a starting place for anyone who is wanting to begin to delve into this area: Tabor's book, *Paul and Jesus*, Fredriksen's books, *When Jews Were Christians, From Jesus to Christ, and Paul the Pagans' Apostle*. These are some of the best books about the historical Jesus and Paul's beliefs, and I encountered them in a continuing search after completing the book. Before I read those, I was gratefully enlightened in my quest for truth by John Meier, N.T. Wright, James Dunn, E.P. Sanders, Dom Crossan, Dale Allison, Philip Yancey and dozens of other noted and respected third quest Bible scholars, as detailed in the book and source notes.

According to John Meier, around 28 A.D., Jesus left his family and close friends in Nazareth, and began a ministry as an "itinerant prophet of the end time." E.P. Sanders points out that Jesus began that ministry after his alliance and association with the ministry of his first cousin, John the Baptist. Sanders says Jesus began his "public career by accepting his baptism."

John the Baptist "was a preacher of repentance in view of the pending judgment" that John believed was soon to come upon the nation of Israel. Jesus, according to most scholars, took up and adapted John's core message of the imminence of the kingdom of God, after John's ignominious death at the hands of Herod Antipas. Jesus' preaching language was remarkably similar to John's in his warnings to the nation. Both speak of a "generation of vipers" and emphasize that the "Kingdom of God is at hand." Fiery judgment was to come upon the nation. John says explicitly, "the ax is now at the root of the tree," bringing this separation of good and evil. Jesus repeatedly said that these events would not only occur in "this generation," but that the generation would not pass until everything written in the Prophets was fulfilled. Clearly, the John the Baptist/Jesus movement was an apocalyptic one to the core.

Paul, who originally opposed the movement, was converted to faith in Jesus as the heavenly Messiah within a decade of his death. He too took up that same imminent apocalyptic message. He told his followers to postpone marriage, any business involvement in the world, because the "appointed time" had grown very short and the form of the world was passing away (1 Corinthians 7). He clearly says he expects to see the return of Christ from heaven in his lifetime, preceded by the coming of a final evil ruler whom Christ would slay at his coming. Paul declares throughout his writings that he got his beliefs and teachings on the subject directly from Jesus (Galatians 1; 1 Thessalonians 4; 1 Corinthians 11).

Fredriksen characterizes Paul's beliefs in her book *Paul—The Pagans' Apostle:*

> "The kingdom of God, Paul proclaimed, was at hand. His firm belief that he lived and worked in history's final hour is absolutely foundational, shaping everything else that Paul says and does. And this conviction is even more remarkable when we consider that, by the time that we hear from him, mid-first century, the Kingdom is already late" (pp xi).

Fredriksen states of the original community of people associated with the message of Jesus and his life's ministry, that the resurrection of Jesus "validated and vindicated both Jesus' message of the coming Kingdom together with his timetable: The kingdom truly was at hand." Fredriksen maintains that, "The point of his particular resurrection, in other words, was not to express Jesus' special status as such. It was to vindicate his prophecy: 'The times are fulfilled, and the Kingdom is at hand! Repent and trust in the good news!'"

In her book titled *When Christians Were Jews*, Fredriksen makes it clear that the early followers of Jesus saw history swiftly drawing to a close:

> "They foresaw no extended future. They passionately believed that God was about to fulfill his ancient promises to Israel; to redeem history, to defeat evil, to raise the dead, and to establish a universal reign of justice and peace" (pp 1).

Before the end was to come, she says in her book *Paul—The Pagans' Apostle*, that as Jewish Christians they believed,

> "...the righteous will suffer persecution at the hands of the wicked...the Day of the Lord will arrive, when the world will be convulsed by celestial and terrestrial catastrophes: earthquakes, plagues, darkness at noon, falling stars....With the resurrection of the dead, the judgment of the wicked, and the vindication of the righteous, Israel will reassemble, all twelve tribes, and return to the Land. God's spirit will pour out onto 'all flesh' (Joel 2:28). The redeemed will gather in Jerusalem, at a rebuilt or renewed temple. Peace unalterably established, the entire world, human and divine, will acknowledge and worship the god of Israel" (pp 27).

James D. Tabor has made a study of Paul's life and letters for over thirty-five years, beginning with his dissertation for his Ph.D. at the University of Chicago in 1981. In his eye opening and paradigm changing book, *Paul and Jesus—How the Apostle Transformed the World*, he writes:

> "Paul operated with a strongly apocalyptic perspective that influenced all he said and did. He was quite sure that he and his followers would live to see the return of Christ from heaven" (pp 15).

E. P. Sanders succinctly summarizes Paul's thoughts in his book *Paul and Palestinian Judaism*,

> "No two elements of Paul's thought are more certain, or more consistently expressed, than his conviction that the full salvation of believers and the destruction of the wicked lay in the near future" (pp 523).

There have been attempts by evangelical Christian scholars to oppose or somehow explain this clear failure of such events to take place in that generation. For example, Ben Witherington's book *Jesus, Paul and the End of the World*. I found his attempts to be weak. There is no way to deny that the whole movement, from John the Baptist, to Jesus, to Paul were profoundly mistaken. History went on, Rome did not fall, it prospered into the next centuries, and the Kingdom of God did not come. Even though Witherington tries to argue, based on 2 Peter, that "a day with the Lord is a thousand years, and a thousand years is a day," the fact is clear. The end of the age failed to arrive as predicted and expected. His appeal to Einstein's theory of time is irrelevant to how we should interpret statements made by individuals 2000 years ago, predictions that clearly failed. Imminent means imminent, not some abstract period of time in the universe, followers of Paul shaped their entire lives around this expectation—that never came about.

Crossan puts things rather succinctly: Jesus words about the end of the age occurring in "this generation" or "soon" didn't mean at most "two thousand years and counting."

One of the most prominent New Testament scholars today, N. T. Wright, wrote a massive 1660 page book titled *Paul and Faithfulness* that drowns the reader with his sources and arguments, trying to avoid the obvious (see pp. 173-175 for a summary of his arguments).

Wright admits that his position that Jesus nor Paul did not believe and teach an imminent second coming, places him within a "minority" of bible scholars and theologians who believe as he does. Dale Allison is probably accurate when he wrote of Wright's position, that Wright would most likely remain among a "beleaguered minority" who cling to his interpretation of our New Testament writings detailing the beliefs of Jesus and Paul.

The late James Dunn, who was a friend and colleague of Wright, believed Wright's interpretation of the New Testament was flawed, particularly his contention that everything Jesus taught referred concretely to events of that time, not the future. This is despite the plain language of both Jesus and Paul.

In the two years since original publication of this book, I have become more convinced, not less convinced, that the writings of the New Testament reflect a Jesus of the gospels who began his ministry, as a human being, capable of error, and born of human parents.

This is my starting point in this book resulting from years of research of the Jesus of history, as told by gospel writers and Paul. Jesus was, as James Dunn states, "proven wrong by the course of history".

The reality of new testament testimony of its writers, is that Jesus' prophesies failed, as did Paul's, and those of John the Baptist, and all the gospel writers. Apparently, contrary to most Christian concepts of Jesus, he wasn't an all-knowing God, omnipresent, omniscient, living in the body and mind of a human being, which if he was, would have made him so utterly unlike us that It would make his suffering for us a mockery as C.S. Lewis and many others have pointed out.

The late James Dunn, in his book *Jesus Remembered*, made a profound statement about Jesus before his death.

> "For Jesus to be fully human he had, for both bio-logical and theological reasons, to have a human father as well as a human mother and the weight of historical evidence strongly indicates that this was so—and that it was probably Joseph. Any theology for a scientific age which is concerned with the significance of Jesus of Nazareth now has to start at this point" (pp 66).

It is a strange theological world in which we live that we find that Paul, the putative founder of Christianity, with all its attendant beliefs of the kingdom of God, atonement theology, the resurrection, the incarnation, the end of the age, and the return of Jesus in a second coming, is built upon the literature and writings of an individual that time and history has shown, by historical events in the world, to be wrong in all he taught and believed relative to most of what he wrote regarding those subjects. This is never realistically confronted.

E.P. Sanders presents for Christianity, in a simple statement, the conundrum it must eventually face in using Paul as a source of Christian beliefs on these subjects when he wrote in *Paul and Palestinian Judaism*:

> "To an appreciable degree, what Paul concretely thought cannot be directly appropriated by Christians today. The form of the present world did not pass away, the end did not come, and believers were not caught up to meet the Lord in the heavens" (pp 524).

It is my firm belief as a lay reader of third quest works, that the writings we have available to us reflect that all the authors and writers of the texts we study, saw themselves as history's last generation before the end of the ages and the establishment of the kingdom of God on earth, and they had no clue they were the first generation, not the last, of what was to become 'Christianity'.

The second coming continues to be pushed forward in time by our generation for Jesus and the kingdom has not yet arrived. The horrors of the book of Revelation remain unfulfilled. Are we to go on believing it will eventually come even though it was to apply to the Roman world? Do we wait with angst for the Great Tribulation? Do we go on in churches in our country teaching our children and generations to come what will occur on this planet one day out of the book of Revelation?

The comments of Philip Yancey were made upon his reading this book previously published under the title—*Was Jesus Potty Trained*. Nothing in that book was changed other than adding the epilogue to this publication of the original book and changing the title as Yancey suggested, to reach a wider audience. The comments of Dale Allison were made after his reading the same. Both Robert Kuhn's comments and those of James D. Tabor were also made after their reading the earlier book publication.

The title used in the previous publication was used to attempt to convey that Jesus was a human being, born of human parents, capable of error, and sorely mistaken about the arrival of the Kingdom of his father, Yahweh.

The front cover pictures the "Western Wall," or Kotel, that many Christians know as the "Wailing Wall," the holiest site in Judaism today. These thousands of massive stones, intact from the time of Jesus, are still in place, forming the compound wall around the enlarged Temple plaza, and part of the Temple buildings referred to in the gospels.

The new title of the book—***The End of All Things is at Hand: A Personal Journey from Apocalyptic Fears to Historical Reality***, is intended to convey my own personal experience in reading and studying and discarding my end of the world beliefs based upon end of the world mythology and most of my concepts of the human being we call Jesus. I have found that history is a much firmer place to stand than apocalyptic fantasy, that for two thousand years has a one-hundred percent failure rate, with countless lives affected as mine was.

I hope this book can be a help and guide to many who have sought to understand early Christianity in its historical roots. And, I hope my grandchildren, and great grandchildren, and great-great-grandchildren, and all grandchildren and great grandchildren and great-great grandchildren of the world, will never experience a religious journey within churches where they live in fear of Armageddon, the End of the World, the Great Tribulation, and a Jesus that is allegedly to appear one day on a white horse, sword in hand, wearing a robe dipped in blood, as he pours out the 7 last plagues and all the horrible events described in the book of Revelation.

APPENDIX
BIOGRAPHIES OF
KEY INDIVIDUALS QUOTED

Raymond Brown
Raymond Edward Brown, S.S., (May 22, 1928–1998) was an American Catholic priest, a member of the Sulpician Fathers and a prominent biblical scholar. He was regarded as a specialist concerning the hypothetical "Johannine community," which he speculated contributed to the authorship of the Gospel of John, and he also wrote influential studies on the birth and death of Jesus. Brown was professor emeritus at Union Theological Seminary in New York where he taught for twenty-nine years. He was the first Catholic professor to gain tenure there, where he earned a reputation as a superior lecturer. (Wikipedia)

N. T. "Tom" Wright
N. T. Wright (1948) is the former bishop of Durham in the Church of England and one of the world's leading Bible scholars. He is now serving as the chair of New Testament and Early Christianity at the School of Divinity at the University of St. Andrews. For twenty years, he taught New Testament studies at Cambridge, McGill, and Oxford Universities. As being both one of the world's leading Bible scholars and a popular author, he has been featured on *ABC News, Dateline, The Colbert Report,* and *Fresh Air.* His award-winning books include *The Case for the Psalms, How God Became King, Simply Jesus, After*

You Believe, Surprised by Hope, Simply Christian, Scripture and the Authority of God, The Meaning of Jesus (coauthored with Marcus Borg), as well as being the translator for *The Kingdom New Testament*. He also wrote the impressive *Christian Origins and the Question of God* series, including *The New Testament and the People of God, Jesus and the Victory of God, The Resurrection of the Son of God*, and most recently, *Paul and the Faithfulness of God* (Amazon books bio). *Time Magazine* called him "one of the most formidable figures in the world of Christian thought." *Newsweek* once labeled him "the world's leading New Testament scholar."

Ben Meyer

Ben Meyer (1927–1995) studied with the Jesuits, his studies taking him to California, Strasbourg, Göttingen, and Rome, where he received his doctorate from the Universita Gregoriana in 1965. He taught briefly at Alma College and at the Graduate Theological Union in Berkeley before joining the faculty at McMaster University in 1969, where he taught in the Department of Religious Studies until 1992. Meyer's areas of specialization included the historical Jesus, the early expansion of the Christian movement, and the hermeneutics of Bernard Lonergan. He authored several important monographs over his thirty-year career (Wikipedia). Both Tom Wright and Ed Sanders have given attribution to Meyer in their books as a source of their understanding of the aims and intents of Jesus.

John Meier

John P. Meier (born 1942) is William K. Warren Professor of Theology (New Testament) at the University of Notre Dame and the author of *A Marginal Jew: Rethinking the Historical Jesus*. He has also written six other books and over seventy articles. At various times, he has been the editor or associate editor of *The Catholic Biblical Quarterly, New Testament Studies*, and *Dead Sea Discoveries*. He is also a catholic priest. Meier was born in New York. He attended St. Joseph's Seminary and College (BA, 1964), Gregorian University Rome (STL, 1968), and the Biblical Institute Rome (SSD, 1976). Meier is William K. Warren Professor of Theology at the University of Notre

Dame, Indiana. His fields include biblical studies and Christianity and Judaism in antiquity. Before coming to Notre Dame, he was professor of New Testament at the Catholic University of America (Wikipedia).

E. P. Sanders

Ed Parish Sanders (born 1937) is a New Testament scholar and one of the principal proponents of the "New Perspective on Paul." He is a major scholar in contemporary scholarship on the historical Jesus, and he contributed to the view that Jesus was part of a renewal movement within Judaism. He has been Arts and Sciences Professor of Religion at Duke University, North Carolina, since 1990. He retired in 2005.

Sanders is a fellow of the British Academy. In 1966, he received a Th.D. from Union Seminary in NYC. In 1990, he received a D. Litt. from the University of Oxford and a Th.D. from the University of Helsinki. He has authored, coauthored, or edited thirteen books and numerous articles. He has received a number of prizes, including the 1990 University of Louisville and Louisville Presbyterian Theological Seminary Grawemeyer Award for the best book on religion published in the 1980s for *Jesus and Judaism* (Wikipedia). Tom Wright has said that Sanders's work on Paul has "towered" above all scholars in the field and it has created a "Sanders' revolution." Coming from Tom Wright, I would think Sanders considers that a great compliment. He is not prone to give them out.

Dale Allison

Dale Allison (born 1955) is a highly lauded professor of Princeton Theological Seminary and a world-class scholar in New Testament studies. Allison's areas of expertise include the historical Jesus, early Jewish and Christian eschatology, Second Temple Judaism, the canonical Gospels (especially Matthew) and the Q source, and the history of the interpretation and application of texts. He has been called the "premier Matthew specialist of his generation in the United States" and "North America's most complete New Testament scholar." Allison has served on many editorial boards including *New*

Testament Studies and the *Journal for the Study of the Historical Jesus*, and he was for many years the main New Testament editor for the multivolume Encyclopedia of the Bible. He is an ordained elder in the Presbyterian Church (USA).

He is a prominent defender of the view of the historical Jesus as an apocalyptic prophet expecting the imminent end of the age. His views are laid out in his books *Jesus of Nazareth: Millenarian Prophet and Constructing Jesus: Memory and Imagination and History* (which the Biblical Archaeology Society named best book relating the New Testament for 2009–2010). His view stands over against those of the Jesus Seminar and such scholars as John Dominic Crossan and Marcus Borg, whose reconstructions of Jesus are largely free of apocalyptic element (Wikipedia).

Richard Hiers

Richard Hiers (born 1932) B.D., M.A., Ph.D., Yale University; J.D., University of Florida College of Law, Professor of Religion and Affiliate Professor of Law. He is currently a member of the Advisory Committee for the *Journal of Law and Religion* (chaired 2005–2010); a member of the Board of Directors for the Florida Free Speech Forum; and a member of the Society of Christian Ethics. Other current memberships: Bar Association of the Fifth Federal Circuit, the Florida Bar, the League of Women Voters, the Natural Resources Defense Council, Save the Redwoods League, Sierra Club, the Society of Phi Beta Kappa, the United Nations Association, and the Yale Whiffenpoofs Alumni Association. Former President of the American Academy of Religion, SE Region, former President of the Society of Biblical Literature, SE Region; member, Danforth Associates in Teaching; recipient of Florida Blue Key Distinguished Faculty Award (Web site).

Hermann Reimarus

Hermann Samuel Reimarus (1694–1768) was a German philosopher and writer of the Enlightenment who is remembered for his Deism, the doctrine that human reason can arrive at a knowledge of God and ethics from a study of nature and our own internal reality, thus eliminating the need for religions based on revelation. He denied the supernatural origin of Christianity and was the first influential critic to investigate the historical Jesus. According to Reimarus, Jesus was a mortal Jewish prophet, and the apostles founded Christianity as a religion separate from Jesus' own ministry (Wikipedia). He is recognized as being the first individual to have written about the Jesus of history contrasted to the theological Jesus all have known. He believed the disciples faked Jesus' death which has all the trappings of the Jesus Seminar.

Edward Schillibeeckx

Edward Schillibeeckx (1914–2009) taught at the Catholic University in Nijmegen. He was a member of the Dominican Order. His books on theology have been translated into many languages, and his contributions to the Second Vatican Council made him known throughout the world. He was considered one of the twentieth century's most important theologians; his influence was worldwide and extended far beyond the confines of his own Roman Catholic Church (Wikipedia).

Albert Schweitzer

Albert Schweitzer (14 January 1875–4 September 1965) was a French-German theologian, organist, writer, humanitarian, philosopher, and physician. A Lutheran, Schweitzer challenged both the secular view of Jesus as depicted by historical-critical methodology current at this time, as well as the traditional Christian view. His contributions to the interpretation of Pauline Christianity concern the role of Paul's mysticism of "being in Christ" as primary and the doctrine of Justification by Faith as secondary (Wikipedia). His seminal book—*Quest for the Historical Jesus*—dominated studies of the historical Jesus by scholars for almost one hundred years. His beliefs of Jesus aims and purposes still live in the works of Wright, Allison, Sanders, Dunn, Hiers, and other conservative Bible scholars who all believe Jesus was an apocalyptic prophet proclaiming the soon coming arrival of the kingdom of God.

James D.G. Dunn

James D. G. "Jimmy" Dunn (born 1939) was for many years the Lightfoot Professor of Divinity in the Department of Theology at the University of Durham. Since his retirement, he has been made Emeritus Lightfoot Professor. He is a leading British New Testament scholar, broadly in the Protestant tradition. Dunn is especially associated with the New Perspective on Paul, along with N. T. "Tom" Wright and E. P. Sanders. He is credited with coining this phrase during his 1982 Manson Memorial Lecture.

Dunn has an MA and BD from the University of Glasgow and a PhD and DD from the University of Cambridge. For 2002, Dunn was the president of the Studiorum Novi Testament Societas, the leading international body for New Testament study. Only three other British scholars had been made president in the preceding twenty-five years (Wikipedia).

Walter Brueggemann

Walter Brueggemann (born March 11, 1933), one of the world's leading interpreters of the Old Testament, Brueggemann is William Marcellus McPheeters professor of Old Testament emeritus at Columbia Theological Seminary. He is the author of more than fifty books, including The Prophetic Imagination, Praying the Psalms: Engaging Scripture, and Reverberations of Faith: A Theological Handbook of Old Testament Themes—as well as commentaries on several Old Testament books, including Genesis, Exodus, Deuteronomy, 1 and 2 Samuel, Isaiah, and Jeremiah. He is an important figure in modern progressive Christianity whose work often focuses on the Hebrew prophetic tradition and sociopolitical imagination of the church. He argues that the church must provide a counternarrative to the dominant forces of consumerism, militarism, and nationalism (Wikipedia).

Larry Hurtado

Larry Hurtado (born 1943) is a New Testament scholar, historian of early Christianity and Emeritus Professor of New Testament Language, Literature and Theology at the University of Edinburgh,

Scotland (professor, 1996–2011). He was the Head of the School of Divinity 2007–2010, and was until August 2011, director of the Centre for the Study of Christian Origins, at the University of Edinburgh (Wikipedia).

John A. T. Robinson

John Arthur Thomas Robinson (16 May 1919–5 December 1983) was an English New Testament scholar, author, and the Anglican Bishop of Woolwich. He was a lecturer at Trinity College, Cambridge, and later dean of Trinity College until his death in 1983 from cancer. Robinson was considered a major force in shaping liberal Christian theology. Along with Harvard theologian Harvey Cox, he spearheaded the field of secular theology, and, like William Barclay, he was a believer in universal salvation (Wikipedia).

Wolfhart Pannenberg

Wolfhart Pannenberg (2 October 1928–4 September 2014) was a German theologian. He has made a number of significant contributions to modern theology, including his concept of history as a form of revelation centered on the Resurrection of Christ, which has been widely debated in both Protestant and Catholic theology, as well as by non-Christian thinkers (Wikipedia).

Marcus Borg

Marcus J. Borg (March 11, 1942–January 21, 2015) was an American New Testament scholar and theologian. He was among the most widely known and influential voices in progressive Christianity. As a fellow of the Jesus Seminar, Borg was a major figure in historical Jesus scholarship. He retired as Hundere Distinguished Professor of Religion and Culture at Oregon State University in 2007 and died eight years later at the age of seventy-two, of idiopathic pulmonary fibrosis (Wikipedia). Borg, like Crossan, has been one of the most published and outspoken members of the Jesus Seminar.

Robert Funk

Robert W. Funk (July 18, 1926–September 3, 2005) was an American biblical scholar, founder of the controversial Jesus Seminar and the nonprofit Westar Institute in Santa Rosa, California. Funk, an academic, sought to promote research and education on what he called biblical literacy. His approach to hermeneutics was historical-critical, with a strongly skeptical view of orthodox Christian belief, particularly concerning the historical Jesus. He and his peers described Jesus' parables as containing shocking messages that contradicted established religious attitudes (Wikipedia).

Alister McGrath

Alister Edgar McGrath FRSA (born 23 January 1953) is a Northern Irish theologian, priest, intellectual historian, scientist, and Christian apologist. He currently holds the Andreas Idreos Professorship in Science and Religion in the Faculty of Theology and Religion at the University of Oxford, and is Professor of Divinity at Gresham College. He was previously Professor of Theology, Ministry, and Education at King's College London and Head of the Centre for Theology, Religion and Culture, Professor of Historical Theology at the University of Oxford, and was principal of Wycliffe Hall, Oxford, until 2005. He is an Anglican priest.

Aside from being a faculty member at Oxford, McGrath has also taught at Cambridge University and is a Teaching Fellow at Regent College. McGrath holds three doctorates from the University of Oxford: a DPhil in Molecular Biophysics, a Doctor of Divinity in Theology and a Doctor of Letters in Intellectual History (Wikipedia).

John Crossan

John Dominic Crossan (born February 17, 1934) is an Irish-American New Testament scholar, historian of early Christianity, and former Catholic priest who has produced both scholarly and popular works. His research has focused on the historical Jesus, on the anthropology of the Ancient Mediterranean and New Testament worlds and on the application of postmodern hermeneutical approaches to the Bible. His work is controversial, portraying the Second Coming as a late corruption of Jesus' message and saying that Jesus' divinity is metaphorical. In place of the eschatological message of the Gospels, Crossan emphasizes the historical context of Jesus and of his followers immediately after his death. He describes Jesus' ministry as founded on free healing and communal meals, negating the social hierarchies of Jewish culture and the Roman Empire (Wikipedia).

John Hick

John Harwood Hick (20 January 1922–9 February 2012) was a philosopher of religion and theologian born in England who taught in the United States for the larger part of his career. In philosophical theology, he made contributions in the areas of theodicy, eschatology, and Christology, and in the philosophy of religion, he contributed to the areas of epistemology of religion and religious pluralism.

In 1948, he completed his MA thesis, which formed the basis of his book *Faith and Knowledge*. He went on to complete a DPhil at Oriel College, Oxford University in 1950 and a DLitt from Edinburgh in 1975. In 1977, he received an honorary doctorate from the Faculty of Theology at Uppsala University, Sweden. In 1953, he married Joan Hazel Bowers, and the couple had four children. After many years as a member of the United Reformed Church, in October 2009, he was accepted into membership of the Religious Society of Friends (Quaker) in Britain. He died in 2012 (Wikipedia).

James D. Tabor (born 1946) is a biblical scholar and Professor of ancient Judaism and early Christianity in the Department of Religious Studies at the University of North Carolina Charlotte, where he has taught since 1989 and served as Chair from 2004–14. Tabor is the founder and director of the Original Bible Project, a non-profit organization aimed to produce a re-ordered new translation of the Bible in English. His bestselling books are the *Jesus Dynasty* and *Paul and Jesus*. Tabor earned his Ph.D. at the University of Chicago in 1981 in New Testament and Early Christian literature with an emphasis on the origins of Christianity and ancient Judaism, including the Dead Sea Scrolls, John the Baptist, Jesus, James the Just, and Paul the Apostle. The author of six books and over 50 articles, Tabor is frequently consulted by the media on these topics and has appeared on numerous television and radio programs. *(Wikipedia)*

Paula F. Fredriksen (born 1951) is an American historian and scholar of religious studies. She held the position of William Goodwin Aurelio Professor of the Appreciation of Scripture at Boston University through 2010 and is now the William Goodwin Aurelio Chair Emerita of the Appreciation of Scripture.

She served as historical consultant for the BBC production *The Lives of Jesus* (1996) and for *US News and World Report's*, "*The Life and Times of Jesus*", and was featured speaker in the *Frontline* documentary From Jesus to Christ: *The First Christians* (1998), based heavily on her book *From Jesus to Christ: The Origins of the New Testament Images of Jesus*. Fredriksen earned her BA degree with Phi Beta Kappa in Religions and History in 1973 from the Wellesley College and a year later got a diploma in theology from Oxford University. In 1979 she earned a Ph.D. in the history of religions from Princeton University and until 1980 was the Andrew W. Mellon Postdoctoral Fellow at Stanford University. *(Wikipedia)*

NOTES

Preface

[1] Wolfhart Pannenberg, *Jesus—God and Man*, Westminster Press 1977, Philadelphia, PA

Introduction

[1] Walter Brueggemann, *Theology of the Old Testament*, Fortress Press 1997, Minneapolis, MN

[2] Peter Berger, *Questions of Faith*, Blackwell Publishing 2004, Malden, MA

[3] Wolfhart Pannenberg, *Jesus—God and Man*, Westminster Press 1977, Philadelphia, PA

[4] N. T. Wright, *Simply Jesus*, Harper Collins 2011, NY, NY

[5] Philip Yancey, *The Bible Jesus Read*, Zondervan Press 1999, Grand Rapids, MI

[6] Brevard Childs, *The Old Testament in a Canonical Context*, Fortress Press 1986, NY, NY

[7] Richard Friedman, *Who Wrote the Bible*, Summit Books 1987, NY, NY

[8] Jack Miles, *God—A Biography*, First Vantage Books 1996, NY, NY

[9] Walter Brueggemann, *Theology of the Old Testament*, Fortress Press 1997, Minneapolis, MN

[10] Ibid, P 629

[11] Ibid, P 740

[12] Ibid, 122

[13] Ibid, P 233

[14] Ibid, P 249

[15] Ibid, P 106

[16] Jack Miles, *God—A Biography*, Vintage Books 1996, NY, NY

[17] Walter Brueggemann, *Theology of the Old Testament*, Fortress Press 1997, Minneapolis, MN

[18] Ibid, P 107

[19] Ibid, P 714

[20] Carey Newman, *Jesus and the Restoration of Israel*, Inter-Varsity Press 1999, Downers Grove, IL

[21] Karen Armstrong, *History of God*, Random House 2000, NY, NY

[22] Thomas Jefferson, *The Jefferson Bible*, Dover Publications 2006, Mineola, NY

[23] David Ray Griffin, *God, Power, and Evil*, Westminster Press 2004, Louisville, KY

Chapter 1

[1] William Miller, Wikipedia

[2] Bart Ehrman, *Jesus—Apocalyptic Prophet of the New Millennium*, Oxford Press 1999, NY, NY

[3] Rudolph Bultmann, *Jesus Christ and Mythology*, SCM Press 1946, London, UK

Chapter 2

[1] David McCullough, *Truman*, Simon and Schuster 1992, NY, NY

[2] Ibid, P 620

[3] Ibid, P 763

[4] Susan Garret, *No Ordinary Angel*, Vail-Ballou 2008, Binghamton, NY

[5] Robert Funk, *Honest to Jesus*, Harper Collins Publishers 1996, NY, NY

[6] Ibid, P 302

[7] Ibid, P 305

[8] N. T. Wright, *Jesus and the Victory of God*, Fortress Press 1996, NY, NY

[9] Ibid, P 302

[10] Ibid, P 426

[11] Raymond Brown, *Death of the Messiah*, Doubleday Publishing 1993, NY, NY

[12] Malcom Muggeridge, *Jesus—the Man Who Lives*, Harper and Row 1975, NY, NY

Chapter 4

[1]   Susan Garrett, *No Ordinary Angel*, Vail-Ballou 2008, Binghamton, NY

[2]   Daniel Taylor, *Myth of Certainty*, Inter-Varsity Press 1992, Madison, WI

Chapter 5

[1]   Jon Levenson, *Creation and the Persistence of Evil*, Princeton University Press 1988, Princeton, NJ

[2]   C.S. Lewis, *Miracles*, Harper Collins 1996, NY, NY

[3]   Philip Yancey, *The Bible Jesus Read*, Zondervan Press 1999, Grand Rapids, MI

[4]   Dale Allison, *The Historical Christ and the Theological Jesus*, Eerdmans Press 2009, Grand Rapids, MI

Chapter 6

[1]   Peter Berger, *Rumor of Angels*, Doubleday Publishiing 1970, Garden City, NY

[2]   E. P. Sanders, *The Historical Figure of Jesus*, Penguin Books 1993, London, UK

[3]   E. P. Sanders, *Studying the Synoptic Gospels*, SCM Press 1989, Philadelphia, PA

[4]   E. P. Sanders, *The Historical Figure of Jesus*, Penguin Books 1989, Philadelphia, PA

[5]   Ibid, E. P. Sanders, P 236

[6]   John Meier, *A Marginal Jew II*, Doubleday 1994, NY, NY

[7]   Harold Bloom, *Jesus and Yahweh*, Penguin Books 2005, London, UK

Chapter 7

[1]   D.A. Carson, *From Sabbath to Lord's Day*, Wipf and Stock Publishers 1999, Eugene, OR

[2]   E.P. Sanders, *The Historical Figure of Jesus*, Penguin Books 1993, London, UK

[3]   E.P. Sanders, *Studying the Synoptic Gospels*, SCM Press 1989, Philadelphia, PA

[4]   James D.G. Dunn, *Jesus and the Spirit*, SCM Press 1975, London, UK

[5]   Larry Hurtado, *Lord Jesus Christ*, Eerdmans Publishing 2003, Cambridge, UK

[6]   Dale Allison, *Jesus of Nazareth Millenarian Prophet*, Fortress Press 1998, Minneapolis, MN

7　Raymond E. Brown, *The Churches the Apostles Left Behind*, Paulist Press 1984, NY, NY

8　John Meier, *A Marginal Jew III*, Doubleday Press 2001, NY, NY

Chapter 8

1　Albert Schweitzer, *The Quest for the Historical Jesus*, Fortress Press 2001, Minneapolis, MN

2　Carey Newman, *Jesus and the Restoration of Israel*, Inter-Varsity Press, 1999, Downers Grove, IL

3　Ibid, P 178

4　N. T. Wright, *Jesus and the Victory of God*, Fortress Press 1996, NY, NY

5　Ibid, P 561

6　Carey Newman, *Jesus and the Restoration of Israel*, Inter-Varsity Press, 1999, Downers Grove, IL

7　Ibid, P 177

8　Ibid, P 178

9　N. T. Wright, *Jesus and the Victory of God*, Fortress Press 1996, NY, NY

10　Albert Schweitzer, *The Quest of the Historical Jesus*, Fortress Press 2001, Minneapolis, MN

11　John Hick, *Metaphor of God Incarnate*, Westminster Press 1993, Louisville, KY

12　James D. G. Dunn, *Jesus and the Spirit*, SCM Press 1975, London, UK

Chapter 9

1　N. T. Wright, *Jesus and the Victory of God*, Fortress Press 1996, NY, NY

2　E. P. Sanders, *Jesus and Judaism*, Fortress Press 1985, Philadelphia, PA

3　Dale Allison, *Jesus of Nazareth—Millenarian Prophet*, Fortress Press 1998, Minneapolis, MN

4　Wolfhart Pannenberg, *Jesus—God and Man*, Westminster Press 1977, Philadelphia, PA

5　James D.G. Dunn, *Christology in the Making*, SCM Press 1989, London, UK

6　Richard Hiers, *Jesus Proclamation of the Kingdom of God*, Fortress Press 1971, Philadelphia, PA

7　N. T. Wright, *The New Testament and the People of God*, Fortress Press 1992, London, UK

8   E. P. Sanders, *The Historical Figure of Jesus*, Penguin Books 1993, London, UK

9   Dale Allison, *The End of the Ages Has Come*, Wipf and Stock Publishers 1985, Eugene, OR

10   James D.G. Dunn, *Jesus and the Spirit*, SCM Press 1975, London, UK

11   Ibid, P 112

12   Dale Allison, *The End of the Ages Has Come*, Wipf and Stock Publishers 1985, Eugene, OR

13   Ibid, P 62–63

14   Richard Hiers, *Jesus and the Future*, John Knox Press 1981, Atlanta, GA

15   Sanders and Davies, *Studying the Synoptic Gospels*, SCM Press 1989, Philadelphia, PA

16   Peter Berger, *Questions of Faith*, Blackwell Publishing 2004, Malden, MA

Chapter 10

1   Ben Meyer, *The Aims of Jesus*, Pickwick Publications, 2002, Eugene, OR

2   Richard Hiers, *Jesus and the Future*, John Knox Press, 1981, Atlanta, GA

3   Ben Meyer, *The Aims of Jesus*, Pickwick Publications, 2002, Eugene, OR

4   Ibid, P 126

5   Ibid, P 154

6   E. P. Sanders, *The Historical Figure of Jesus*, Penguin Books, 1993, London, UK

7   John Dominic Crossan, *The Historical Jesus*, Harper Collins Publishers 1999, NY, NY

8   E. P. Sanders, *The Historical Figure of Jesus*, Penguin Books, 1993, London, UK

9   John A. T. Robinson, *In the End God*, Wipf and Stock Publishers, 2011, Eugene, OR

10   Wolfhart Pannenberg, *Jesus—God and Man*, Westminster Press, 1977, Philadelphia

Chapter 11

1   John A.T. Robinson, *In the End God,* Wipf and Stock Publishers, 2011, Eugene, OR

2   E. P. Sanders, *Paul and Palestinian Judaism*, Fortress Press, 1977, Philadelphia, PA

3   N. T. Wright, *What Saint Paul Really Said*, Eerdmans Press, 1977, Grand Rapids, MI

4   Shirley Jackson Case, *Jesus—A New Biography*, University of Chicago Press, Chicago, IL

5   John Meier, *A Marginal Jew II*, Doubleday, 1994, NY, NY

Chapter 12

1   James D.G. Dunn, *Christology in the Making*, SCM Press, 1989, London, UK

2   C. S. Lewis, *World's Last Night*, Harcourt Brace and Company, 1960, NY, NY

3   Ibid, P 98

4   Ibid, P 98

5   Raymond Brown, *Jesus—God and Man*, Macmillan Publishing Company, 1967, NY, NY

6   Raymond Brown, *Jesus—God and Man*, Macmillan Publishing Company, 1967, NY, NY

7   N. T. Wright, *Jesus and the Victory of God*, Fortress Press 1996, NY, NY

Chapter 13

1   E. P. Sanders, *The Historical Figure of Jesus*, Penguin Books 1993, London, UK

2   Wolfhart Pannenberg, *Jesus—God and Man*, Westminster Press 1977, Philadelphia, PA

3   John Hick, *The Metaphor of God Incarnate*, Westminster Press 1993, Louisville, KY

4   Wolfhart Pannenberg, *Jesus—God and Man*, Westminster Press 1977, Philadelphia, PA

5   Raymond E. Brown, *Birth of the Messiah*, Doubleday 1977, NY, NY

6   Dale Allison, *Resurrecting Jesus*, T & T Clark 2005, NY, NY

7   E. P. Sanders, *Jesus and Judaism*, Fortress Press 1985, Philadelphia, PA

8   Albert Schweitzer, *The Quest for the Historical Jesus*, Fortress Press 2001, Minneapolis, MN

Chapter 14

1   Dale Allison, *Resurrecting Jesus*, T & T Clark 2005, NY, NY

2   Raymond E. Brown, *Death of the Messiah*, Doubleday Publishing 1993, NY, NY

3   Ben Meyer, *The Aims of Jesus*, Pickwick Publications, 2002, Eugene, OR

4   Raymond E. Brown, *Death of the Messiah*, Doubleday Publishing 1993, NY, NY

5   E. P. Sanders, *The Historical Figure of Jesus*, Penguin Books 1993, London, UK

6   Gregory Boyd, *The Jesus Legend*, Baker Publishing Group 2007, Grand Rapids, MI

7   Ibid, P 437

8   Raymond E. Brown, *Death of the Messiah*, Doubleday Publishing 1993, NY, NY

9   N. T. Wright, *The New Testament and the People of God*, Fortress Press 1992, London, UK

10   George Eldon Ladd, *Theology of the New Testament*, Eerdmans 1974, Grand Rapids, MI

11   Raymond E. Brown, *Death of the Messiah*, Doubleday Publishing 1993, NY, NY

12   E.P. Sanders, *Studying the Synoptic Gospels*, SCM Press 1989, Philadelphia, PA

Chapter 15

1   Raymond E. Brown, *The Community of the Beloved Disciple*, Paulist Press 1979, Mahwah, NJ

2   A. T. Robertson, *Harmony of the Gospels*, Harper and Row 1922, NY, NY

3   Larry Hurtado, *Lord Jesus Christ*, Eerdmans Press, Grand Rapids, MI

4   Edward Schillibeeckx, *Jesus—An Experiment in Christology*, Crossroad Publishing 1991, NY, NY

5   John Meier, *A Marginal Jew III*, Doubleday 1994, NY, NY

6   Raymond E. Brown, *Death of the Messiah*, Doubleday Publishing 1993, NY, NY

7   Edward Schillibeeckx, *Jesus—An Experiment in Christology*, Crossroad Publishing 1991, NY, NY

8   Bart Erhman, *Misquoting Jesus*, Harper One 2005, NY, NY

9   Dale Allison, *Constructing Jesus*, Baker Publishing Group 2010, Grand Rapids, MI

Chapter 16

1   Raymond Brown, *Death of the Messiah*, Doubleday Publishing 1993, NY, NY

2   Ibid

3   Ben Meyer, *The Aims of Jesus*, Pickwick Publications, 2002, Eugene, OR

4   James D. G. Dunn, *Christology in the Making*, SCM Press 1989, London, UK

5   Richard Hiers, *Jesus and the Future*, John Knox Press 1981, Atlanta, GA

6   E. P. Sanders, *The Historical Figure of Jesus*, Penguin Books 1993, London, UK

7   James D.G. Dunn, *Christology in the Making*, SCM Press 1989, London, UK

8   James D.G. Dunn, *Jesus Remembered*, Eerdmans 2003, Grand Rapids, MI

9   Albert Schweitzer, *The Quest for the Historical Jesus*, Fortress Press 2001, Minneapolis, MN

10   N.T. Wright, *Jesus and the Victory of God*, Fortress Press 1996, London, UK

11   N.T. Wright, *The New Testament and the People of God*, Fortress Press 1992, London, UK

12   James G.D. Dunn, *Christology in the Making*, SCM Press 1989, London, UK

13   Raymond Brown, *The Community of the Beloved Disciple*, Paulist Press 1979, Chicago, IL

14   George Eldon Ladd, *Theology of the New Testament*, Eerdmans 1974, Grand Rapids, MI

15   Ben Meyer, *The Aims of Jesus*, Pickwick Publications 2002, Eugene, OR

16   Raymond Brown, *The Community of the Beloved Disciple*, Paulist Press 1979, Chicago, IL

17   Carey Newman, *Jesus and the Restoration of Israel*, Inter-Varsity Press 1999, Downers Grove, IL

Chapter 17

1   Dale Allison, *Constructing Jesus*, Baker Publishing Group 2010, Grand Rapids, MI

2   Raymond E. Brown, *Jesus—God and Man*, Macmillan Publishing Company 1967, NY, NY

3   Ibid, 69–70

4   E. P Sanders, *The Historical Figure of Jesus*, Penguin Books 1993, London, UK

5   N. T. Wright, *Jesus and the Victory of God*, Fortress Press 1996, NY, NY

6   E. P. Sanders, *The Historical Figure of Jesus*, Penguin Books 1993, London, UK

7   Marcus Borg & Tom Wright, *The Meaning of Jesus*, Harper Collins 1999, NY, NY

Chapter 18

1   Edward Schillibeeckx, *Jesus—An Experiment in Christology*, Crossroad Publishing 1991, NY, NY

2   Dale Allison, *Jesus of Nazareth—Millenarian Prophet*, Fortress Press 1998, Minneapolis, MN

3   Reimarus (Fragments) Wikipedia

4   Ben Meyer, *The Aims of Jesus*, Pickwick Publications, 2002, Eugene, OR

5   John Meier, *A Marginal Jew II*, Doubleday 1994, NY, NY

6   Dale Allison, *Jesus of Nazareth—Millennarium Prophet*, Fortress Press 1998, Minneapolis, MN

7   E. P. Sanders, *Jesus and Judaism*, Fortress Press 1985, Philadelphia, PA

8   Ibid, P 310

9   John Hick, *Metaphor of God Incarnate*, Westminster Press 1993, Louisville, KY

10 E. P. Sanders, *Jesus and Judaism*, Fortress Press 1985, Philadelphia, PA

11 Ben Meyer, *The Aims of Jesus*, Pickwick Publications, 2002, Eugene, OR

12 Carey Newman, *Jesus and the Restoration of Israel*, Inter-Varsity Press 1999, Downers Grove, IL

13 N. T. Wright, *Simply Jesus*, Harper Collins 2011, NY, NY

14 Carey Newman, *Jesus and the Restoration of Israel*, Inter-Varsity Press 1999, Downers Grove, IL

15 Ibid, P 168

16 N. T. Wright, *The New Testament and the People of God*, Fortress Press 1992, London, UK

17 N. T. Wright, *Simply Jesus*, Harper Collins 2011, NY, NY

18 Carey Newman, *Jesus and the Restoration of Israel*, Inter-Varsity Press 1999, Downers Grove, IL

19 Richard Hiers, *Jesus and Ethics*, Westminster Press 1973, Philadelphia, PA

20 James D.G. Dunn, *Jesus Remembered*, Eerdmans 2003, Grand Rapids, MI

21 Richard Hiers, *Jesus and the Future*, John Knox Press 1981, Atlanta, GA

22 Carey Newman, *Jesus and the Restoration of Israel*, Inter-Varsity Press 1999, Downers Grove, IL

23 Ibid, P 239

24 Dale Allison, *The Historical Christ and the Theological Jesus*, Eerdmans Press 2009, Grand Rapids, MI

25 Ibid, P 89

26 Ibid, P 118

27 Richard Hiers, *Jesus and the Future*, John Knox Press 1981, Atlanta, GA

Chapter 19

[1] E. P. Sanders, *Paul—A Very Short Introduction*, Oxford University Press 1981, Oxford, UK
[2] Ibid, P 139
[3] Ibid, P 147
[4] Ibid, P 149
[5] Raymond E. Brown, *The Churches the Apostles Left Behind*, Paulist Press 1984, NY, NY

Chapter 20

[1] Raymond E. Brown, *Birth of the Messiah*, Doubleday 1977, NY, NY
[2] Walter Brueggemann, *Theology of the Old Testament*, Fortress Press 1997, Minneapolis, MN
[3] Raymond E. Brown, *Birth of the Messiah*, Doubleday 1977, NY, NY
[4] James D. G. Dunn, *Christology in the Making*, SCM Press 1989, London, UK
[5] Shirley Jackson Case, *Jesus—A New Biography*, University of Chicago Press 1927, Chicago, IL
[6] James D. G. Dunn, *Jesus Remembered*, Eerdmans 2003, Grand Rapids, MI
[7] Wolfhart Pannenberg, *Jesus—God and Man*, Westminster Press 1977, Philadelphia, PA
[8] Albert Schweitzer, *The Quest for the Historical Jesus*, Fortress Press 2001, Minneapolis, MN
[9] Wolfhart Pannenberg, *Jesus—God and Man*, Westminster Press 1977, Philadelphia, PA
[10] Raymond E. Brown, *Introduction to New Testament Christology*, Paulist Press 1994, Chicago, IL
[11] E. P. Sanders, *Paul and Palestinian, Judaism*, Fortress Press 1977, Philadelphia, PA
[12] Bart Erhman, *Misquoting Jesus*, Harper One 2005, NY, NY
[13] Suarez, Mills and Stewart, *Sanity, Insanity, and Common Sense*, Ballantine Books, NY, NY
[14] Dale Allison, *The Historical Christ and the Theological Jesus*, Eerdmans Press 2009, Grand Rapids, MI
[15] Richard Hiers, *Jesus and the Future*, John Knox Press 1981, Atlanta, GA
[16] Dale Allison, *Constructing Jesus*, Baker Publishing Group 2010, Grand Rapids, MI

17   Daniel Taylor, *The Myth of Certainty*, Inter-Varsity Press 1992, Madison, WI

18   Robert W. Funk, *Honest to Jesus*, Harper Collins Publishers 1996, NY, NY

19   Ben Meyer, *The Aims of Jesus*, Pickwick Publications, 2002, Eugene, OR

20   Ben Meyer, *Critical Realism and the New Testament*, Pickwick Publications, Eugene, OR

21   Harold Bloom, *Jesus and Yahweh*, Penguin Books 2005, London, UK

22   Walter Brueggemann, *Theology of the Old Testament*, Fortress Press 1997, Minneapolis, MN

23   E. P. Sanders, *Paul and Palestinian Judaism*, Fortress Press 1977, Philadelphia, PA

24   Wolfhart Pannenberg, *Jesus—God and Man*, Westminster Press 1977, Philadelphia, PA

About the Author

Jack Pyle is happily married for 53 years, father of three children, and seven grandchildren. He was an ordained minister in the Worldwide Church of God, pastor of churches in the south and Midwest USA, and spent twenty years proclaiming the return of Jesus in 1975. Upon resignation from the ministry in 1979, he got into the property and casualty insurance business and made a career in insurance sales, management, and agent training and development, until his retirement in 2010 from Zurich Insurance Group. He resides with his wife in Lakewood Ranch, Florida.

CPSIA information can be obtained
at www.ICGtesting.com
Printed in the USA
LVHW021329310721
694125LV00002B/146